Maryland Bible Records

VOLUME 1: BALTIMORE AND HARFORD COUNTIES

Henry C. Peden, Jr.

HERITAGE BOOKS
2019

HERITAGE BOOKS
AN IMPRINT OF HERITAGE BOOKS, INC.

Books, CDs, and more—Worldwide

For our listing of thousands of titles see our website at
www.HeritageBooks.com

Published 2019 by
HERITAGE BOOKS, INC.
Publishing Division
5810 Ruatan Street
Berwyn Heights, Md. 20740

Copyright © 2003 Henry C. Peden, Jr.

All rights reserved. No part of this book may be reproduced or transmitted in any form or by any means, electronic or mechanical, including photocopying, recording or by any information storage and retrieval system without written permission from the author, except for the inclusion of brief quotations in a review.

International Standard Book Number
Paperbound: 978-1-68034-712-8

CONTENTS
of Maryland Bible Records, Volume 1

PREFACE	
CLAYTON AARONSON BIBLE	1
THOMAS AIREY BIBLE	2
ALLISON-BROWN BIBLE	6
DANIEL C. AMMERMAN BIBLE	9
OLIVER H. AMOS BIBLE	9
JOHN ARCHER, JR. BIBLE	12
JOHN ATWELL FAMILY RECORD	13
BENJAMIN F. AULD BIBLE	14
THOMAS AULD BIBLE	14
CHARLES W. BAKER BIBLE	16
JOHN HANSON BAKER BIBLE	18
NICHOLAS BAKER BIBLE	19
BARNES-HUGHES BIBLE	21
RICHARD BARNES BIBLE	23
JOHN BAUER BIBLE	27
THOMAS C. BAYARD BIBLE	29
JOHN S. BEAVEN BIBLE	30
JOHN W. BEAVEN BIBLE	31
BILLINGSLEY-SHERTZER BIBLE	31
WILLIAM R. BISSELL BIBLE	33
HUGH BLAIR BIBLE	36
GEORGE W. BLANEY BIBLE	38
EPHRAIM BORING BIBLE	40
ISAAC H. BOTTS BIBLE	40
ISAAC THOMAS BOTTS BIBLE	41
SAMUEL BRADFIELD BIBLE	42
JOHN A. BURKINS BIBLE	43
JOSEPH BREVITT BIBLE	44
LLOYD CANN BIBLE	45
GEORGE CAREINS BIBLE	46
BISHOP CARNAN BIBLE	47
LIDA VALIANT CARNAN BIBLE	48
WILLIAM CARRICK FAMILY RECORD	49
JOHN WESLEY CARTER BIBLE	50

GEORGE CHARITON BIBLE	51
JAMES CHESNEY BIBLE	52
SUMMERFIELD CHILDS BIBLE	54
DANIEL CLAYTON BIBLE	55
WELLS CLAYTON BIBLE	56
GEORGE W. CLOMAN BIBLE NO. 1	58
GEORGE W. CLOMAN BIBLE NO. 2	59
THOMAS B. COCKEY BIBLE	61
THOMAS BEALE COCKEY BIBLE	63
MOSES PARLETT COE BIBLE	65
JAMES C. COLE BIBLE	66
JOHN MARCHBORN COOLEY BIBLE	67
JOSHUA COOPER BIBLE	68
GEORGE CREVENSTEN BIBLE	69
GEORGE A. CREVENSTEN BIBLE	69
CROMPTON-DAVIS BIBLE	70
BENJAMIN CRONIN BIBLE	72
JOHN W. CRONIN BIBLE	72
FRANK DAVIS BIBLE	73
DILL-HUTTON BIBLE	74
DORSEY-LEWIS BIBLE	75
WILLIAM DOSH BIBLE	76
FREDERICK ELLENDER BIBLE	77
JOHN HENRY EMMORD BIBLE	79
FERGUSON-PRICE BIBLE	80
JAMES W. FORWOOD BIBLE	82
JOHN FORWOOD BIBLE	82
WILLIAM FORWOOD BIBLE	85
FULFORD-MITCHELL BIBLE	87
GALLOWAY-KNAUFF BIBLE	88
HARRIET GALLOWAY BIBLE	90
GEORGE W. GALLUP BIBLE	93
GILLESPIE-HUGHES BIBLE	94
JOHN GRAPE BIBLE	96
MICAJAH GREENFIELD BIBLE	97
JOHN HENRY GRENINGER BIBLE	98
STEPHEN B. HANNA BIBLE	100
HERMAN HANSON BIBLE	101

HENRY E. HARKINS BIBLE	102
HARKINS-ROBINSON BIBLE	103
HASTINGS-RICHARDSON BIBLE	104
NATHANIEL W. S. HAYS BIBLE	105
HARRY DAVID HANWAY BIBLE	106
HENRY HERRING BIBLE	107
GEORGE HESS FAMILY BIBLE	109
THEODORE J. HETRICK BIBLE	110
HIGGINS-GUEST BIBLE	111
GEORGE W. HOPKINS BIBLE	112
JOSEPH R. HOPKINS BIBLE	116
WILLIAM HOPKINS BIBLE	118
MATTHEW HOWLETT BIBLE	119
JOHN M. HUFF BIBLE	122
JOHN HUGHES BIBLE	122
JOHN S. HUTCHINS BIBLE	124
ANNA D. HUTSON BIBLE	126
MICHAEL HUTSON BIBLE	127
BENJAMIN JEFFERS BIBLE	130
ELISHA JOHNSON BIBLE	133
EMORY JOHNSON BIBLE	133
JOHNSTON-JOHNSON BIBLE	134
JOHN FLETCHER JONES BIBLE	136
JOHN A. KECK BIBLE	138
EMANUEL KENT BIBLE	139
GEORGE A. KIMBLE BIBLE	139
ABRAM (ABRAHAM) KING BIBLE	142
PIERSON D. KLAIR BIBLE	143
WILLIAM KNIGHT BIBLE	144
JOHN S. LAGAN BIBLE	145
LAMDIN-FOX-HUGG BIBLE	146
BENEDICT LEE BIBLE	149
EDMOND LEE BIBLE	150
ISAAC I. LEITHISER BIBLE	151
JAMES NEWTON LITTLE BIBLE	152
ROBERT S. LIVEZEY BIBLE	153
THOMAS N. LIVEZEY BIBLE	155
JOSEPH LOBACH (LOBAUGH) BIBLE	156

WILLIAM C. LOCKARD BIBLE	157
ALBERT R. MAGNESS BIBLE	158
THOMAS MAGNESS BIBLE	158
THOMAS H. MAGNESS BIBLE	160
MARTIN-SLEE BIBLE	161
McCOMAS-GILBERT BIBLE	162
EDWARD DAWES McCONKY BIBLE	164
SARAH ANN McMULLEN BIBLE	164
HENRY C. MICHAEL BIBLE	166
JACOB MICHAEL BIBLE	168
JOHN M. MICHAEL BIBLE	169
EDMUND MITCHELL BIBLE	170
EDWARD T. MONKS BIBLE	171
JAMES P. MONKS BIBLE	173
HERRMANN MOOG BIBLE	174
THOMAS E. MORGAN BIBLE	175
WILLIAM MORRIS BIBLE	176
HAMILTON MORRISON BIBLE	177
DAVID M. MURRAY BIBLE	178
MARTIN MYERS FAMILY BOOK	179
ELIZABETH H. NAGLE BIBLE	180
JOHN NAGLE BIBLE	183
JOHN H. NAGLE BIBLE	186
SAMUEL O. NAGLE BIBLE	187
JAMES NOBLE BIBLE	188
SAMUEL W. PALMER BIBLE	188
PETER PARKS BIBLE	189
PARSONS-FRENCH BIBLE	190
HENRY CLINT PEDEN, JR. BIBLE	192
RICHARD POOLE BIBLE	193
WILLIAM PRITCHARD BIBLE	196
MITCHEL MARTIN PUGH BIBLE	196
ISAAC L. PYLE BIBLE	197
JOSHUA HARLAN PYLE BIBLE	199
JOHN READ BIBLE	201
WILLIAM H. REASIN BIBLE	201
REESE-PRICE BIBLE	204
WILLIAM B. RICHARDSON BIBLE	207

THOMAS M. RICKETTS BIBLE	208
THOMAS W. RICKETTS BIBLE	210
HENRY RUFF BIBLE	211
RUTLEDGE-FITZPATRICK BIBLE	212
RUTLEDGE-PRICE BIBLE	213
THOMAS SCAGGS BIBLE	215
GEORGE T. SHANNON BIBLE	215
ASBURY SHERIDAN BIBLE	216
LUTHER SHERIDAN BIBLE	217
REBECCA SHERIDAN BIBLE	217
RICHARD SHERIDAN BIBLE	218
JACOB SHERTZER BIBLE	219
JOHN H. SHORT BIBLE	220
GEORGE W. SLEE BIBLE	221
JOHN LEWIS UPPERCO BIBLE	222
WILLIAMS-NEILSON FAMILY BIBLE	225
INDEX	227

PREFACE

This volume of bible records contains information about families in Baltimore and Harford Counties. These bible records have been collected by individuals and organizations, notably the Sons and Daughters of the American Revolution, over many years and typescript copies or photocopies of the original bible pages have been deposited at the Maryland Historical Society in Baltimore and in local historical and genealogical societies.

The bible records herein have been arranged alphabetically by the last name of the family and any title page information has been included when available. Vital records have been gleaned from each bible and rearranged into four major groups: Marriages, Births, Deaths and Family Records. Thus, the information in this book will not appear in the same arrangement as in the original. Notes and comments by various named donors have been included within the text when appropriate.

Some of the missing and incomplete bible entries have been annotated by the compiler [in brackets] with information from various primary and secondary sources. The names of the bible owners have been withheld except when permission was granted.

Bibles are important in genealogical research because they may contain information about families that might not be found anywhere else, especially before the enactment of state laws establishing vital records (birth and death certificates) in 1875 for Baltimore City and 1898 for the counties of Maryland. This volume of bible records should prove to be a useful tool for genealogical researchers and family historians.

Henry C. Peden, Jr.
Bel Air, Maryland

MARYLAND BIBLE RECORDS, VOLUME ONE
BALTIMORE AND HARFORD COUNTIES

CLAYTON AARONSON BIBLE

Bible published in 1853 by John B. Perry Company. Family data gleaned from a typescript of records copied by Jon Harlan Livezey in 1974. Bible presented to Russell T. Aaronson, Jr. of Harford County, MD by his grandfather Francis Anderson.

Marriages:
Clayton Aaronson and Mary Ann Folwell m. 15 Nov 1843
Alfred E. Aaronson and Emmalenda Austin m. 20 Feb ---- [*Ed. Note:* The year was not given, but Harford County marriage records indicate Alford E. Aaronson and Emma L. Austin were married in 1867].
William F. Aaronson and Martha J. Numbers m. 27 Oct 1870
Ambrose P. Aaronson and Annie J. Pennington m. 25 May 1870
Bennett Arnold and Hope Aaronson m. 26 Apr 1871
Russell Taylor Aaronson and Edna Dickey Jamison m. 27 Apr 1940
Ann Jamison Aaronson and Edwin Burton Kelbaugh, Jr. m. 18 Jan 1864 at Grove Presbyterian Church in Aberdeen, MD
Russell Taylor Aaronson, Jr. and Joan Rosemary Farr m. 20 Jun 1964 at St. Ann's Church in Washington, D.C.
Ann J. Kelbaugh and Thomas Allen Bender m. 4 Jul 1970 at Grove Presbyterian Church in Aberdeen, MD

Births:
Clayton Aaronson, son of Ezra and Hope Aaronson, b. 24 Mar 1821
Mary Ann Aaronson, dau. of William and Ann Folwell Aaronson, b. 8 Jul 1812
Russell Taylor Aaronson, son of Frank (Francis) Folwell and Henrietta Morris Aaronson, b. 30 Jan 1910

Children of William F. and Martha J. Aaronson:
1. Mary Emmeline Aaronson, b. 1 Nov 1871
2. Francis Folwell Aaronson, b. 21 Mar 1874

Children of Clayton and Mary Ann Aaronson:
1. Alfred Ezra Aaronson, b. 4 Dec 1844
2. Anna Elizabeth Aaronson, b. 9 Aug 1846
3. William Folwell Aaronson, b. 1 Feb 1848

4. Ambrose Palmer Aaronson, b. 13 Apr 1849
5. Hope Aaronson, b. 27 Sep 1850
6. Samuel Clayton Aaronson, b. 21 Dec 1851
7. Mary Elizabeth Aaronson, b. 28 Oct 1853

Children of Russell T. and Edna D. Aaronson:
1. Russell Taylor Aaronson, Jr., b. 20 Jul 1941 at University Hospital in Baltimore City
2. Ann Dickey Jamison Aaronson, b. 22 Jun 1944 at Union Memorial Hospital in Baltimore City

Children of Edwin B. and Ann D. Kelbaugh:
1. Michael Burton Kelbaugh, b. 15 Apr 1965
2. Brendan Kelbaugh, b. 30 Nov 1967

Children of Russell T. and Joan R. Aaronson:
1. Russell Taylor Aaronson 3rd, b. 8 Jun 1965
2. Jennifer Lynn Aaronson, b. 21 Sep 1967

Deaths:
Anna Elizabeth Aaronson, d. -- Aug 1847, age 1 year and 5 days
Clayton Aaronson, d. 11 Jul 1868, age 47 years, 3 months and 17 days
Mary Ann Aaronson, d. 21 Sep 1886, age 74 years, 3 months and 13 days

THOMAS AIREY BIBLE

Bible published in 1844 by Jesper Harding, No. 57 South Third Street, Philadelphia. Family data gleaned from a photocopy at the Maryland Historical Society.

Marriages:
James Airey and Jemima Carroll m. 11 May 1837
John B. Airey and Miss Laura J. Cline, of Baltimore, m. 6 Apr 1859 by Rev. Shreeves

Charles Grant Rhoads and Emma Airey m. 1 Aug 1900

Helen Hayes Rhodes and Robert Caruth Stevenson m. 8 Apr 1928

William Carroll Airey, son of St. Clare Airey, and Buelah Walters m. 2 Sep 1908

Hyacinth Ella Virginia Airey and Ray Clinton Hylton m. 10 Aug 1936 and divorced

1 Jan 1943; remarriage of Hyacinth to Raymond B. White on 14 Jun 1946

Norma Valentine Airey and Joseph McKinley Quade m. 26 Jan 1941

Dawn Virginia Hylton and Charles Frederick Willner, Jr. m. 14 Jan 1956

Ronald Ray Hylton and Mildred JoAnn Geist m. 21 Feb 1964 in Merced, CA

Nancy Carroll Quade and Paul Martin Kaplan m. 1 Aug 1975

Births:
Ann Payne, wife of Francis A. Airey, b. 22 Jan 1793

Susannah Carroll, b. 13 Jul 1793
Jemima Carroll, dau. of Susannah and John Carroll, b. 19 Dec 1819

Francis Asbury Airey, son of Thomas Hill Airey and wife Mary, b. 14 May 1791
Joseph Airey, son of Francis and Ann Airey, b. 9 Nov 1828
James Airey, son of Francis Asbury Airey, b. 17 Jul 1816(?)
Mary E. Airey, consort of Joseph Airey, b. 24 Jun 1845
George Washington Wilson Airey, b. 30 Sep 1855
Emma Airey, b. 13 Jun 1876
William Carroll Airey, son of Sinclair Carroll Airey, b. 16 Mar 1885

Children of William and Buelah Airey:
1. William Howard Airey, b. 18 Jun 1909 in Princess Anne, VA
2. Hyacinth Ella Virginia Airey, b. 8 Feb 1918 in Baltimore
3. Norma Valentine Airey, b. 14 Dec 1921 in Baltimore
Children of Hyacinth and Ray Hylton:
1. Dawn Virginia Hylton, b. 24 May 1937 in Baltimore
2. William Ernest Hylton, b. 18 Oct 1938
3. Ronald Ray Hylton, b. 11 Jul 1941

Children of James and Jemima Airey:
1. William Francis Airey, b. 28 Jan 1838
2. John Bond Airey, b. 20 Dec 1839
3. Mary Susan Airey, b. 5 Jun 1842
4. James K. Polk Airey, b. 9 Nov 1844

5. Charles Carroll Airey, b. 8 Feb 1847
6. Joseph Edward Airey, b. 13 May 1849
7. Sinclair Carroll Airey, b. 13 Sep 1851
8. George Washington Wilson Airey, b. 30 Sep 1855 in Wrightsville, PA

Children of John and Laura Airey:
1. Carroll Bell Airey, b. -- Nov 1860
2. John William Airey, b. 28 Jan 1863

[Children of Dawn and Charles Willner]:
1. Brian Lee Willner, b. Tues., 7 May 1956 at 1:55 p.m.
2. Wayne Lawrence Willner, b. 6 Jan 1959
3. JoAnn Gail Willner, b. 15 Dec 1960
4. Glenn Alan Willner, b. 5 Mar 1962

Children of Norma and Joseph (Joe) Quade:
1. Melody Page Quade, b. 16 Apr 1947 at a 1/4 of 10 o'clock Wed. morning
2. Nancy Carroll Quade, b. 10 Sep 1949

Helen Rhodes, b. 12 Dec 1901
Augustus Churchill Rhodes, b. 20 Aug 1903

Ronald Dion Hylton, son of Ronald and Mildred Hylton, b. 15 Oct 1968

Deaths:
Susannah Carroll, d. 11 Dec 1882, age 89 years, 4 months and 28 days

Samuel P. Airey, d. on the Mississippi River, 60 miles from St. Louis where he resided, on 9 Jul 1853, age 28 years, 6 months and 17 days

Francis A. Airey, d. at Wrightsville, PA on 23 Jul 1854, age 63 years, 2 months and 9 days

Mrs. Ann Airey, d. at Wrightsville, PA on 9 Nov 1855, age 62 years, 9 months and 17 days

John Bond Airey, son of James and Jemima Airey, d. in Baltimore on 20 Jul 1864, age 24 years and 7 months

John William Airey, son of John B. and Laura Airey, d. in Baltimore on 31 Jan 1865, age 2 years and 3 days

Jemima Airey, wife of James Airey, d. in Baltimore on 8 Mar 1865, age 45 years, 2 months and 18 days

James Airey, consort of Jemima Airey, d. in Baltimore on 4 Apr 1867, age 50 years, 8 months and 18 days

Carroll Bell Airey drowned in Baltimore on 14 May 1868, age 7 years

Joseph Airey, son of Francis and Ann Airey, d. 31 Mar 1868 of softening of the spine; b. 19 Nov 1828

Mary E. Airey, consort of Joseph Airey, d. suddenly on Sunday night 25 Jan 1869; b. 24 Jun 1845

Charles C. Airey, d. of consumption on 22 Jun 1876, age 29 years and 4 months

James K. Polk Airey, son of James and Jemima Airey, d. 19 Mar 1900, age 55 years, 4 months and 10 days

Talitha A. Jack, dau. of Susanna and John Carroll, d. at 3033 St. Paul Street in Baltimore on 6 Apr 1907 at 7:10 p.m., age 88 years, 8 months and 2 days; she was the last of ten children.

Joseph E. Airey, d. in Baltimore on 24 Nov 1916, age 67 years, 6 months and 11 days

George Washington Wilson Airey, d. 1898

Sinclair C. Airey, d. from an accident on 29 Mar 1918, age 67 years, 6 months and 16 days

William Francis Airey "died suddenly of hardening of the arteries. Left 300,000 thousand to Womens Christian Association. age 82 January 5th 1920"

Susan Airey Watson, age 82, the last of James and Jemima Airey's children, d. of hardening of the arteries on 1 Feb 1923

A. Churchill Rhodes, d. 17 Jul 1924, age 20 years and 11 months; mother Emma

A. Rhodes

Charles Grant Rhodes, d. Wed., 11 Apr 1928, age 58 years; wife E. Airey Rhodes

George E. Airey, son of Sinclare Airey, killed in action in France on 18 Sep 1918

Eugene Howard Airey, son of Sinclare Airey, d. of rabbit fever on 8 Feb 1940, age 53

William Howard Airey, son of W. Carroll and Beulah Airey, d. 8 Oct 1935, age 26 years, 3 months and 20 days, at his home in Catonsville, MD, a suicide (left wife Emma Jones Airey, school teacher)

Adelaide Airey, wife of Sinclair Airey, d. 16 Jul 1918

Melody Paige Quade, dau. of Norma Airey and Joseph Quade, d. of lympo sarcoma (cancer) on 20 Nov 1947, age 7 months

Hyacinth Ella Virginia Airey (neé White), d. of cancer on 12 Oct 1958, age 40

Family Records:
Rev. Thomas Airey, rector of Christa [sic] Church, Cambridge, Dorchester County [MD], was born at Kendal, Yorkshire, England 1701. He came to this province in 1726 and was inducted in the office of Minister to the Great Choptank Parish, Dorchester County, by a letter received from the Lord Proprietary Charles Calvert, Governor of Maryland.

Rev. T. Airey married Elizabeth Pitt and they had 6 children [only 4 named here]: Thomas Hill Airey, Joseph Airey, Mary Airey Martin, and Louisa Airey Gilmore (married 1771)

Thomas Hill Airey married Mary Thomson and they had 5 children [only 3 named here]: Francis Asbury Airey, Robert Airey, Joseph Airey

Francis Asbury Airey married Ann Payne and they had 6 children: James Airey, Joseph Airey, Samuel Airey, Edward Airey, Louisa Airey, and Mary Airey

ALLISON-BROWN BIBLE

No publication date given. Bible printed by Mathew Carey, No. 118 Market Street, Philadelphia. Family data gleaned from a typescript in Filing Case A at the

Maryland Historical Society submitted in 1946 by Mrs. R. E. L. Marshall (address not given).

Marriages:
Patrick Allison and Mary Buchanan m. 13(?) Mar 1787(?). [*Ed. Note:* The copyist was uncertain about the date, but Maryland marriage records indicate they were married by Rev. Isaac S. Keith at the First Presbyterian Church in Baltimore on 15 Mar 1787].

George I. Brown and Esther Allison m. 7 Mar 1810

George William Brown and Clara M. Brune, m. 29 Oct 1839 by Rev. Dr. William E. Wyatt

Nathaniel Holmes Morison and Sidney B. Brown m. 22 Dec 1842 by Rev. George W. Burnap

Sanderson Robert and Mary Buchanan Brown m. 28 Mar 1848 by Rev. George W. Burnap

John Cumming Brown and Mary Riddell m. 11 Apr 1848 by Rev. Henry V. F. Johns

Francis Tiffany and Esther Allison Brown m. 14 Oct 1852 by Rev. George W. Burnap

Robert D. Brown and Mary D. Dobbin m. -- Oct 1860 by Rev. W. F. Jackson

Births:
George I. Brown, son of George and Rose Brown, b. 4 Oct 1787
Esther Allison, b. 17 Feb 1792

Children of George I. and Esther Brown:
1. Mary Buchanan Brown, b. 2 Jan 1811, bapt. by Rev. Inglis [*Ed. Note:* Church records state she was baptized at First Presbyterian Church in Baltimore on 7 Mar 1811]
2. George William Brown, b. 13 Oct 1812, bapt. by Rev. Inglis [*Ed. Note:* Church records state he was baptized at First Presbyterian Church in Baltimore on 15 Mar 1813]

3. Rose Ann Brown, b. 28 Nov 1814
4. Sidney Buchanan Brown (dau.), b. 15 Jan 1818, bapt. by Dr. Inglis [*Ed. Note:* Church records state she was baptized at First Presbyterian Church in Baltimore on 27 Feb 1818]
5. Allison Brown (son), b. 26 Sep 1819, bapt. by Dr. Glendy on 23 Nov 1819
6. John Cumming Brown, b. 14 Jan 1821, bapt. by Mr. Sparks
7. Robert Davison Brown, b. 8 Dec 1823, bapt. by W. Greenwood on 17 Jun 1824
8. Jane Brown, b. 25 Jun 1825, bapt. by Mr. Walker of Charleston, MA on 29 Jan 1827
9. Esther Allison Brown, b. 12 Dec 1826, bapt. by Mr. H. Walker of Charleston, MA on 29 Jan 1827

Deaths:

Patrick Allison, d. 21 Aug 1802 [Written in another handwriting: "Born in Lancaster County, TN in 1740"]

Rose Ann Brown, dau. of George and Esther Brown, d. 10 Apr 1822

George I. Brown, son of George and Rose Brown, d. 4 Jun 1829

Mary Allison, widow of Patrick Allison, d. 23 Aug 1832 [Written in another handwriting: "Born about 1760 in Carlisle, PA"]

Jane Brown, dau. of George and Esther Brown, d. 26 Jun 1840

Allison Brown, lost at sea in Lat. 33⸍? N., Long. 177⸍? W., on 27 Mar 1846 at 1 p.m.

Esther Brown, relict of George I. Brown, d. 27 Oct 1849 in New York City on her way from Cincinnati to her home in Baltimore [Written in another handwriting: "Buried in Greenmount"]

Sanderson Robert, d. 5 Jan 1864 in Cincinnati [Written in another handwriting: "Buried in Greenmount"]

John Cumming Brown, d. 25 Dec 1864 in Boston [Written in another handwriting: "Buried in Greenmount"]

Allison A. Brown, d. 12 May 1872 in Baltimore

Mary B. Robert, d. 5 Mar 1886 in West Newton, MA at the residence of her brother-in-law Francis Tiffany [Written in another handwriting: "Buried in Greenmount"]

DANIEL C. AMMERMAN BIBLE

No publication information available. Family data gleaned from a typescript at the Maryland Historical Society.

Marriage:
Daniel C. Ammerman and Katherine Kinslowe m. 19 Aug 1841

Births:
Daniel C. Ammerman, b. 11 Jan 1822

[Children of Daniel and Catherine Ammerman]:
1. Elmira Ammerman, b. 1 Dec 1842
2. Miles G. Ammerman, b. 3 May 1845
3. Josephine Ammerman, b. 31 Jan 1848
4. Mary M. Ammerman, b. 2 Apr 1850
5. Emma Ammerman, b. 22 Jun 1852
6. Catherine E. Ammerman, b. 14 Nov 1855
7. Oceanna Ammerman, b. 8 Nov 1857
8. James Y. Ammerman, b. 17 Aug 1861

Deaths:
Daniel C. Ammerman, d. 24 Mar 1872 in Wernersville, Berks County, PA, and bur. near Water Cure on Cushen Mountain

Catherine Kinslowe Ammerman d. ---- [date not given], age 96, Philipsburg, PA

OLIVER H. AMOS BIBLE

Bible published in 1829 by C. Omer, T. Bedlington and J. H. A. Frost of Boston, MA. Family data gleaned from a typescript at the Maryland Historical Society.

Marriage:
---- [page cut] and Elizabeth Ann King m. 18 Mar 1829 [*Ed. Note:* Part of the bible page was missing, but Harford County marriages indicate a license was issued to Oliver H. Amos and Elizabeth Ann King on 16 Mar 1829].

Births:

[Children of Oliver and Elizabeth Amos]:
1. George King Amos, b. 4 Apr 1830
2. Rebecca Lee Amos, b. 17 Apr 1834
3. James Oliver Amos, b. 21 Jun 1836
4. Elizabeth T. Amos, b. 31 Aug 1838
5. Mary Rebecca Amos, b. 10 May 1845

Children of James and Hannah Amoss:
1. Mary T. Amoss, b. 2 Mar 1792
2. Oliver H. Amoss, b. 18 Sep 1801

Deaths:
Abraham King, d. Sun., 11 Dec 1836 about half past 1 o'clock a.m. in Baltimore County, in his 77th year

Jane King, dau. of William King, d. 7 Dec 1833 about half past 1 o'clock a.m., supposed to be 47 years old

Hannah Amoss, dau. of David Lee and wife Rebecca, d. 11 May 1839 at half past 12 o'clock at night, in her 68th year

James Amos, son of William and Hannah Amos, d. 10th month 30, 1845, age 82

Elizabeth King, wife of Abraham King and dau. of John and Elizabeth Taylor, d. 17 Nov 1853 at half past 4 p.m., in her 84th year

Children of Abraham and Elizabeth King:
1. George King, d. 5 Jun 1869 in his 79th year
2. Dr. David King, d. 18 Jan 1874 in his 75th year
3. Elizabeth A. (King) Amoss, wife of Oliver H. Amoss, d. 8 Dec 1884 in her 79th year

Children of James and Hannah Amoss:
1. Mary T. (Amoss) Calwell, d. 31 Dec 1862, age 70 years, 9 months and 29 days
2. Oliver Huff Amoss, d. 9 Apr 1864 in his 63rd year

Children of Oliver H. and Elizabeth A. Amoss:
1. Rebecca Lee Amoss, d. 8 Nov 1842 at 2 o'clock a.m. in her 8th year

2. George K. Amoss, d. Fri., 9 Aug 1878 at half past 6 o'clock a.m., in his 49th year
3. James O. Amoss, d. Thurs., 9 Oct 1879 at half past 8 o'clock in the morning in his 43rd year
4. Mary R. (Amoss) Lee, d. Tues., 26 Apr 1881 at half past 12 o'clock in the morning, in her 36th year

Ralph Charles Lee, son of David and Barbara Lee and husband of Mary R. Lee, d. Thurs. night, 30 Mar 1904, at 25 minutes to 11, in his 70th year

Family Records (Clippings in Bible):

1. William Amos, 1717-1814, of Harford County, d. 26th of 2nd month, 1814 in the 97th year of his age. He was a minister and leaves 16 children, 92 grandchildren, 133 great-grandchildren and 8 great-great-grandchildren.

2. Dr. Richard D. Lee, of Bel Air, d. Tues., 4th instant, age 64 [no month or year indicated] and bur. at Rock Spring. Brother of Col. Otho S. Lee. Survived by wife ne Mary Moore, sister of John Moore of this [Harford] county.

3. Garrett Amos, age 80, d. at his home at Benson [date not indicated]. Member of Little Falls [Friends] Meeting. Survived by one son William L. Amos and three daughters: Mrs. Frank Taylor, of Wilmington, Miss Martha Amos and Miss Josephine Amos.

4. Silver wedding of Mr. and Mrs. William T. Watson celebrated on 9 Mar 1890. Mrs. Watson was Miss Elizabeth Amoss, a daughter of the late Oliver Amoss of this [Harford] county.

5. Ralph Charles Lee, d. 31 Mar 1904 in his 70th year and bur. in Friends Burying Ground at Fallston. Two sons were David Lee and Oliver Lee, former of New York. His wife was the only daughter of the late Charles Broadway Rouss, one of New York's most prominent men. He leaves three sisters: Mrs. William Price, Mrs. Sallie Downe and Miss Lee.

6. Mrs. Elizabeth Amoss, widow of the late Oliver Amoss, d. ---- [date not indicated], age 79

7. George K. Amoss, d. ---- [date not indicated], bur. at Friends Meeting in Fallston.
8. Mrs. Rebecca Wilson, wife of Dr. Joshua Wilson, d. ---- [date not indicated] at her home near Emmorton, age 75, and bur. at Mt. Carmel in Emmorton. Her

son-in-law was Dr. E. Hall Richardson. She was the sister of Mrs. David Lee of Jerusalem Mills and sister of the wife of Col. John Carroll Welsh. She had been married 56 years.

9. Mary R. Lee, wife of R. Charles Lee and daughter of the late Oliver H. Amoss of Harford County, d. 26 Apr 1881, age 36.

10. Oliver H. Amoss, d. 9th instant [date not indicated] near Fallston, in his 63rd year, leaving a wife and four children [not named].

11. Garrett Amoss, of Harford County, d. ---- [date not indicated]. His is the ancestral Amoss home he loved. He being the 6th in line from the original settler James Amos. The great grand sire of the subject, William Amoss, die 1814, age 97. Eleven years after his death, Garrett Amoss was born upon this spot.

12. Elizabeth King, wife of Abraham King and daughter of John Taylor and Elizabeth his wife, d. 19 Nov 1853 at half past 4 in the afternoon in her 84th year. Elizabeth King Amoss' mother was a Taylor and her grandmother a Minehart. [*Ed. Note:* Another undated obituary stated she was the widow of Abraham King and she died at the residence of her son-in-law George King in Baltimore County].

13. Mrs. Jane Worthington, d. 26th instant [date not indicated] in her 94th year and bur. from residence of Evans Rogers in West Chester on Tues., 30th instant.

14. John Taylor, a native of Chester County, PA, formerly practiced law in our [Harford County, MD] courts, died on Thurs. last [obituary dated 13 Jun 1820] at his residence in the city of Natchez [MS]. Hon. John Taylor, Chief Justice of the Supreme Court of this State, buried in PA. He emigrated to this county [Harford] when 17 years old.

JOHN ARCHER, JR. BIBLE

Bible was printed for Thomas Dobson, at the Stone House, No. 41, South Second Street, Philadelphia, 1799. Family data gleaned from a photocopy of the bible records in Filing Case A at the Maryland Historical Society. Written on a page in the front of the bible was the name "Mary Archer" which was followed by "Henry Wilson Archer, son of ---- [name scratched out], 19 Dec 1882."

Marriage:
John Archer, Jr. and Ann Stump m. Tues., 10 Nov 1802

Births:
John Archer, Jr., b. Thurs., 9 Oct 1777 at a quarter past 12 o'clock
Ann Stump, b. 29 Jan 1786

Children of John and Ann Archer:
1. George Archer, b. Fri., 9 Sep 1803 at 4:30 a.m.
2. Hannah Archer, b. Thurs., 1 Aug 1805 at 5 p.m.
3. Mary Archer, b. 2 Apr 1808 at 1 a.m.
4. Catharine Cassandra Archer [#1], b. 2 Apr 1809 at 1 a.m.
5. Catharine Cassandra Archer [#2], b. 25 Sep 1810 at 3 p.m.
6. Henry Wilson Archer, b. Sun., 18 Apr 1813 at 8 a.m.
7. John Archer, b. Sun., 16 Jul 1815 at 11 p.m.
8. James Archer, b. Fri., 19 Dec 1817 at 1 p.m.
9. Robert Archer, b. Sat., 20 May 1820 at 2 a.m.
10. Ann Archer, b. Tues., 1 Oct 1822 at 8 a.m.
11. Marion Archer, b. Sat., 22 Oct 1825 at 8 p.m.

Deaths:
Children of John and Ann Archer:
1. George Archer, d. 16 Oct 1822
2. Hannah Archer, d. 24 Jan 1871
3. Mary Archer, d. 19 Dec 1882 at 8(?) a.m.
4. Catharine Cassandra Archer [#1], d. 31 Oct 1809 at 6 p.m.
5. Catharine Cassandra Archer [#2], d. Sun., 1 Oct 1893 at 6 a.m.
6. Henry Wilson Archer, d. Fri., 8 Jul 1887 at 5 p.m.
7. John Archer, d. 31 Aug 1835
8. James Archer, d. 24 Oct 1864
9. Robert Archer, d. 12 Mar 1878
10. Ann Archer, d. 30 Jun 1882
11. Marion Archer, d. Sun., 12 Aug 1827 at 9 a.m.

JOHN ATWELL FAMILY RECORD

These Atwell family records were gleaned from a typescript at the Maryland Historical Society (which was undated and identified as Accession No. 58708 in their Filing Case A). The information had been copied from "flyleaves of unidentified volume" by Mrs. Lee Reely of Baltimore, MD (no date was given). There were no marriages or deaths recorded, only a list of births in Baltimore.

Births:

John Atwell, b. 20 Feb 1814
Rebeckah Ann Atwell, b. 15 Jul 1817
Catherine Atwell, b. 5 Feb 1820
Joseph Henry Atwell, b. 19 Jul 1822
William Atwell, b. 26 Jun 1824
Ann Maria Atwell, b. 21 May 1826
George Atwell, b. 15 Jan 1828
Sary Elisibeth Atwell, b. 12 Mar 183-(?)
James Richard Atwell, b. 14 Sep 1834
Cathern Leienary Atwell, b. 2 Mar 1836

BENJAMIN F. AULD BIBLE

No publication information available (title page missing). Family data gleaned from a photocopy of the bible filed in Filing Case A at the Maryland Historical Society (no date given).

Marriage:
Benjamin F. Auld and Kate A. W. Clark m. 6 Jul 1860 by Rev. Guyer at the High Street Parsonage

Births:
Benjamin F. Auld, son of Hugh and Sophia Auld, b. 27 Dec 1828
Catherine A. W. Clark, dau. of Benjamin J. and Mary Jane Clark, b. 19 Jan 1841
Children of Benjamin and Catherine Auld:
1. Hugh Auld, b. Thurs., 5 Dec 1861 at 7:20 p.m.
2. Ella Virginia Auld, b. Mon., 7 Sep 1863 at 8 a.m.
3. Benjamin Franklin Auld, b. Sat., 13 Jan 1866 between 11 and 12 p.m.
4. Edward Wesley Auld, b. Sun., 5 Jan 1868 at noon
5. Wilson C. Auld, b. Mon., 13 Feb 1871
6. John Summerfield Deale Auld, b. Thurs., 27 Feb 1873 at 8 p.m.
7. Catherine A. Auld, b. Sat, 10 Jul 1875 at 1 a.m.
8. Wilson Auld, b. Wed., 5 Dec 1877 at 6:40 p.m.

Deaths:
Hugh Auld, d. 23 Dec 1861, age 62
Wilson C. Auld, d. Wed., 3 Jul 1872, age 16 months and 20 days

THOMAS AULD BIBLE

Bible published in 1850 by the American Bible Society in New York. "1850, Sept. 10th" was handwritten at the top of the Family Record page. Family data gleaned from a photocopy filed in Filing Case A at the Maryland Historical Society.

Marriages:
Col. Hugh Auld and Zipporah Willson m. 26 Jul 1792 in Baltimore
Thomas Auld and Lucretia P. Anthony m. 16 Jan 1823
John L. Sears and Arianna Amanda Auld m. 6 Dec 1843 in Baltimore
Thomas Auld and Rowena Hambleton m. 21 May 1829
Thomas Auld and Ann Harper m. 16 May 1844
William H. Bruff and Sarah Louisa Auld m. 21 Dec 1854
John C. Harper and Rowena H. Auld m. 23 Nov 1858 in Philadelphia
Thomas Auld and Amanda M. Thompson m. 23 May 1865 in Baltimore

Births:
Col. Hugh Auld, son of Edward and Sarah Auld, b. 20 Jul 1767
Zipporah Willson, afterwards the wife of Hugh Auld, b. 26 Aug 1775
Children of Hugh and Zipporah Auld:
1. Elizabeth Auld (1st dau.), b. 9 Sep 1794
2. Thomas Auld (1st son), b. 10 Sep 1795
3. Arrianna Auld (2nd dau.), b. 4 Mar 1797
4. Edward Auld (2nd son), b. 9 Jul 1798
5. Hugh Auld (3rd son), b. 10 Sep 1799
6. Sally Auld (3rd dau.), b. 23 Nov 1800
7. Edward Auld (4th son), b. 26 Feb 1802
8. Zipporah Auld (4th dau.), b. 24 Mar 1804
9. Willson Auld (5th son), b. 26 Jun 1806
10. Haddaway Auld (6th son), b. 5 Apr 1808
11. Washington Auld (7th son), b. 21 May 1810
12. Sarah Auld (5th dau.), b. 26 Jun 1811
13. Haddaway Auld (8th son), b. 4 Mar 1813

Lucretia P. Anthony, only dau. of Aaron and Ann Anthony, b. 7 Dec 1804

Rowena R. Hambleton, first dau. of William and Lydia Hambleton, b. 11 Jul 1811

Ann Baggs, third dau. of Isaac and Nancy Baggs, b. 28 Mar 1806

Arrianna Amanda Auld, first dau. of Lucretia Auld, b. 26 Jan 1826

Children of Thomas and Rowena Auld:
1. William H. Auld, b. 4 Mar 1831 (Died Fifth?)
2. Sarah Louisa Auld, b. 13 Jul 1833
3. Rowena Hambleton Auld, b. 29 Oct 1835 at 3 a.m.

Deaths:
Edward Auld, second son of Hugh and Zipporah Auld,, d. 16 Nov 1801

Sally Auld, third dau. of Hugh and Zipporah Auld, d. 25 Nov 1807

Col. Hugh Auld, son of Edward and Sarah Auld, d. 3 Nov 1820 of pleurisy, age 53 years, 3 months and 13 days

Zipporah Auld, wife of Hugh Auld, d. 12 Jan 1859 of asthma in Baltimore in her 84th year

Thomas Auld, d. 8 Feb 1880 in his 85th year, at "Beverly" residence of J. C. Harper

Lucretia P. Auld, wife of Thomas Auld, d. 6 Jul 1827 with dropsy, age 22 years and 7 months

Rowena R. Auld, wife of Thomas Auld, d. 24 Nov 1842 with consumption, age 31 years, 3 months and 28 days

Zipporah Drummond, formerly Z. Auld, d. 27 Dec 1848 in Lafayette County, MO, age 44 years, 9 months and 3 days

Arrianna W. Deale, formerly Auld, wife of William G. Deale, d. 31 Oct 1849 in Washington City, age 52 years, 7 months and 27 days

Mrs. Ann Auld, wife of Thomas Auld, d. 1 Aug 1863 with cancer in the breast

Mrs. Amanda M. Auld, wife of Thomas Auld, d. 13 Feb 1874

Mrs. Arianna Amanda Sears, dau. of Capt. Thomas and Lucretia P. Auld, and wife of John L. Sears, d. at her residence in Baltimore on Thurs. evening 31 Jan 1878

CHARLES W. BAKER BIBLE

Bible published in 1872 by A. J. Holman & Co., 930 Arch Street, Philadelphia, PA. Family data gleaned from a typescript at the Maryland Historical Society.

Marriages:

Charles W. Baker and Emma F. Michael m. 11 Jun 1874
Pendleton Tevis Baker and Ethel Lee Ridgely m. 19 Nov 1903
Frank E. Baker and Edith C. Kimmell m. 31 Oct 1905
A. Lynn Baker and Reba Charshee m. 19 Jan 1915
Beulah Baker and J. Victor Adams m. 26 Aug 1918
Frank S. Baker and Edythe Rogers m. 11 Oct 1917
Charles W. Baker and Susan O. Pritchard m. 29 Jan 1914
Emerson Baker and Nancy Worthington m. 19 Jul 1941
Margaret Grace Baker and Dick Liles m. 27 Sep 1941
Charles W. Baker and Barbara Harward m. 24 Apr 1944
Ridgely Baker and Helen Wescott m. 28 Apr 1945
Helen Baker and Peter Kendrick Kelly m. 7 Apr 1926
Emma Baker and Kai Rasmussen m. 16 Aug 1930
Frances Adele Baker and Harry Addison Bechtol m. 2 Dec 1950

Births:
Children of C. W. and Emma F. Baker:
1. Pendleton Tevis Baker, b. 11 Aug 1875
2. Frank Emerson Baker, b. 13 Oct 1877
3. Beulah Baker, b. 10 Dec 1886
4. Austin Lynn Baker, b. 9 Nov 1893

Children of P. T. and E. R. Baker:
1. Helen Lee Baker, b. 1 Aug 1905
2. Emma Franklin Baker, b. 2 Nov 1907
3. Ridgely Baker, b. 2 Apr 1911
4. Charles Winfield Baker, b. 9 Feb 1921

Children of Frank E. and Edythe R. Baker:
1. Frances Baker, b. 30 Dec 1918
2. Margaret Grace Baker, b. 28 Jan 1924

Children of Emma and Kai Rasmussen:
1. Ann Baker Rasmussen, b. 27 Dec 1931
2. Kai Rasmussen, Jr., b. 26 Nov 1937

Children of Helen and P. K. Kelly:
1. John Luke Kelly, b. 7 Oct 1934
2. Mary Lee Kelly, b. 2 Mar 1943

Children of Ridgely and Helen Baker:
1. Ann Ridgely Baker, b. 13 Aug 1948
2. Gwendolyn Wescott Baker, b. 11 Nov 1950

Children of Harry and Frances Bechtol:
1. Carol Ann Bechtol, b. 2 Mar 1952
2. Eleanor Marie Bechtol, b. 20 Sep 1954
C. Emerson Baker, son of F. E. and E. C. Baker, b. 11 Jul 1907

Marion Lynn Baker, dau. of A. Lynn and Reba Baker, b. 6 Mar 1917

Joan Worthington, dau. of Emerson and Mary Worthington, b. 20 May 1943

Alton Bruce MacDonald, son of A. Bruce and Marian Baker MacDonald, b. 18 Sep 1945

Ann Elizabeth Baker, dau. of Emerson and Nancy Baker, b. 5 Aug 1946

Susan Baker Liles, dau. of John Richardson and Margaret Grace Liles, b. 9 Jul 1947

Patricia Vandergrift Baker, dau. of Charles and Barbara Baker, b. 31 Mar 1951

Neal Pendleton Baker, b. 27 Nov 1954

Deaths:
Emma F. Baker, wife of Charles W. Baker, d. 19 Aug 1907
Charles W. Baker, d. 18 Jun 1918
Edith C. Baker, wife of Frank E. Baker, d. 21 Aug 1907
P. Tevis Baker, husband of Ethel Ridgely Baker, d. 19 Apr 1943
Frank E. Baker, husband of Edythe A. Baker, d. 12 Jul 1957
Beulah Baker Adams, wife of J. Victor Adams, d. 22 Oct 1953

JOHN HANSON BAKER BIBLE

Bible published by American Bible Company, 621 S. 11th Street, Philadelphia, PA (undated). The cover is inscribed "E. J. Smith." Family data gleaned from a typescript at the Maryland Historical Society.

Marriage:
John H. Baker and Miss Lizzie J. Smith m. 27 Feb 1873 at the bride's residence by Rev. B. Peyton Brown in the presence of James L. Carmine and Susie E. Baker.

Births:
John Hanson Baker, son of Elizabeth and George W. Baker, b. 21 Sep 1849

Elizabeth Jane Smith, dau. of William J. and Margaret B. Smith, b. 19 Feb 1853

Children of John H. and Elizabeth J. Baker:
1. Viola Estelle Baker, b. 13 Dec 1873
2. Margaret Littleton Baker, b. 27 Aug 1786
3. Warren LeRoy Baker, b. 29 Nov 1878
4. William Reid Baker, b. 28 Mar 1886

Helen Elizabeth Pyle, dau. of G. P. and Viola E. Pyle, b. 14 Feb 1897 (originally written 1896)

Deaths:
William Reid Baker, son of John H. and Elizabeth J. Baker, d. 19 Jul 1887

Elizabeth Jane Baker, wife of J. H. Baker, d. 29 May 1892

John Hanson Baker, husband of Elizabeth Smith and Katie Kimmel Baker, d. 1 May 1930

Viola Estelle Baker, wife of Granville P. Pyle, d. 12 Mar 1949

Warren LeRoy Baker, husband of Mary Albaugh, d. 13 Jul 1954

Margaret B. Baldwin, wife of William J. Baldwin, d. 3 Jul 1955

Family Records:
"Portrait section contains three unidentified portraits and notations in blank spaces: Wm. J. Smith, Margaret Hand[?] Smith, parents of Lizzie Baker; Elizabeth Greenland Baker, mother of John H. Baker.

NICHOLAS BAKER BIBLE

No publication information available. Family data gleaned from a typescript at the Maryland Historical Society. Bible originally owned by Nicholas Baker, Jr. of Harford County.

Marriages:
Nicholas Baker and Elizabeth Carsins m. 2 Nov 1837
Nicholas Baker and Mary B. Greenland m. 12 Apr 1859
Charles H. Baker and Martha F. Mills m. ---- [date not given]

John C. Baker and Martha L. C. Wells m. 5 Dec ---- [*Ed. Note:* Their marriage certificate states John C. Baker and Mattie C. Wells m. 5 Dec 1867].

Frank F. Bruce and Mary J. Baker m. 20 Jun 1871
Martin L. Gilbert and Sarah F. Baker m. 13 Dec 1877
George H. Baker and Libbie Wells m. 29 Oct 1879

[*Ed. Note:* The marriage record was not shown in the bible, but Elizabeth Baker married George T. Everist circa 11 Apr 1859 (date of license) in Harford County. Their children are listed below].

Births:
Nicholas Baker, son of Nicholas and Elizabeth Baker, b. 27 Jan 1810
Elizabeth Carsins, b. 13 Sep 1819

Children of Nicholas and Elizabeth Baker:
1. Elizabeth Ann Baker, b. 18 Aug 1839
2. John Carsins Baker, b. 18 Jun 1841
3. Charles Henry Baker, b. 6 Mar 1843
4. Mary Jane Baker, b. 29 Jan 1845
5. ---- Baker (unnamed), b. 21 Sep 1846
6. George Hildt Baker, b. 13 Aug 1850

Children of Nicholas and Mary B. Baker:
1. Winfield Lee Baker, b. 12 Apr 1861
2. Edmund Monroe Baker, b. 26 Jul 1859
Children of George and Elizabeth Everist:
1. Elmer N. Everist, b. 25 May 1864
2. Mary Oleita Everist, b. 8 Sep 1869
3. Ellen E. Everist, b. 7 Oct 1872
4. Ava M. and Annie Everist, b. 6 Apr 1874

5. Lily J. Everist, b. 2 May 1876
6. George C. Everist, b. 12 Aug 1879

George T. Everist, b. 13 Sep 1833

Harry Baker, son of F. P. and Mary J. Baker, b. 21 Nov 1872

Deaths:
Elizabeth Baker, wife of Nicholas Baker, d. 27 Feb 1853
Edmund Monroe Baker, son of Nicholas and Mary Baker, d. 1 Feb 1871

Children of Nicholas and Elizabeth Baker:
1. Mary Jane Bruce, d. 5 Jan 1873
2. Charles Henry Baker, d. 23 Jul 1875
3. Sarah Frances Gilbert, d. 2 Jul 1878
4. George Hildt Baker, d. 7 Sep 1880

BARNES-HUGHES BIBLE

Bible published by Hubbard Brothers, Philadelphia, PA (date not indicated). Family data gleaned from a typescript at the Maryland Historical Society.

Marriages:
Clifford Colfax Barnes and Hannah Elizabeth Hughes m. 28 Aug 1902 at Grove Presbyterian Church in Aberdeen, Harford County, MD.

Morgan Mitchell Hughes and ---- m. 19 Jan 1900 [*Ed. Note:* "The Hughes Genealogy" by Renna Craig Ambrose (p. 27) states Morgan Mitchell Hughes married Jesse Bruce Fulton].

William Oliver Hughes, Jr. and ---- m. 20 Oct 1909 [*Ed. Note:* "The Hughes Genealogy" by Renna Craig Ambrose (p. 27) states William Oliver Hughes, Jr. married Ellen Belle Hunter].

Kate Silver Hughes and ---- m. 12 Feb 1908 [*Ed. Note:* "The Hughes Genealogy" by Renna Craig Ambrose (p. 27) states Kate Silver Hughes married Samuel Rickey Mitchell].

Robert Leslie Hughes and ---- m. 12 Jan 1915 [*Ed. Note:* Their marriage license dated 11 Jan 1915 states R. Leslie Hughes married Mabel C. Mitchell].

Robert Fulton Hughes and ---- m. 5 Aug 1926 [*Ed. Note:* Their marriage license dated 4 Aug 1926 states Robert Fulton Hughes of Aberdeen, MD, married Helen Gertrude Schrader of Washington, PA. "The Hughes Genealogy" by Renna Craig Ambrose (p. 55) spells her last name "Schroeder"].

Joseph Lee Hughes and ---- m. 1 Jan 1936 [*Ed. Note:* Their marriage certificate states Joseph Lee Hughes of Perryman, MD, married Elizabeth Odessa Johnson of Perryman, MD].

Amos Hollis Hughes and ---- m. -- May 1924 [*Ed. Note:* "The Hughes Genealogy" by Renna Craig Ambrose (p. 56) states Amos Hollis Hughes married Frances Marian Hayes on 27 May 1924].

Harry Edmund Mitchell and ---- m. 21 Jun 1933 [*Ed. Note:* "The Hughes Genealogy" by Renna Craig Ambrose (p. 56) states Harry Edmund Mitchell married Alma Blake and she was his first wife].

Edith C. Mitchell and ---- m. 7 Jun 1947 [*Ed. Note:* "The Hughes Genealogy" by Renna Craig Ambrose (p. 56) states Edith Catherine Mitchell married Norman Earl Tindal].

William Oliver Hughes and Estelle Morgan m. 12 Sep 1873

Births:
[Children of William O. and Estelle Hughes]:
1. Frank Lee Hughes, b. at Lapidum, 14 Apr 1874
2. Hannah E. Hughes, b. at Lapidum, 26 Aug 1876
3. John Adams Hughes, b. at Rock Run, 14 Nov 1878
4. Morgan Mitchell Hughes, b. at Rock Run, 23 Jan 1881
5. William Oliver Hughes, Jr., b. at Rock Run, 11 Apr 1883
6. Kate Silver Hughes, b. at Lapidum, 15 May 1885
7. Robert Leslie Hughes, b. at Lapidum, 6 Jul 1886
8. George VanBibber Hughes, b. at Lapidum, 7 Jul 1887

[Children of Morgan M. and Jesse B. Hughes]:
1. Robert Fulton Hughes, b. at Aberdeen, 17 Apr 1902
2. Joseph Lee Hughes, b. at Aberdeen, 4 Feb 1904
3. Amos Hollis Hughes, b. at Spesutia, 23 Sep 1905
4. Jesse Bruce Hughes, b. at Havre de Grace, 2 Aug 1907

Harry Edmund Hughes, b. at Boothby Hill, 25 Sep 1910
Jessie Fulton Hughes, b. at Philadelphia, 19 Dec 1878
Francis H. Hughes, b. ---- [date not given]
A. Hollis Hughes, b. at Washington, PA, 11 Aug 1925
Donald Hughes, b. ---- [date not given]
Rosella Jessie Hughes, b. 10 May 1930
William Oliver Hughes, b. 19 Sep 1843
Odessa Hughes, b. 24 Jun 1913
Sandra Sue Hughes, b. 6 Apr 1939
Jo Ann Hughes, b. 10 May 1942

Edith C. Mitchell, b. at Aberdeen, 7 Oct 1920
Shirley Blake Mitchell, b. at Havre de Grace, 16 Jun 1934

Estelle Morgan, b. at Aberdeen, 11 Sep 1853

William Colfax Barnes, b. at Belcamp, 3 May 1908
Estelle B. Barnes, b. at Bradshaw, 15 Mar 1911
Richard Amos Barnes, b. at Baltimore, 25 Jul 1912
Mary Elizabeth Barnes, b. at Boothby Hill, 31 Jul 1912
Beverly L. Barnes, b. at Joppa, ---- [date not given]

Deaths:
Morgan Mitchell, d. 8 Dec 1908
George VanBibber Hughes, d. 29 Nov 1888
Jesse Bruce Hughes, d. 15 Aug 1907
Jessie Fulton Hughes, d. 1 Feb 1911
Hannah E. Hughes, d. 16 Mar 1919
Estelle Morgan Hughes, d. 2 Dec 1927
Frank Lee Hughes, d. 28 Aug 1932
William Oliver Hughes, d. 11 Sep 1935
Odessa Hughes, d. 1 Jan 1936
John Adams Hughes, d. 21 Mar 1936
William Oliver Hughes, Jr., d. 11 Aug 1947

Mary Elizabeth Barnes, d. 17 Aug 1912

RICHARD BARNES BIBLE

Bible published in 1809 by Mathew Carey, 122 Market Street, Philadelphia. Inscribed on first page: "Richard Barnes, Sr., his Bible, 1 Sep 1811. Price: $9.00." Family data gleaned from a typescript at the Maryland Historical Society.

Marriages:
Richard Barnes and Sarah Gilbert m. 19 Dec 1782
Richard Barnes and Mary Bayless m. 25 Feb 1812
Asael Bayley and Polly Barnes m. 3 Mar 1808
Mordecai G. Barns and Sarah Bailey m. 1 Jan 1818
Richard Barns and Susannah Osborn m. 24 Jan 1832
Aquila E. Treadway and Sarah A. Barnes m. 14 Jun 1855
Richard A. Barnes and Frances Noble m. 14 Mar 1861
Richard A. Barnes and Mary V. Parker m. 7 Nov 1894
Wilmer L. Barnes and Ellen R. Chesney m. 7 Jun 1894
Clifford C. Barnes and Hannah E. Hughes m. 28 Aug 1902
Charles F. Barnes and Minnie Eason m. 14 Nov 1907
Asael Bailey and Mary ---- m. 3 Mar 1808 [*Ed. Note:* Asael Bailey and Mary Barnes obtained a marriage license in Harford County on 29 Feb 1808].

Births:
Children of Richard and Sarah Barns:
1. Winstone Barns, b. 5 Sep 1784
2. Mary Barns, b. 7 Sep 1787
3. Mordecai G. Barns, b. 13 Aug 1791
4. Elizabeth Barns, b. 16 Jun 1795
5. Richard Barns, Jr., b. 24 Jan 1805

Richard Barns, Sr., b. 4 Oct 1767
Averilla Barns, b. 6 Dec 1759
Susannah Barns, wife of Richard Barns, Jr., b. 4 Jun 1808

Children of Gregory and Elizabeth Barns:
1. Ford Barns, b. 4 Apr 1761
2. Richard Barns, b. 25 Jun 1762
3. Rachel Barns, b. 23 Mar 1764
4. Gregory Barns, b. 17 Dec 1765
5. Mary Barns, b. 14 Jun 1767
6. Sarah Barns, b. 6 Mar 1769
7. Farmer Barns, b. 25 Apr 1772
8. John Barns, b. 5 May 1774, d. -- Mar 1778

9. Arabella Barns, b. 6 Dec 1775, d. 12 Mar 1819
10. Elizabeth Barns, b. 30 Aug 1778
11. Ann Barns, b. 4 Apr 1782

Children of Mordecai G. and Sarah Barns:
1. Elizabeth Barns, b. 14 Jan 1819
2. Winstone Barns, b. 24 Jul 1820
3. Richard Barnes, b. 27 Mar 1822
4. Edwin Barnes, b. 4 Dec 1823
5. Sarah Barnes, b. 5 Jan 1832, d. about 1912
6. Asail Barnes, b. about 1838

Children of Richard and Susannah Barnes:
1. Sarahann Barnes, b. 6 Dec 1832
2. Richard Amos Barnes, b. 12 Feb 1834
3. Mary Barnes, b. 16 Apr 1835, d. 17 Jul 1835
4. William Harrison Barnes, b. 21 Feb 1837, d. 19 Aug 1837
5. Mary Elizabeth Barnes, b. 29 Dec 1838
6. William Henry Barnes, b. 3 Nov 1840
7. Frances Cordelia Barnes, b. 21 Jul 1843

Children of Aquila E. and Sarah A. Treadway:
1. Ellen B. Treadway, b. 19 Mar 1860
2. Clayton Seward Treadway, b. 9 Apr 1862, d. 11 Feb 1865

Children of Richard A. and Frances Barnes:
1. Wilmer Lewis Barnes, b. 4 Apr 1862
2. Charles Barnes, b. 27 Jun 1865
3. Clifford C. Barnes, b. 19 May 1868

Children of Wilmer L. and Ellen R. Barnes:
1. Richard Randolph Barnes, b. 25 Feb 1896, d. 11 Aug 1896
2. Wilmer Noble Barnes, b. 22 Aug 1902

Children of Clifford C. and Hannah E. Barnes:
1. William Colfax Barnes, b. 3 May 1908
2. Estelle B. Barnes, b. ---- [date not given]
3. Richard A. Barnes, b. ---- [date not given]
4. Beverly L. Barnes, b. 12 Mar 1914

Children of Asael and Mary Bailey:
1. Elizabeth Bailey, b. 10 Dec 1808
2. William Bailey, b. 29 Sep 1816
3. James H. Bailey, b. 10 May 1820
4. Charles L. Bailey, b. 14 Nov 1824

Aquila E. Treadway, b. 4 Apr 1826

Frances Barnes, wife of Richard A. Barnes, b. 18 Jul 1829
Frances Eason Barnes, dau. of Charles F. and Amelia Gertrude Barnes, b. 26 Mar 1909
Elizabeth R. Barnes, dau. of Charles F. and Minnie E. Barnes, b. 19 Feb 1912

Deaths:
John Barns, d. -- Mar 1778
Arabella Barns, d. 12 Mar 1819
Gregory Barns, Sr., d. 26 Mar 1808
Ford Barns, d. 5 Feb 1798
Sarah Barns, wife of Richard Barns, d. Wed. morning at 7 o'clock on 13 Feb 1811 in the 49th year of her age

Winstone Barns, son of Richard and Sarah Barns, d. 12 Aug 1796, age 11 years, 11 months and 7 days
Elizabeth Barns, dau. of Richard and Sarah Barns, d. 24 Nov 1801, age 6 years, 5 months and 1 week
Richard Barns, Sr., d. Mon. morning at 5 o'clock and 40 minutes, 29 Nov 1830, age 68 years, 5 months and 4 days
Mary Barns, wife of Richard Barns, Sr., d. 8 Dec 1848 in the 81st year of her age

Elizabeth Barnes, wife of Gregory Barnes, Sr., d. Wed., 18 Apr 1832 in the 93rd year of her age
Gregory Barnes, d. 6 Nov 1846 in the 81st year of his age
Richard Barnes, Sr., d. Mon. evening, 10 Sep 1840, age 44 years, 7 months and 17 days
Mordecai G. Barnes, d. 30 Apr 1866 in the 75th year of her age
Sarah Barnes, wife of Mordecai G. Barnes, d. 23 Aug 1873 in the 81st year of her age
Susan Barnes, wife of Richard Barnes, d. 27 Oct 1892, age 84 years, 4 months and 23 days

Mary Barnes, d. 17 Jul 1835
William Harrison Barnes, d. 19 Aug 1837
Winston Barnes, son of Mordecai G. and Sarah Barnes, d. 5 Nov 1863
Edwin Barnes, son of Mordecai and Sarah Barnes, d. 1882
Frances Barnes, wife of R. A. Barnes, d. 17 Dec 1887
Richard Barnes, son of Mordecai and Sarah Barnes, d. 20 Mar 1893
Richard Randolph Barnes, son of Wilmer and Ellen R. Barnes, d. -- Aug 1896
Frances Barnes, wife of Richard A. Barnes, d. 17 Dec 1887
Hannah E. Barnes, wife of Clifford C. Barnes, d. 19 Mar 1919
Sarah Barnes, d. about 1912
William Henry Barnes, d. 21 Jul 1928
Frances Cordelia Barnes, d. 21 Feb 1906 in her 63rd year
Richard Amos Barnes, d. 21 May 1913 in his 80th year
Mary E. Barnes, d. 31 Aug 1918 in her 80th year

Elizabeth Fletcher, dau. of Mordecai G. and Sarah Barnes, d. 25 Apr 1882

Aquila E. Treadway, d. 9 Nov 1887
Sarah Ann Treadway, wife of Aquila E. Treadway and dau. of Richard and Susanna Barnes, d. 25 Aug 1901 in her 69th year

Ellen Barnes Treadway, dau. of Aquila E. and Sarah A. Treadway, d. 3 Oct 1906 in her 47th year
Clayton Seward Treadway, son of A. E. Treadway and Sarah A. Barnes, d. -- Feb 1865
Asael Bailey, d. at 7 o'clock in the evening on 21 Sep 1825, age 47 years and 22 days [*Ed. Note:* Another entry in the bible stated he was aged 47 years, 3 weeks and 3 days].
Mary Bailey, wife of Asael Bailey, d. about 5 o'clock in the afternoon on 3 Sep 1828, age 41 years wanting 4 days.

Elizabeth Bailey, d. -- Feb 1854
William A. Bailey, d. 3 Mar 1873
J. Harvey Bailey, d. 22 Jul 1883
Charles L. Bailey, d. 2 Jun 1895

JOHN BAUER BIBLE

No publication information available (title page missing). Family data gleaned from a typescript at the Maryland Historical Society.

Marriages:

John Bauer, of Harford County, MD, and Sarah Jane Clayton, of Baltimore County, MD, m. 10 Feb 1862 by Rev. I. Mapier Husted in the presence of James M. Magraw and Henry Bauer. [*Ed. Note:* A marriage license was issued to John Bauer and Sarah Jane Claydon *[sic]* on 8 Feb 1862 in Harford County].

J. W. Bauer and Alice French m. -- Jan ---- [no date]
Nannie Bauer and J. M. Anderson m. Sat., 10 Nov 1887 in Baltimore

George H. Bauer and Lydia Jones m. ---- [*Ed. Note:* George H. Bauer, age 24, of Baltimore City, and Lydia E. Jones, age 27, of Harford County, obtained a marriage license in Harford County on 20 Feb 1889].

Alverta Bauer and Chapin Alexander Ferguson m. 28 Nov 1900
Hettie Bauer and Dr. Francis Herbert Poole m. 27 Apr 19--
Lawrence S. Bauer and Mary Ford m. ---- [no date]
John Milton Bauer and Frances Barnard m. 9 Dec 1912
Bessie Mae Anderson and Howard L. A. Border m. 29 Nov 1911
Effie O. Anderson and W. Edgar Rhodes m. 21 Jun 1914
Rebecca May Bauer and Murray V. Lawder m. 1915

Births:
John Bauer, b. 16 Mar 1834 in Lauterbach, Hessen Darmstadt, Germany
Sarah Jane (Clayton) Bauer, b. 6 Nov 1836 in Baltimore County, MD

Children of John and Sarah Jane Bauer:
(All were born in Bel Air, MD)
1. John William Bauer, b. 15 Oct 1862
2. George Henry Bauer, b. 3 Mar 1864
3. Clara May Bauer, b. 24 May 1866
4. Nanny Bauer, b. 19 Nov 1867
5. Lena Jane Bauer, b. 13 Nov 1869
6. Mary Bauer, b. -- Jun 1871
7. Hettie Bauer, b. 23 Oct 1872
8. Alverta Bauer, b. 6 Feb 1875
9. James Fulton Bauer, b. 16 Feb 1878
10. Effie Bauer, b. 25 Nov 1879

Lawrence Edward Bauer, b. Thurs., 23 Sep 1887, 12:30 a.m.
John Milton Bauer, b. Sat., 15 Mar 1890
Rebecca May Bauer, b. Sat., 30 Jul 1893, 12:30 p.m.
Howard Andrew Bauer, b. 27 Feb 1894
Linwood French Bauer, b. Sat., 19 Sep ----
Arthur Lee Clayton Bauer, b. ---- [blank]

Effie Ogilvin Anderson, b. Sat., 3 Nov 1888, 8 a.m.
Bessie Mae Anderson, b. 27 Feb 1892, 8:20 a.m.
Jane Currie Anderson, b. 8 Jan 1906, Baltimore

Sarah Frances Ferguson, b. 26 Oct 1901
Chapin Alexander Ferguson, b. 28 Nov 1902

William Clayton Poole, b. 6 Feb 1905
John Knox Poole, b. 2 Dec 1906

Deaths:
Mary Bauer, d. -- Aug 1871
Effie Bauer, d. Fri., 22 Feb 1884
George Henry Bauer, d. Fri., 22 Apr 1892
John Bauer, d. Sat., 12 Oct 1907, 11:30 p.m.
Sarah Jane Bauer, d. Fri., 12 Oct 1894, 10:55 a.m.

THOMAS C. BAYARD BIBLE

No publication information available. Family data gleaned from a typescript at the Maryland Historical Society.

Marriages:
[*Ed. Note:* None were listed in the bible, but Catherine Bayard, widow of Thomas C. Bayard, m. Thomas Davis on 18 Nov 1860 in Harford County; marriage license obtained on 17 Nov 1860].

Births:
Thomas C. Bayard, b. 19 Nov 1819
Catherine L. Bayard, b. 18 Aug 1827

Children of Thomas and Catherine Bayard:
1. Lewis H. Bayard, b. 15 Apr 1851
2. Samuel T. Bayard, b. 18 Jan 1853
3. Catharine A. Bayard, b. 22 Aug 1857
Emma Davis, b. 4 Oct 1871
Onidia Davis, b. 14 Sep 1864
George H. Howlett, son of Richard and Annie Howlett, b. 6 Nov 1868

Deaths:
Thomas C. Bayard, d. 12 Jun 1858
Catherine Davis, wife of Thomas Bayard, d. at noon on 26 Jan 1910

Children of Thomas and Catherine Bayard:
1. Lewis H. Bayard, d. 15 Jan 1865
2. Samuel T. Bayard, d. 15 Mar 1873

Margaret Annie Howlett, wife of Richard Howlett, d. at 3 o'clock in the morning on 23 Apr 1909

JOHN S. BEAVEN BIBLE

Family data gleaned from a typescript at the Maryland Historical Society. Written at top of transcript: "Holman Bible, 1887."

Marriages:
John Sterrett Beaven and Emma Elizabeth Stebbing m. 4 Nov 1886
Arthur Beaven and Elsie A. Patterson m. 17 Nov 1915 by Rev. F. X. Moore
Walter Crothers Beaven and Bertha L. Mitchell m. 21 Dec 1916
Sterrett Patterson Beaven, grandson of Emma Elizabeth and John Sterrett Beaven, and Doris May Susemihl m. 2 Jun 1942 by Rev. Hugo Schroeder

Births:
John Sterrett Beaven, b. 25 May 1860
Emma Elizabeth Beaven, b. 2 Sep 1862

Children of John S. and Emma E. Beaven:
1. Arthur Beaven, b. 16 Sep 1887, bapt. 18 Oct 1887 by Rev. Barrett
2. Walter Crothers, b. 23 Aug 1889, bapt. 21 Jul 1890 by Rev. J. P. Otis

Death:
John Sterrett Beaven, d. 31 May 1937, age 77 years and 6 days

JOHN W. BEAVEN BIBLE

No publication information available. Family data gleaned from a typescript at the Maryland Historical Society. Written at top of the transcript: "Lippincott Bible 1857 of John Wood Beaven - emigr. 1852."

Marriages:
John W. Beaven and Mary Jane Sterrett m. 21 Jan 1852
Margaret Rachel Beaven and Alonzo McNulty m. 23 May 1876
John Sterrett Beaven and Emma Elizabeth Stebbing m. 4 Nov 1886

Births:
John W. Beaven, b. 14 Jan 1821
Mary Jane Sterrett, b. -- Aug 1819

Children of John W. and Mary J. Beaven:
1. Margaret Rachel Beaven, b. 14 Jan 1855
2. Sarah Elizabeth Beaven, b. 23 Jun 1857
3. John Sterrett Beaven, b. 25 May 1860

Harry Beaven McNulty, son of Margaret and Alonzo McNulty, b. 13 Mar 1879

Deaths:
Sarah Elizabeth Beaven, dau. of John W. and Mary J. Beaven, d. 24 Dec 1861
Mary Jane Beaven, wife of John W. Beaven, d. 8 Aug 1891
John W. Beaven, d. 14 Jan 1895
John Sterrett Beaven, d. 31 May 1937

John Sterrett, father of Mary Jane (Sterrett) Beaven, d. 13 Dec 1871, age 82

Alonzo McNulty, husband of Margaret Beaven, d. 6 Dec 1881
Margaret Beaven McNulty, d. 10 Oct 1897
Harry Beaven McNulty, son of Margaret McNulty, d. 29 Mar 1898

BILLINGSLEY-SHERTZER BIBLE

Bible published in 1870 by The National Publishing Company, Ziegler & McCurdy, Jones Brothers & Company, and M. A. Parker & Company. A transcript was published in the *Maryland Genealogical Society Bulletin* (Vol. 23, No. 2) in Spring, 1982.

Marriages:

Paul A. Moore, of Kingsville, MD, and Alma Billingsley, of Perry Hall, MD, m. 22 Jun 1913 at St. John's Rectory, Kingsville, MD

Price I. Shertzer, of Bel Air, MD, and Myrtle Billingsley, of Perry Hall, MD, m. 28 Sep 1911 at the M. E. Parsonage, Gardenville, MD

Guy Lee Upperco, of Baltimore, and Marian E. Shertzer m. 10 Oct 1934 at Lutheran Church, Ellicott City, MD

Martin W. Krepp, Jr. and Alma Shertzer m. 14 Jun 1841 at Overlea M. E. Church

Price L. Shertzer and Lola Kittridge m. Fri., 19 Sep 1948 at St. John's Methodist Church, Hamilton, MD

Theodore P. Shertzer and Linda Kreisel m. 8 Aug 1971 at Zion Lutheran Church

Norman L. Shertzer and Nancy B. Canapp m. 18 Jun 1972 at Kenwood Presbyterian Church

Debra Lee Shertzer and Lee B. Hohlbein m. 23 Sep 1974 at Overlea U. M. Church

Denise L. Shertzer and Richard A. Brewer m. 23 Sep 1974 at Overlea U. M. Church

Births:
Paul C. Moore, d. 17 May 1913, Bel Air, MD

Marian Elizabeth Shertzer, b. 6 Aug 1916, Perry Hall, MD
Alma Mildred Shertzer, b. Sat., 13 Jul 1918, Perry Hall, MD
Price Leslie Shertzer, b. Sat., 20 Aug 1927, Perry Hall, MD
Theodore Price Shertzer, b. 15 Jun 1949 at MD General Hospital
Leslie Norman Shertzer, b. 20 Dec 1950 at MD General Hospital
Debra Lee Shertzer, b. 18 Aug 1953 at MD General Hospital
Denise Lynn Shertzer, b. 28 Sep 1954 at MD General Hospital
Diane Lisa Shertzer, b. 3 Aug 1957 at MD General Hospital
Norman Edward Shertzer, son of Norman and Nancy Shertzer, b. 28 Dec 1973 at MD General Hospital

Lee Dixon Upperco, b. Wed., 19 Jan 1938 at 5:20 a.m. at West Baltimore General Hospital
Leslie Martin Upperco, b. Sun., 25 Oct 1942 at 8:15 p.m. at St. Joseph's Hospital
Karen Elizabeth Upperco, b. 8 Mar 1945 at St. Joseph's Hospital

Martin W. Krepp, III, b. Wed., 10 May 1943 at 11:59 p.m. at Maryland General Hospital
Patricia Lynn Krepp, b. Fri., 10 Oct 1947 at 6:45 p.m. at Maryland General Hospital

Deaths:
David G. Billingsley, d. 16 Feb 1905 in his 47th year
Mattie E. Billingsley, d. Thurs., 15 Feb 1945 at 9:10 a.m., age 80, and bur. Sun., 18 Feb 1945 at 2 p.m. at North Bend Cemetery
Daisey L. Billingsley, d. 17 Jul 1955
John Billingsley, d. 27 Jul 1959
S. Streett Billingsley, d. 15 Mar 1961
Clarence Billingsley, d. 19 Nov 1969

Paul A. Moore, d. Thurs., 17 Oct 1918 at 12:45 a.m. and bur. Sat., 19 Oct 1918 at 2:30 p.m.
Alma Billingsley Moore, d. 6 Feb 1974

James Ayres, husband of Mattie E., d. 8 Nov 1943 and bur. 11 Nov 1943 at 11 a.m. at Cooptown Church

Price I. Shertzer, d. 9 Apr 1957

WILLIAM R. BISSELL BIBLE

Holy Bible by Hervery Wilbur, A.M., American Bible Society; stereotyped by James Conner, New York; published by N. &. J. White, 108 Pearl Street, New York, in 1833. Family data gleaned from a typescript at the Maryland Historical Society.

Marriages:
William R. Bissell and Margaret Webster m. 11 Sep 1834
Elizabeth Rombaugh Bissell, dau. of William and Margaret Bissell, and William S. Richardson m. 8 Feb 1864

John Holland and Rachel Virginia Bissell m. 17 Dec 1871
Joseph S. Baldwin and Nannie Bissell m. 9 Dec 1874
Benjamin Bissell and Bessie A. Henshaw m. 18 Oct 1876
Mary Jarrett Bissell and John N. Wilkinson m. 13 Feb 1884
Hargraves Spalding and Martha Wilkinson Bissell m. 18 Nov 1885

Births:
William Rombaugh Bissell, b. 19 Aug 1811
Margaret Bissell, wife of William Bissell, b. 13 Dec 1817

Children of William and Margaret Bissell:
1. Elizabeth Rombough Bissell, b. 24 Jul 1835
2. John Adams Webster Bissell, b. 27 Oct 1837
3. Margaret Ann Bissell, b. 18 Dec 1842
4. Rachel Virginia Bissell, b. 6 Aug 1845
5. William Thomas Bissell, b. 31 Oct 1847
6. Benjamin Bissell, b. 31 Dec 1852
7. John Adams Bissell, b. 14 Dec 1854
8. Josephine D. Bissell, b. 19 Mar 1856
9. Martha Wilkinson Bissell, b. 21 Aug 1859
10. Mary Jarrett Bissell, b. 30 Nov 1861

Children of William and Elizabeth Bissell:
1. William Bissell, b. 12 Nov 1864
2. John Adams Webster Bissell, b. 31 Jul 1866
Children of William and Georgia Bissell:
1. Mary Lillie Bissell, b. 21 Aug 1872
2. William Ridgely Bissell, b. 28 Jul 1874
3. Margaret Webster Bissell, b. 19 Sep 1876
4. Emma Walker Bissell, b. ---- [blank]
5. Wilson Cleveland Bissell, b. 4 Mar 1885

Children of William and Elizabeth Richardson:
1. Elihu Hall Richardson, b. 5 Nov 1867
2. Bessie May Bissell, b. 8 Apr 1876
Children of Joseph S. and Nannie Baldwin:
1. Blanche Paxton Baldwin, b. 6 Oct 1875
2. Joseph Salling Baldwin, b. 25 May 1877
3. Nannie Bissell Baldwin [#1], b. 1 Apr 1879
4. Nannie Bissell Baldwin [#2], b. 26 May ----

Children of Benjamin and Bessie Bissell:
1. Bessie Webster Bissell, b. 19 Feb 1878
2. Benjamin Bissell, b. 13 Oct 1879
3. Phoebe Ann Bissell, b. 8 Oct 1881
4. Fannie Henshaw Bissell, b. 13 Nov 1883
5. William Jacques Bissell, b. 30 Aug 1885
6. Harry Reiche Bissell, b. -- Dec 1888

Children of John N. and Mary J. Wilkinson:
1. Mary Archer Wilkinson, b. 17 Sep 1885
2. John Nicholas Wilkinson, b. 4 Jun 1889

Children of Hargraves and Martha Spalding:
[*Ed. Note:* Her name was also listed as "Mattie"]
1. William Hargraves Spalding, b. 13 Mar 1887
2. Basil Dennis Spalding, b. 13 Jul 1890
3. Martha Bissell Spalding, b. 21 Apr 1892
4. Elizabeth Rombough Spalding, b. 30 Apr 1894
5. Margaret Webster Spalding, b. 3 Apr 1899

Elizabeth Webster, dau. of ---- [blank]

Oletia Holland, dau. of John and R. Virginia Holland, b. 29 Nov 1866

Elihu Hall Richardson, son of E. Hall and Charlotte R. Richardson, b. 12 May 1896 in Bel Air

Deaths:
Children of William and Margaret Bissell:
1. John Adams Webster Bissell, d. 17 Jun 1839, age 7 years, 1 month and 21 days
2. John Adams Bissell, d. 25 Dec 1854, age 11 days

William R. Bissell, husband of Margaret Bissell, d. 17 Jul 1863 in his 52nd year
Oletia Holland, dau. of John and R. Virginia Holland, d. 23 May 1867, age 5 months and 24 days

--hn Holland, d. -- Aug 1867, age 30 [*Ed. Note:* "John" was handwritten in for his first name and "11" for the day he died in August, followed by "b. 14 Jan 1838, buried Churchville Pres."]

Nannie Bissell Baldwin, dau. of Joseph S. and Nannie Baldwin, d. 16 Apr 1879, age 16 days

Elizabeth R. Richardson, wife of William S. Richardson, d. 29 Oct 1890, age 55

William S. Richardson, husband of E. R. Richardson, d. -- Apr 1894 [*Ed. Note:* "23" was handwritten in for the day he died in April]

Children of William and Elizabeth Richardson:
1. William B. Richardson, d. -- May, 1894 [*Ed. Note:* "1" was handwritten in for the day he died in May]
2. E. Hall Richardson (son), d. ---- [blank]

E. Hall Richardson, Jr., son of W. H. and Charlotte E. Richardson, d. 6 Feb 1898

Margaret Bissell, wife of William R. Bissell, d. 12 Feb 1906, age 88

Benjamin Bissell, Jr., son of Benjamin and Bessie A. Bissell, d. -- Jan 1908

Dr. Joseph Baldwin, husband of Nannie Bissell, d. ---- 1914

Nannie Bissell Baldwin, wife of Joseph Baldwin, d. 1 Feb 1922
Joseph S. Baldwin, son of Nannie Bissell Baldwin, d. -- Feb 1922

Hargraves Spalding, husband of Mattie Bissell, d. 23 Jun 1926

William T. Bissell, d. -- Mar 1912
Mary Bissell Wilkinson, d. 9 May 1924
Virginia Bissell Holland, d. 25 Oct 1926
Josephine Dallam Bissell, d. 2 Dec 1928
Benjamin Bissell, d. 28 Sep 1930

HUGH BLAIR BIBLE

Bible published in 1704 by J. Nuttall, 21 Duke Street, Liverpool, England ("The Christian Complete Family Bible"). Family data gleaned from a typescript at the Maryland Historical Society.

Marriages:
James Blair and Jane Campbell m. 11 Feb 1817
Eliza Jane Blair and Rev. James L. Mackey m. ---- [no date]
Esabella WoodwardBlair and Clarkson H. West m. ---- [no date]
Alexander Ross Blair and Cassandra M. Small m. ---- [no date]

Births and Deaths:
Hugh Blair, b. 1 Mar 1706, d. 8 Jul 1796, age 90
Jane Ray, b. 11 Jul 1710, d. 4 Nov 1790, age 80
James Blair, b. 6 Dec 1730, d. 10 May 1798, age 64
Elizabeth Sparrow(?), b. 6 Jun 1731, d. 6 Aug 1791, age 60
John Blair, b. 5 Feb 1750, d. 6 Feb 1837, age 87
Jane Taggart, b. 25 Dec 1747, d. 31 Dec 1835, age 88, dau. of Fernando Taggart and Jane Knox
James Blair, b. 2 Feb 1790, d. 26 Oct 1877, age 87 years, 8 months and 24 days
Jane Campbell, b. 2 Jun 1793, d. 8 Nov 1871, age 78 years, 5 months and 6 days
Eliza Jane Blair, b. 18 Dec 1818, d. 11 Mar 1850, age 31 years, 2 months and 23 days, on the Island of Corsica in Africa
Ann Maria Blair, b. 16 Sep 1820, d. 18 Nov 1894
James Blair, b. 23 Jul 1822, d. 5 Feb 1839, age 16 years, 6 months and 12 days
Esabella Woodward Blair, 21 Jan 1824, d. 15 Feb 1914
Alexander Ross Blair, b. 25 Dec 1826, d. 16 Jul 1889
Margaret C. Blair, b. 25 Oct 1828, d. 24 Dec 1914, age 86
William E. Blair, b. 9 Feb 1830, d. 2 Nov 1894
Sarah Catherine Blair, b. 26 Nov 1832, d. 24 Dec 1835, age 3 years and 28 days
Elleanor Blair, b. 27 Nov 1834, d. 5 Sep 1836, age 1 year and 10 months
Thaddeus C. Blair, b. 27 Feb 1844, d. 19 Mar 1910

Edward Campbell, b. ---- [date not given]
Alexander Campbell, b. ---- [date not given]
Jane Campbell, b. ---- [date not given]
Mary Macready, b. ---- [date not given]
Jane Chambers, b. ---- [date not given]

Deaths:
Catherine Stout, dau. of Richard and Mary Stout, d. 7 May 1777, age 65
Charity Stout, d. 24 Jul 1778, age 36
John Stout, son of Josuf and Ruth Stout, d. at 10 o'clock at night on 27 Jul 1761, age 54 years, 10 months and 20 days

John Stout, Sr., son of Daniel and Charity Stout, d. 1 Aug 1778, age 11 years and 8 months

Polley Stout, dau. of Daniel and Charity Stout, d. 25 -- 1778, age 13 months and 6 days

Family Records:
Jane Chambers, the mother of Jane Campbell, was the dau. of John Chambers, and Jane Ross was the dau. of William Ross and Rebecca Orr.

Lancaster County: I hereby certify that John Blair, a native of Ireland, was naturalized in the Court of Common Pleas of this County on the 11th day of August 1802. Attest: R. S. Rouch, Prothonotary.

GEORGE W. BLANEY BIBLE

Bible published in 1881. Family data gleaned from a typescript at the Maryland Historical Society. Bible originally owned by George W. Blaney of The Rocks, Harford County.

Marriages:
George W. Blaney and Susan Jane Nagle m. 17 Mar 1870 in the presence of Thomas F. Nagle and Emma Blaney

Lester C. Blaney and Fannie Walton Hutcheson m. 4 Sep 1898 by Rev. C. N. Wolfe

Josias Bleany and Mary Streett m. 10 Apr 1801

Births and Deaths:
Elizabeth Nagle, b. ---- [date not given]
Emanuel Nagle, b. 14 Nov 1823, d. 7 Jan 1906

Julia Blaney, b. 11 Sep 1825, d. 5 Nov 1903
William J. Blaney, b. 28 Aug 1810, d. 5 Aug 1871
William T. Blaney, b. 16 Feb 1849, d. 9 Nov 1906
George David Blaney, b. 2 May, 1901, Granville, NY

Josias Bleany, b. 23 Jul 1776, d. 26 Nov 1823
Mary Streett, b. 5 Aug 1776, d. 4 May 1844

Children of Josias and Mary Bleany:
1. Melissa Bleany, b. 15 Feb 1802
2. Thomas S. Bleany, b. 11 Mar 1804
3. William Bleany, b. 7 May 1806
4. James W. Bleany, b. 2 Dec 1807
5. William J. Bleany, b. 28 Aug 1810
6. Sarah Bleany, b. 6 Sep 1813
7. Ann Bleany, b. 2 Nov 1816

Family Records:

George W. Blaney, b. 24 Oct 1842, Harford County, d. 8 Aug 1902, m. 17 Mar 1870

Susan Jane Blaney, b. 2 May 1853, Harford County, d. 23 Apr 1930, m. 17 Mar 1870

Lizzie Blaney, b. 8 May 1870 (changed in Bible to 1871), Harford County, d. 9 Dec 1953, m. 15 Jan 1887

John W. Blaney, b. 14 Apr 1872, Harford County, d. 22 May 1920, m. 9 Nov 1896

Samuel G. Blaney, b. 14 Dec 1873, Harford County, m. 10 Sep 1905

Lester C. Blaney, b. 21 Dec 1875, Harford County, m. 4 Sep 1898

Emanuel Blaney, b. 9 Dec 1877, Harford County, d. 16 Oct 1935, m. 16 Dec 1903

Stillie W. Blaney, b. 15 Jun 1880, Harford County, m. 10 Nov 1902

Charles Archer Blaney, b. 24 Dec 1885, Harford County, d. 20 Jan 1951, m. 16 May 1912

Edith Zachary Blaney, b. 18 Dec 1885, Washington, D.C., m. 16 May 1912

Edith Louise Blaney, b. 28 Apr 1913, Baltimore, m. 11 Nov 1943

Charles Archer Blaney, b. 8 Jul 1915, Baltimore, m. -- Nov 1942

Betty Blaney, b. 28 Nov 1922, Baltimore

EPHRAIM BORING BIBLE

No publication information available. Family data gleaned from a 1980 typescript in the *Notebook* (No. 3) of the Baltimore County Genealogical Society.

Births:

Ephraim Boring, b. 21 Jul 1836 [*Note:* Ephraim Boring is placed as a son of Isaac Boring and Elizabeth Cole in *Descendants of John Boreing, Maryland Planter*, by Hecklinger & Boring (1950), p. 14]

Mary V. Boring, wife of Ephraim, b. 20 May 1841

Children of Ephraim and Mary Boring:
1. Edward E. Boring, b. 14 Sep 1860
2. Emma V. Boring, b. 8 May 1862
3. Mary Boring, b. 23 Feb 1866
4. Minnie Boring, b. 1 Apr 1869
5. Corra B. Boring, b. 31 Jul 1872
6. Ephraim A. Boring, b. 1 Sep 1873
7. Clarra Boring, b. 20 Jun 1877
8. Howard Boring, b. 3 Apr 1882

Deaths:
Ephraim Boring, d. 31 Jan 1914, age 77 years, 6 months and 10 days
Mary V. Boring, his wife, d. 20 Mar 1913, age 72

Children of Ephraim and Mary Boring:
1. Emma V. Boring, d. 27 Jun 1864, age 2 years, 1 month and 21 days
2. Corra P. Boring, d. 4 Nov 1872, age 3 months and 4 days
3. Mary Boring, d. 18 Nov 1901, age 35 years, 8 months and 25 days
4. Minia Boring, d. 13 Oct 1903, age 34 years, 6 months and 13 days
5. Howard Boring, d. at Baltimore on 13 Oct 1918, age 36 years, 7 months and 10 days
6. Edward E. Boring, d. at Louisville, KY on 31 Aug 1921, age 60 years, 11 months and 17 days

ISAAC H. BOTTS BIBLE

Bible was published in 1866 by the American Bible Society. The front cover is inscribed "Mary J. Botts, 1883." Family data gleaned from a typescript of records at the Maryland Historical Society. The unnamed submitter of the typescript indicated that "a number of inconsistencies in the dates and ages of death of children of Isaac and May [Mary] Botts will be noted."

Marriages:
Isaac H. Botts and Mary Sheridan m. 11 Apr 1837
Daisy Botts and MacDonald Garrettson m. 31 Aug 1929

Births:
Isaac H. Botts, b. 1812
Irvin C. Botts, b. 10 Jul 1877
Daisy L. Botts, b. 24 Dec 1889
Mary E. Botts, b. 3 Mar 1839
George F. Botts, b. 4 Jun 1840
John E. Botts, b. 10 Mar 1843
William H. Botts, b. 6 Nov 1846
David O. Botts, b. 13 Sep 1853
Susan R. Botts, b. 18 Jan 1855
Isaac T. Botts, b. 6 Oct 1858
Sarah Smith, b. 2 Mar 1854
Joseph Cassell, b. 5 May 1957

Deaths:
Susan R. Botts, d. 21 Aug 1855, age 3 years, 6 months and 7 days
Joseph G. Botts, d. 14 Mar 1857, age 1 year and 10 months
William H. Botts, d. 3 Jun 1862, age 16 years, 5 months and 27 days
Mary E. Botts, d. -- 1870, age 52
Isaac H. Botts, d. 5 Sep 1887 in his 75th year
David O. Botts, d. 14 Apr 1909
Irvin C. Botts, d. 29 Sep 1913
Sarah Botts, d. 1 Aug 1936

MacDonald Garrettson, d. 29 Dec 1935

ISAAC THOMAS BOTTS BIBLE

Bible was published after 1895 (no further details were given) and purchased by Mr. Botts around 1916. Family data gleaned from a typescript of records at the

Maryland Historical Society. The unnamed submitter of the typescript noted that "family records prior to that time [1916] were entered by his brother Edgar from another source."

Marriages:
Isaac Thomas Botts and Lovenia Ellen Jones m. 10 Nov 1886
Annie Adelle Botts and William Kilgore m. 23 Jul 1914
George Thomas Botts, of Street, MD, and Julia Elvira McNutt, of Darlington, MD, m. 19 Sep 1921 at Parksburg, PA by Rev. W. T. Dunkle, Minister of the Gospel, in the presence of Mrs. Elsie Meeler and Mr. Russell Meeler.

Births:
Isaac Thomas Botts, b. 6 Oct 1858
Lovenia Ellen Jones, b. 23 Jul 1859

[Children of Isaac T. and Lovenia Botts]:
1. Isaac H. Botts, b. 17 Aug 1887
2. Edgar Grady Botts, b. 2 Aug 1889
3. Albert Nelson Botts, b. 24 Aug 1891
4. Annie Adelle Botts, b. 22 May 1893
5. George Thomas Botts, b. 7 Aug 1894
6. Mary Valeria Botts, b. 15 Sep 1898
7. Bertha Wheeler Botts, b. 25 Jan 1906

Theda Mae Botts, b. 14 Jun 1923

John Michael Fitzgerald, b. 7 Nov 1947
John William Fitzgerald, b. 11 May 1949
Patricia Kathleen Fitzgerald, b. 18 Mar 1953

Deaths:
Isaac H. Botts, d. 2 Oct 1887
Albert Nelson Botts, d. 2 Jul 1914
Isaac Thomas Botts, d. -- Feb 1935, age 77
L. Ellen Botts, d. -- Jul 1935, age 76
Bertha Wheeler Botts, d. -- 1939, age 33
Edgar G. Botts, d. 22 Jun 1949, age 59

SAMUEL BRADFIELD BIBLE

Bible published in 1854 and inscribed "To Samuel Bradfield from John F. Preston, April 5, 1855." Family data gleaned from a typescript at the Maryland Historical Society.

Births:
Children of Enos and Rebecca Bradfield:
1. Mary Bradfield, b. 3 May 1807
2. William Bradfield, b. 4 May 1809
3. Samuel and Benjamin Bradfield, b. 22 May 1810
4. Alice Bradfield, b. 11 May 1812
5. Louisa Bradfield, b. 18 Oct 1814

Children of George and Louisa Foard (Ford):
1. Malcolm Ford, b. 26 Jan 1858
2. Albert Malcolm Ford, b. 26 Jan 1868
3. Anna Kate Foard, b. 6 Feb 1870
4. Carrie V. Foard, b. 8 Feb 1873
5. Dora E. Foard, b. 8 Sep 1874
6. Bennett S. Foard, b. 22 Oct 1876
7. Charley Foard, b. 26 Feb 1882

Children of J. E. and Dora (Ford) Ricketts:
1. G. Walter Ricketts, b. 24 Oct 1905
2. Martha Irene Ricketts, b. 26 Jun 1909

Deaths:
Sammie C. Bradfield, d. 3 Mar 1865, age 54 years, 9 months, 1 week and 2 days
Martha Louisa Shay, dau. of Bennett and Alice Shay, b. 26 Feb 1837
George Michael Ford, son of James and Susannah Ford, b. 22 Oct 1837
Martha Louise Ford, d. 20 Dec 1908
George Michael Ford, d. 31 Jan 1913

JOHN A. BURKINS BIBLE

No publication information available. Family data gleaned from a typescript at the Maryland Historical Society.

Marriage:
John A. Burkins and Mary Ellen Logan m. 29 Nov 1864 at Dublin [in Harford County] by Rev. Jonathan H. Lemmon in the presence of Catharine Ann Lemmon.

Births:
John A. Burkins, son of Jacob and Catharine Burkins, b. 7 Dec 1840
Mary E. Burkins, dau. of Patrick and Jane Logan, b. 7 Mar 1841

Children of John A. and Mary E. Burkins:
1. Claranda Burkins, b. 22 Sep 1865
2. Edward R. Burkins, b. 27 Dec 1867
3. Nettie Burkins, b. 13 Jul 1870
4. Granville S. Burkins, b. 15 Jul 1874
5. Mamie Burkins, b. 5 Oct 1877

Deaths:
Jacob Burkins, d. 5 Mar 1869
Catheren Burkins, d. 15 May 1882
John A. Burkins, d. 14 Jan 1912
Mary E. Burkins, d. 27 Apr 1915

Children of John A. and Mary E. Burkins:
1. Edward R. Burkins, d. 19 Nov 1928
2. Granville S. Burkins, d. 24 Sep 1937
3. Mamie H. Magness, d. 22 Oct 1948

Jane Logan, d. 15 Oct 1890

JOSEPH BREVITT BIBLE

Bible published in 1769 in Cambridge, England. Family data gleaned from a typescript by Mary K. Meyer in 1974 which was deposited at the Maryland Historical Society. It was subsequently included in the *Notebook* (No. 62) of the Baltimore County Genealogical Society in 1993. The words "Dr. Joseph Brevitt, 1801" and "$5.00" were inscribed on the title page.

Marriages:
John Brevitt and Elizabeth Skatt m. ---- [no date], of Wolverhampton, Staffordshire, England.

Joseph Brevitt [son of John] m. 2nd to Ann Wilkes of Autherly near

Wolverhampton "of the blood of John Wilkes the English patriot."

Elizabeth Brevitt [dau. of John] and George Boraston of Edge Hill near Kidderminster, m. ---- [no date].

Mary Brevitt [dau. of John] and John Power of Wolverhampton, m. ---- [no date].

Dr. Joseph Brevitt [son of Joseph] and Cassandra Woodland m. 29 Nov 1798 [*Notebook Ed. Note:* They were married by Rev. John Allen, Minister of the Church of England, at Abingdon, Harford County, MD. She was born 2 Apr 1762, dau. of Jonathan Woodland and Cassandra Webster of Harford County. Cassandra Brevitt died 13 Apr 1841].

Births:
Children of John and Elizabeth Brevitt:
1. Sarah Brevitt, b. 28 Jun 1717
2. John Brevitt, b. 15 Jul 1718
3. James Brevitt, b. 17 Aug 1719
4. Elizabeth Brevitt, b. 17 Mar 1720
5. Mary Brevitt, b. 28 Oct 1722
6. James Brevitt, b. 22 Jan 1724/5
7. Simon Brevitt, b. 29 Aug 1727
8. Joseph Brevitt, b. 20 Mar 1729

Four sons of Joseph and Ann Brevitt:
(All born at Wolverhampton, England)
1. John Brevitt, b. 29 Nov 1760
2. Joseph Brevitt, b. 26 Jun 1763
3. James Wilkes Brevitt, b. 18 Jan 1765
4. William Brevitt, b. ---- [*Notebook Ed. Note:* A note in the bible stated that Dr. Joseph Brevitt had two brothers, James and William, but the birth date of William is not recorded].

[*Ed. Note:* Additional information about this family was included in the aforementioned *Notebook* by Robert W. Barnes. The information was also published in his book *British Roots of Maryland Families* in 1999].

LLOYD CANN BIBLE

New Testament Bible published in Edinburgh in 1800. This transcript was published in the *Maryland Genealogical Society Bulletin* (Vol. 30, No. 4) in Fall, 1989. Information was submitted by Cecil C. Alton of Dumfries, VA, who stated that "This is the bible of his great-grandfather Lloyd Cann. Lloyd was a fisherman and lived with his family in the Federal Hill area of Baltimore City on Johnson Street from 1827 till 1888. Beginning in 1851, while living at 9 Johnson Street, his family name appeared off and on as McCann in the Baltimore City directory. After 1860 the change to 'McCann' became fast and was used by Lloyd, his brothers and all their descendants." It should also be noted that the title of this transcript was "Bible Transcript: Benjamin and Nancy (Wamsley) Cann."

Births:
[*Noted in Bible transcript:* "Entries in parenthesis are added for clarity and corrections to spelling" and "John Wamsley is probably Nancy Wamsley's nephew"].

John Wolmsey (Wamsley), b. 12 Apr 1790
Elizabeth Can(n), b. 4 Oct 1796
Ruben (Reuben) Can(n), b. 14 Apr 1798
Nathan Can(n), b. 2 Jan 1800
Loyed (Lloyd) Can(n), b. 1 Jan 1802
Noah Can(n), b. 6 Apr 1805
Michael Can(n), b. 30 Jan 1815 [*Note:* "This entry was written in a different color ink and is just barely discernible"].

GEORGE CAREINS BIBLE

Bible published in 1834 (name of published not given). Family data gleaned from a typescript at the Maryland Historical Society.

Marriages:
George Careins and Mary Ann Bay m. 7 Apr 1836
James A. Careins and Susan R. Johnson m. 6 Feb 1868
William G. Cairnes and Belle A. Patterson m. 21 Oct 1869
George R. Cairnes and Belle Nelson m. 11 Feb 1869
Mary A. Cairnes, dau. of James Cairnes, and Emory A. Burton, son of Edward Burton, of Hereford, m. ---- 1907

Births:
George Careins, b. 1 Oct 1812
Mary A. Bay, b. 17 Jan 1809

Children of George and Mary A. Careins:
1. James Andrew Careins, b. 10 Apr 1837
2. William Glasgow Careins, b. 18 Feb 1839
3. Martha Jean Careins, b. 16 Jan 1841
4. George Richard Careins, b. 11 Apr 1843
5. Rebecca Elizabeth Careins, b. 7 Dec 1845
6. Robert Quilish Careins, b. 1 Jan 1858

Deaths:
George Careins, d. 8 Aug 1861
Mary A. (Bay) Careins, d. 21 Sep 1872

Children of George and Mary A. Careins:
1. James Andrew Careins, d. 1 Feb 1906
2. William Glasgow Careins, d. 1 Sep 1918
3. Martha Jean Careins, d. 23 May 1893
4. George Richard Careins, d. 28 Nov 1924
5. Rebecca Elizabeth Careins, d. 3 Nov 1848
6. Robert Quilish Careins, d. 2 Oct 1867

BISHOP CARNAN BIBLE

Bible published by The American Bible Society, New York, in 1866. Family data gleaned from a photocopy of the bible records in Filing Case A at the Maryland Historical Society.

Marriages:
Charles Walter Carnan and Lida Valiant m. 9 Nov 1904
Charles Walter Carnan, Jr. and Emily St. Claire Brown m. 24 Jun 1939

Births:
Bishop Carnan, b. 1831
Catherine Carnan, b. 1842
Walter Carnan, b. 1872
Margaret Carnan, b. 1874
Florence Carnan, b. 1876
Agnes Carnan, b. 1880
Charles Walter Carnan, b. 20 May 1872
Charles Walter Carnan, Jr., b. 13 Jan 1908
Alice Humphreys Carnan, b. 4 May 1940

Lida Valiant Carnan, b. 25 Jan 1943
Christopher Bruce Carnan, b. 20 Apr 1947

John Behr, b. 22 Jan 1865
Lida Valiant, b. 28 Sep 1883
Emily St. Claire Brown, b. 7 Jun 1914

Deaths:
Bishop Carnan, d. 1 May 1899
Margaret Dettus (grandmother) d. 27 Nov 1885
John Dettus (grandfather) d. -- Nov 1887

LIDA VALIANT CARNAN BIBLE

Red Letter Edition of The Holy Bible published by The World Publishing Company, New York City and Cleveland, OH (no date given). "Presented to Grandmother Carnan by Alice, Val and Chris, on her Seventieth Birthday, September 28, 1953." Family data gleaned from a photocopy of the bible records in Filing Case A at the Maryland Historical Society.

Marriages:
Charles Walter Carnan and Lida Valiant m. 9 Nov 1904 at Mount Holly Inn, Hotel Walbrook in Baltimore, MD at 7 p.m. by Dr. William Wright

Charles Walter Carnan, Jr. and Emily St. Claire Brown m. 24 Jun 1939 at Glendale, OH

Alice Humphreys Carnan and Washington Carlyle Winn m. 27 May 1967 at Grace Church in Newport News, VA

Lida Valiant Carnan and James Anthony Holloway m. 16 Dec 1972 in White Hall, VA

Christopher Bruce Carnan and Carolyn Adele Maxwell m. 14 Apr 1973 at Chester United Methodist Church in Chester, VA

Births:
Martha Robinson Carnan, b. 29 Nov 1905
Charles Walter Carnan, Jr., b. 13 Jan 1908
Alice Humphreys Carnan, b. 4 May 1940

Lida Valiant Carnan, b. 25 Jan 1943
Christopher Bruce Carnan, b. 20 Apr 1947

Washington Carlyle Winn III (grandson), b. 15 May 1970, St. Louis, MO

Charles McIntyre Winn (grandson), b. 2 May 1974, Charlottesville, VA

Valerie Leigh Holloway (granddaughter), b. 12 Apr 1974, Richmond, VA
Deaths:
Martha Robinson Carnan, d. 29 Nov 1905
Charles Walter Carnan, d. 10 Feb 1944
Lida Valiant Carnan, d. 2 Jan 1958

WILLIAM CARRICK FAMILY RECORD

A transcript was published in the *Maryland Genealogical Society Bulletin* (Vol. 23, No. 2) in Spring, 1982, by the late Shirley L. Reightler of Bel Air, MD. This information was found in a trunk purchased at the Bel Air Auction Gallery sometime during the 1970s.

Births:
William Isaac Carrick, b. 9 Oct 1841 [*Ed. Note:* It is interesting that all the records except this one give his name as William J. Carrick. His marriage date is not recorded in the bible, but the marriage of William J. Carrick and Virginia Miller took place on 1 Nov 1864 and the notice appeared in the *Baltimore Sun* on 2 Nov 1864].

Virginia Rosten Miller, b. 27 Sep 1844

Mary Elizabeth Carrick, b. Wed., 7 Aug 1867 at 7:15 p.m.; bapt. by James E. Alford
Lydia Charlotte Carrick, b. Tues., 30 Nov 1869 at 5 a.m.; bapt. by James France
Ridia Minnerva Carrick, b. Fri., 30 Aug 1872 at 12:15 a.m.; bapt. by James E. Alford
William Alford Downs Carrick, b. Wed., 11 Nov 1874 at 9:45 p.m.; bapt. by James E. Alford
Charles Howard France Carrick, b. 26 Feb 1877 at 8:45 a.m.; bapt. by Rev. Woods
Emmie Virginia Carrick, b. Fri., 28 Apr 1879; bapt. by ---- [blank]
Louisa Adinia Carrick, b. 29 Nov 1883

Gorman Carrick, b. Sun., 25 Mar 1886
Grace Carrick, b. Sun., 9 Jun 1889 at 6 a.m.

Death:
Lydia A---? Miller, d. 16 May 1897

Family Records:
(Notes by the late Shirley L. Reightler)

1. Among the other items in the trunk included a certificate from the Board of Police Commissioners for the City of Baltimore "William J. Carrick, a policeman fo the Permanent Police Force for the City of Baltimore for the term of 4 years from the 7th of March 1896" (in an envelope addressed to Miss Lulu Carrick, 2041 E. Fayette St., City, postmarked Baltimore, Md. 1910) and a promissory note dated 1 Jul 1908 to Colonial Park Estates for purchase of lot - signed R. Minerva Carrick.

2. Sgt. William J. Carrick was born in Prince George's County, MD on 9 Oct 1841, was appointed to the [Baltimore] police force on 14 Dec 1872, and served until the autumn of 1873 when he resigned; he was reappointed on 26 Jul 1876 and was made sergeant on 4 Aug 1883.

JOHN WESLEY CARTER BIBLE

A photocopy and typescript of these Bible records were submitted by Ross W. Smith of Fallston, MD in 2002: "The following Bible record is from the family Bible of John Wesley Carter (born 18 May 1842 in Anne Arundel Co., MD - died 12 Nov 1897 in Baltimore City) and his wife Emma Theresa Carter neé Boteler (born 24 Nov 1841 in District of Columbia - died 14 Feb 1883 in Baltimore City). Resident of Baltimore City, John Wesley Carter was a Commission Merchant (Carter Brothers & Co.) and was twice elected to the Baltimore City Council. The bible record has been passed down through generations and is now in the possession of Ross W. Smith, great-great-grandson of John W. and Emma T. Carter. Evidently, even though the family record was saved, and is in good condition, the remainder of the bible has deteriorated and was discarded by a previous owner."

Marriage:
J. W. Carter and Emma T. Boteler m. 22 Mar 1864

Births:
John Wesley Carter, son of William H. and Caroline Carter, b. 18 May 1842

Emma Theresa Boteler, dau. of Joseph Issac Boteler and Ellen Williams, b. 24 Jan 1841

Children of John and Emma Carter:
1. Carrie Emma Carter, b. 29 Jan 1865
2. William H. Carter, b. 5 Mar 1866
3. Charles Wesley Carter, b. 27 Jan 1868
4. Milton Irwin Carter, b. 3 Dec 1869
5. Lewellyn Carter, b. 21 Apr 1872
6. Nettie Estelle Carter, b. 30 Sep 1873
7. Florence Hellen Carter, b. 23 Jul 1875
8. Grace Addie Carter, b. 23 Oct 1877
9. John Edgar Carter, b. 14 Feb 1881
10. James Garfield Carter, b. 11 Dec 1882

Deaths:
Caroline Carter, wife of William H. Carter, d. 14 Jun 1863
Emma T. Carter, wife of J. W. Carter, d. 14 Feb 1883

Children of John and Emma Carter:
1. Carrie Emma Carter, d. 17 Feb 1865
2. Charles Wesley Carter, d. 29 May 1877
3. James Garfield Carter, d. 15 Dec 1882

Ellen Williams Boteler, wife of Joseph I. Boteler, d. 21 Mar 1872
Joseph I. Boteler, husband of Ellen W. Boteler, d. 29 Aug 1871

GEORGE CHARITON BIBLE

No publication information available. A transcript was published in the *Maryland Genealogical Society Bulletin* (Vol. 32, No. 2) in Spring, 1991 and placed in Filing Case A at the Library of the Maryland Historical Society in Baltimore.

Marriages:
George Chariton and Mary Ann Phillips m. 28 Jul 1836
Charles Luis Chariton and Elizabeth Jones m. 2 Jun 1872
George Washington Chariton and Mary Ann Gardner m. 6 Jul 1880
William Nicoll and Sarah A. Chariton m. 13 Jul 1849

Births:
George Washington Chariton, b. 28 Jul 1800
Alabama Louisa Chariton, b. 19 Oct 1837 about 2 o'clock Thurs. afternoon
Emily Jane Chariton, b. 13 Oct 1839 about half past 4 on Sun. afternoon
George Washington Chariton, b. 16 Feb 1842 at 12 o'clock in the morning
James Nathaniel Chariton, b. 19 Sep 1845
William Henry Chariton, b. 13 Feb 1847 about 8 o'clock in the morning
Alabama Ann Chariton, b. 6 Jul 1849
Charles Lewis Chariton, b. 3 Dec 1851
George Washington Chariton, b. 1 Jul 1854 at 11 o'clock Saturday nit
Elizabeth McDonald Chariton, b. 27 Oct 1855 at half after 11 o'clock
Luisa Fisher Chariton, b. 12 Jan 1859 on Wed. afternoon at half past 1
Lotus Lee Ashby, b. 2 ----ber 1867, ---- Street in Baltimore City [*Ed. Note:* A later entry stated Lotta Lee Ashby, b. 2 Oct 1867].

Mary Ann Phillips, b. 19 May 1817

Deaths:
Nathaniel Phillips, d. 23 Jul 1818
Mary A. Phillips, d. 30 Nov 1865, age 79

Emley Jean Chariton, d. 8 Sep 1843 in her 4th year
James Nathaniel Chariton, d. 22 Mar 1846
George Washington Chariton, d. 16 Feb 1844, age 2 years
Ruhanna L. Chariton, d. 30 Oct 1856 at half past 3 o'clock on Tues. morning, age 18 years, 4 months and 10 days
Emily Fisher Chariton, d. 22 Feb 1859 at half past 1 o'clock on Wed. afternoon
Mary Ann Chariton, d. 9 Oct 1880, age 64 years, 4 months and 21 days
George W. Chariton, d. 14 Aug 1885, age 85 years and 17 days

JAMES CHESNEY BIBLE

Bible published in 1845 by S. Andrus & Son, Hartford, CT. Family data gleaned from a typescript at the Maryland Historical Society.

Marriages:
James Chesney and Ann McCauley m. 10 Mar 1812
Isaac Fletcher and Mary E. Chesney m. 2 Oct 1838
Henry Foster and Lydia R. Chesney m. 3 Dec 1840

Daniel B. Chesney and Martha R. Osborn m. 13 Feb 1845
William H. Chesney and Frances Hawkins m. 7 Nov 1847
James S. Gorrell and Cordelia A. Chesney m. 28 Dec 1847
James R. Chesney and Sarah R. Thompson m. 23 Jan 1855
Ellen Randolph Chesney and Wilmer Lewis Barnes m. 7 Jun 1894

Births:
James Chesney, b. 9 Aug 1785
Ann McCauley, wife of James Chesney, b. 10 Jan 1789
Mary E. Chesney, b. 12 Jun 1814
D. B. Chesney, b. 13 Feb 1816
Sarah R. Chesney, wife of J. R. Chesney, b. 22 Jan 1832
Children of J. R. and S. R. Chesney:
1. Annie Mollie Chesney, b. 3 Apr 1856
2. Elizabeth Guest Chesney, b. 3 Jul 1858
3. Marion Rebecca Chesney, b. 24 Jun 1867
4. Ellen Randolph Chesney, b. 21 Aug 1875

Children of James and Ann Chesney:
1. Lydia R. Chesney, b. 24 Sep 1819
2. William H. Chesney, b. 24 Nov 1821
3. Cordelia A. Chesney, b. 26 Jan 1824
4. Henrietta P. Chesney, b. 12 Sep 1826
5. James R. Chesney, b. 11 Dec 1828
6. Jesse M. Chesney, b. 2 Mar 1834

From William Chesney, Sr.'s notebook:
1. Thomas Chesney, son of William, b. 8 May 1784
2. James Chesney, b. 9 Aug 1785
3. William Chesney, b. 9 Sep 1787
4. Anne Chesney, b. 7 Jun 1789
5. Benjamin Chesney, b. 4 Feb 1791
6. John Chesney, b. 27 Apr 1793
7. Mary Chesney, b. 24 Feb 1795
8. Susanne Chesney, b. 29 May 1797
9. Jesse Chesney, b. 23 Sep 1802

Deaths:
H. P. Chesney, d. 6 Nov 1834

Jesse M. Chesney, d. -- Aug 1835
Annie Mollie Chesney, d. 2 Sep 1856
James Chesney, d. 22 Dec 1868
Ann Chesney, d. -- Dec 1874
James R. Chesney, d. 9 Oct 1881
William H. Chesney, d. 22 Nov 1886
Daniel B. Chesney, d. -- Sep 1891
Fransiney Ann Chesney, d. -- Jan 1894
Sarah R. Chesney, d. 17 Aug 1911
Marion R. Chesney, d. 25 Feb 1926
Elizabeth G. Chesney, d. 12 Nov 1943
Cordelia A. Gorrell, d. -- Feb 1874
Mary E. Fletcher, d. -- Feb 1885
Ellen Randolph Barnes, d. 8 Mar 1953

SUMMERFIELD CHILDS BIBLE

No publication information available. A typescript of the bible records was submitted by Carleton L. Weidemeyer of Clearwater, FL in 2002, noting that this family resided at Randallstown in Baltimore County. He also prepared the notes presented herein and listed the following chain of possession of the family bible: G. Summerfield Childs, Clementine A. Childs Keck, John Alfred Keck, Walter Winfield Keck, Winifred Keck Snyder, and Ronald Francis Snyder of Palmetto, FL (current owner).

Marriage:
John A. Keck and Clementine Childs of Baltimore m. 4 Mar 1888 in Frankford, Philadelphia, PA, 4620 James Street, by Rev. R. D. Naylor

Births:
Summerfield Childs, b. 8 Mar 1842
Harry Ellsworth Childs, b. 8 May 1862
Maria Elizabeth Childs, b. 1 Oct 1865
Clementine Adelade Childs, b. 16 Jul 1868
Lulu Maybel Childs, b. 30 Jun 1871
Emma Lavanna Childs, b. 2 Apr 1874
Lemuel Levi Childs, b. 5 Apr 1877

Ruth Elizabeth Keck, b. 8 Jul 1842
John Alfred Keck, b. 5 Mar 1868

Lulu Lavanna Keck, b. 13 May 1890
Walter Winfield Keck, b. 27 Feb 1893
John Alfred Keck, b. 6 Dec 1895
Ruth Elizabeth Keck, b. 8 Jul 1900

John Younger, b. 22 Aug 1800
Maria Younger, b. 22 Feb 1806
Susanna C. Younger, b. 6 Aug 1844

Deaths:
Lulu Maybel Childs, d. 15 Apr 1876
Emma Lavanna Childs, d. 20 Apr 1876
G. Summerfield Childs, d. 21 Kan 1891

Lemuel Younger, d. 29 Feb 1896
John Younger, d. 19 Mar 1850
Maria Younger, d. 16 Jul 1865

Lulu Lavanna Keck, d. 24 Sep 1890
Clementine Adelade Keck, d. 28 Sep 1911

Family Records:
(Notes prepared by Carleton L. Weidemeyer)

1. The Childs Family Bible is in possession of Ronald F. Snyder, of Palmetto, FL.

2. Walter Winfield Keck died 12 Feb 1951. Buried in unmarked grave, Mt. Olive Cemetery, Randallstown, MD.

3. Summerfield Childs (born 8 Mar 1842) same as George Summerfield Childs who died 21 Jan 1891 and was buried in Powhatan Cemetery in the n.e. corner of present Woodlawn Cemetery.

4. Clementine Adelade Keck buried in Mt. Olive Cemetery, Randallstown, MD.

DANIEL CLAYTON BIBLE

No publication information available. Bible pages are in Filing Case A at the Library of the Maryland Historical Society in Baltimore.

Marriages:
Daniel Clayton, son of Joseph and Sarah Clayton, and Sarah Sewell, dau. of Richard and Rebecca Sewell, m. 4 Mar 1813 by Rev. C. W. Ryland

William Poits, eldest son of Isaac and Ann Poits, and Rebecca Clayton, eldest dau. of Daniel and Sarah Clayton, m. 23rd day of 3rd month, 1830 by Rev. James Sewell

Births:
Children of Daniel and Sarah Clayton:
1. Rebecca Clayton, b. 26 May 1814
2. Sarah Ann Clayton, b. 3 Nov 1816
3. Daniel Clayton, b. 18 Apr 1819
4. Joseph Clayton, b. 15 Oct 1820
5. James Clayton, b. 8 Apr 1823
6. Mary Clayton, b. 22 Dec 1824
7. Anietta Clayton, b. 5 Jun 1827

WELLS CLAYTON BIBLE

Bible published in 1844 by Jesper Harding, No. 57 South Third Street, Philadelphia. Family data gleaned from a typescript at the Maryland Historical Society. The bible was originally owned by Wells and Mary Elizabeth Clayton of Reckordville, Baltimore County, MD.

Marriages:
Wells Clayton and Mary Elizabeth Lukens m. 6 Nov 1845 by Rev. March

Joseph Clayton and Sarah Wells m. 18 Aug 1796
Elwood Thomas Grier and Ethel Archer m. 8 Jul 1916
George Archer, of Wilna P.O., Harford County, and Mary E. Clayton, of Reckord P.O., Baltimore County, m. 13 Mar 1897 at the Mountain Christian Church by Rev. J. B. Crane

Births:
Joseph Clayton, son of Joseph and Priscilla Clayton, b. 1 Mar 1778
Sarah Wells, dau. of John and Susannah Wells, b. 26 Jun 1782

Mary Elizabeth Lukens, dau. of Benjamin and Hannah Lukens, b. 23 Jul 1827

Ethel Archer, b. 13 May 1885

Children of Elwood and Ethel Grier:
1. George Archer Grier, b. 23 Oct 1918
2. Mary Alice Grier, b. 26 May 1921
3. Jane Thomas Grier, b. 20 Oct 1923
4. John Walter Grier, b. 9 Mar 1925

Children of Wells and Mary Clayton:
1. Augustus Lukens Clayton, b. 30 May 1847
2. Howard Cooper Clayton, b. 15 Apr 1849
3. Wells Orvis Clayton, b. 30 Aug 1851
4. Mary Elizabeth Clayton, b. 18 Mar 1854

George Archer, b. 30 Feb *[sic]* 1854
Mary E. Clayton, b. 18 Mar 1854

Children of George and Mary Archer:
1. Hannah Elizabeth Archer, b. 6 Aug 1880
2. Cheyney Hoskins Archer, b. 6 Apr 1882
3. Ethel Archer, b. 13 May 1885
4. Walter Henry Archer, b. 11 Sep 1887
5. Mary Trainor Archer, b. 26 Aug 1889
6. George Trainor Archer, b. 28 Aug 1893
7. Edwin Smallwood Archer, b. 8 Jan 1896
8. Augustus C. Archer, b. 12 Mar 1898

Deaths:
Mary Elizabeth Clayton, dau. of Wells, d. 23 Nov 1946 at 3:05 p.m.
Joseph Clayton, son of Joseph and Priscilla, d. 9 Feb 1854
Wells Clayton, son of Joseph and Sarah, d. 8 Dec 1857
Howard Cooper Clayton, son of Wells, d. 23 Dec 1888
Mary E. Clayton, d. 7 Mar 1905
A. L. Clayton, d. 11 Jan 1907
Children of George and Mary Archer:
1. Cheyney Hoskins Archer, d. 21 Jun 1917
2. George Trainor Archer, d. -- May 1953
3. Augustus C. Archer, d. 14 Feb 1919

4. Hannah Elizabeth Archer, d. 5 Feb 1898 at 6 a.m., age 17 years, 5 months and 27 days

GEORGE W. CLOMAN BIBLE NO. 1

Bible was published by W. N. Farrar, Davenport, Iowa (no date was given). Family data gleaned from a typescript of records at the Maryland Historical Society. The unnamed submitter of the typescript noted that "these Bibles record the family history of George W. Cloman of Harford County who moved to Baltimore with his family about 1860." It should also be noted that there are some inconsistencies in the second bible record below.

Marriage:
George Washington Cloman and Eliza Agnes Nagle m. 20 Jan 1843 in York County, PA by Rev. Samuel Parke, Pastor of Slate Ridge Church, in the presence of Benjamin Nagle and Rebecca Kane.

Births:
George Washington Cloman, son of William and Elizabeth Cloman, b. 12 Mar 1819 in Harford County, MD

Eliza Agnes Nagle, dau. of John and Sarah Nagle, b. 12 Mar 1824 in York County, PA

Children of George and Eliza Cloman:
    Born in Harford County:
1. Emanuel Edward Cloman, b. 18 Apr 1844
2. Charlotte Rebekah Cloman, b. 1 Dec 1845
3. Sarah Elizabeth Cloman, b. 18 Oct 1850
4. George Clifford Cloman, b. 16 Jul 1852
5. James William Cloman, b. 27 Jul 1854
6. George Robert Cloman, b. 25 Aug 1856
    Born in York County:
7. Leah Jane Cloman, b. 15 Dec 1859
    Born in Baltimore:
8. Elmer Ellsworth Cloman, b. 16 Apr 1861

Deaths:
George Clifford Cloman, d. 20 Jul 1853 in Harford County, age 1 year and 4 days
Emanuel Edward Cloman, d. 27 Jan 1872 in Baltimore, age 27 years, 9 months and 9 days

George W. Cloman, d. 31 May 1877 in Baltimore, age 67 years, 2 months and 17 days

GEORGE W. CLOMAN BIBLE NO. 2

Bible was published by Charles H. Yost, Market Street, Philadelphia (no date was given). Family data gleaned from a typescript of records at the Maryland Historical Society. The unnamed submitter of the typescript noted that "these Bibles record the family history of George W. Cloman of Harford County who moved to Baltimore with his family about 1860." It should also be noted that there are some inconsistencies in the first bible record above.

Marriage:
George Cloman and Eliza Noggle m. 17 Jan 1843

Births:
George Cloman, b. 12 Mar 1819
Eliza Noggle, b. 12 Mar 1824

Children of George and Eliza Cloman:
1. Emanuel Edward Cloman, b. 18 Apr 1844
2. Charlotte Rebecca Cloman, b. 1 Dec 1845
3. Elizabeth Sarah Cloman, b. 18 Oct 1850
4. George Clifford Cloman, b. 16 Jul 1852
5. James William Cloman, b. 27 Jul 1854
6. George Robert Cloman, b. 25 Aug 1856
7. Leah Jane Cloman, b. 10 Dec 1859
8. Elmore Ellsworth Cloman, b. 18 Apr 1861

Deaths:
George Clifford Cloman, d. 20 Jul 1853, age 1 year and 4 days
Emanuel Edward Cloman, d. 27 Jan 1872, age 27 years, 9 months and 9 days

OTHER DATA IN ABOVE CLOMAN BIBLES

Births on pages from another bible:
Margarette Nagle, b. 29 Oct 1809
John Nagle, b. 4 Aug 1811
Rebecca Nagle, b. 22 Dec 1812
Daniel Nagle, b. 17 Apr 1814
Michael Nagle, b. 13 Aug 1815
Henry Nagle, b. 12 Apr 1817
William Nagle, b. 14 Aug 1819
Emaniel Nagle, b. 14 Dec 1822
Elizabeth Nagle, b. 12 Mar 1824
Leah Nagle, b. 23 Feb 1826
Charlotte Nagle, b. 27 Apr 1828
Mary Ann Nagle, b. 14 May 1830
Sarah Jane Nagle, b. 8 Nov 1831
Isaac Nagle, b. 18 Jan 1833
James Nagle, b. 18 Apr 1835
Netty C. Arnett, b. 11 Oct 1873

Deaths on pages from another bible:
Margarette Nagle, d. 27 Sep 1810
John Nagle, d. 3 Jan 1845
Sarah Nagle, d. 8 Sep 1864
William Nagle, d. 25 Nov 1866
Mary Ann Nagle, d. 8 Aug 1874
Daniel Nagle, d. 16 Mar 1894
Rebecca Nagle, d. 20 Mar 1894
Netty C. Arnett, d. 24 Apr 1878
Two letters to Dear Aunt Eliza from Lena & Betty in Lebanon, PA:

1. On 18 Oct 1896 mentions Virgie, Aunt Sarah, Mr. and Mrs. Nagle, Lena (a single girl), and that Mrs. Nagle stopped at Steelton.

2. On 5 Nov 1896 mentions Aunt Kate's grandchild will be buried tomorrow, Edith Garret is sick at Coateville with "typing fever" and Frank Nagle's wife has a baby.

Card in the Bible:
George Cloman, Harford County, MD and Miss Eliza Agnes Nagle, York County, PA, were married January 17th 1843 by the Rev. Samuel Parks

"Our Jewels"
Emanuel Edward Cloman, b. 15 Apr 1844

Charlotte Rebecca Cloman, b. 1 Dec 1845
Elizabeth Sarah Cloman, b. 18 Oct 1850
George Clifford Cloman, b. 16 Jul 1852
James William Cloman, b. 27 Jul 1854
George Robert Cloman, b. 26 Aug 1856
Leah Jane Cloman, b. 15 Dec 1859
Elmore Ellsworth Cloman, b. 16 Apr 1861

Summary of Obituary Notices:

Laura Bertha Akehurst, age 4 years, 8 months and 7 days, dau. of George T. and Sarah E. Akehurst, d. 19 Feb ---- [blank] at 4:30 p.m. Verse by grandmother E. Cloman - parents residence at 1638 Fort Ave.

Martha Ann Callahan, wife of Michael M. Callahan, age 19 years, 1 month and 10 days, dau. of Daniel and Rebecca Nagle, d. 28 Jun ---- [blank]. Verse by her sister S. R. Oliver.

Emma Callahan, dau. of Martha Ann and Michael M. Callahan, d. 28 Aug ---- [blank], age 1 year, 2 months and 5 days. Verse by S. R. O. "Do not weep, grandpa & grandma, I've gone to meet Anna, my sister."

Sarah Elizabeth Nagle, dau. of Emanuel and Charlotte R. Nagle, d. -- Apr 1873 at Locust Point in Baltimore, age 2 years, 8 months and 20 days. Verse to "Sarah Lizzie" by grandma E. Cloman. (Cecil County and Cumberland papers please copy).

Florence Alvertia Akehurst, dau. of George T. and Sarah E. Akehurst of 1638 Fort Avenue, d. 22 Mar ---- [blank], age 2 years, 1 month and 24 days. Verse by her uncle.

Eliza Agnes Akehurst, dau. of George T. and Sarah E. Akehurst, d. ---- [no date given], age 1 year, 10 months and 10 days. Verse by grandma E. Cloman. (Cecil County papers please copy).

THOMAS B. COCKEY BIBLE

Bible published in 1819 (no further information given). This transcript was published in the *Maryland Genealogical Society Bulletin* (Vol. 26, No. 2) in Spring, 1985.

Marriages:
Thomas B. Cockey and Mary A. Worthington m. 9 Apr 1816

Edward A. Cockey, son of Charles and Urath Cockey, and Urath Cromwell Owings, dau. of Samuel and Ruth (Cockey) Owings, m. 26 Oct 1824

Charles Cockey, son of Thomas and Prudence (Hill) Cockey, and Urath Cockey, his cousin, dau. of Col. Edward and Elinor (Pindall) Cockey, m. 4 Nov 1786

Charles Thomas Cockey, son of Edward A. and Urath (Cromwell) Cockey, and Susannah D. Brown, dau. of William and Anne (Perry) Brown, m. 18 Mar 1852

Urath Cromwell (Owings) Cockey, widow of Edward A. Cockey and dau. of Samuel and Ruth (Cockey) Owings, m. David Carlisle ---- (no date given). [*Ed. Note:* David Carlisle and Ureth C. Cockey married on 2 Nov 1837 and their marriage notice appeared in the *Baltimore Sun* on 6 Nov 1837].

Births:
Children of Charles and Urath Cockey:
1. Thomas B. Cockey, b. 2 Oct 1787
2. Edward A. Cockey, b. 19 Jun 1791
3. ---- [daughter] Cockey, b. 18 Nov 1793 and d. 15 Jul 1795 "without name"

Mary A. Cockey, dau. of John and Ann Worthings *[sic]*, b. 25 Feb 1791

Mary Anne Worthington, dau. of John and Penelope Worthington, b. 5 Feb 1835

Mary Ann Heston, dau. of William and Susan Hooten *[sic]*, b. 11 Jan 1827

John Worthington, son of Thomas, b. 16 Jan 1763

Children of Samuel and Sarah Cockey:
1. Stephen D. Cockey, b. 12 Jan 1824
2. Emela Jane Cockey, b. 17 Feb 1827
3. Thomas B. Cockey, b. 17 Jan 1829

Charles Thomas Cockey, son of Edward S. and Urath Cromwell (Owings) Cockey, b. 6 Dec 1829

Susannah D. Brown, his wife, dau. of William and Ann (Perry) Brown, b. 12 May 1831

Charles Cockey, son of Thomas and Prudence Cockey, b. 14 Feb 1762

Urath Cockey, his wife, dau. of Col. Edward and Elinor Cockey, b. 27 Apr 1754

Deaths:
Charles Cockey, d. 23 Apr 1823 in his 62nd year
Urath Cockey, wife of Charles, d. 10 Oct 1824 in her 71st year
Edward A. Cockey, son of Charles and Urath (Cockey) Cockey, d. 21 Aug 1834, age 43

Mary A. Cockey, wife of Thomas B. Cockey and dau. of John and Ann Worthington, d. 31 Dec 1859 in her 69th year

Thomas B. Cockey, son of Charles and Urath Cockey, d. 27 Apr 1868 in her 81st year

Urath Cromwell (Owings) (Cockey) Carlisle, dau. of Samuel and Ruth (Cockey) Owings, d. 2 Jun 1886 in her 90th year

Mrs. Ann Worthings *[sic]*, wife of June *[sic]* Worthington of Thomas, d. 13 Dec 1820

John Worthington, of Thomas, d. 19 Mar 1829

Edward A. Cockey, son of Charles and Urath Cockey, d. 21 Aug 1834 and bur. in family graveyard in Worthington Valley; his remains were removed and interred beside those of his wife in Loudon Park [in Baltimore] in November, 1897.

Worthington C. Cockey Carlisle, d. 2 Jun 1886 in his 30th year

Susannah D. (Brown) Cockey, of Pikesville, wife of Charles T. Cockey and dau. of William and Ann (Perry) Brown, d. Fri. morning, 30 Jul 1897, at 6:45 a.m., age 66

THOMAS BEALE COCKEY BIBLE

Bible published in 1884 in Philadelphia. This transcript was published in the *Maryland Genealogical Society Bulletin* (Vol. 26, No. 2) in Spring, 1985. The Cockey and Warfield families lived in Baltimore and Howard Counties, MD.

Marriages:
Thomas Beale Cockey and Mary Thomas Warfield m. 17 Nov 1885 at the Franklin Street Presbyterian Church in Baltimore by Rev. Thomas J. Shepherd

Eva Warfield Cockey and Henry S. Regester m. 28 Dec 1910
Sally Anne Warfield Cockey and M. F. Maury Werth m. 18 Jun 1914

Dr. Evan W. Warfield, of Longwood, Howard County, MD, and Sallie Anne Warfield, of Bushey Park, m. 9 Nov 1848 by Rev. Thomas J. Shepherd

Thomas Beal Cockey, of Garrison, Baltimore County, and Mary Thomas Warfield, of Woodlawn, Howard County, m. 17 Nov 1885 by Rev. Thomas J. Shepherd

Emma Shepherd Cockey and Bruce H. Helfrich m. 14 Oct 1914 at Lyal Park

Thomas Beale Cockey, Jr. and Sarah Bradley m. 24 Jun 1925

Charles Thomas Cockey and Helene Halling m. 20 Jan 1926 in New York

Births:
Thomas Beale Cockey, b. 19 Oct 1856
Mary Thomas Warfield, b. 13 Jun 1855

Children of Thomas B. and Mary T. Warfield:
(All were born at Lyal Park)
1. Eva Warfield, b. 22 Oct 1886
2. Sally Anne Warfield, b. 22 Feb 1889
3. Emma Shepherd Warfield, b. 11 Jun 1891
4. Charles Thomas Warfield, b. 23 Nov 1893
5. Thomas Beal Warfield, b. 28 Apr 1897
Children of Sallie Ann Warfield Cockey and M. F. Maury Werth:
1. Virginia Lee Maury Werth, b. 8 Jun 1915
2. Sallie Anne Warfield Werth, b. 8 Sep 1917
3. Matthew Fontaine Maury Werth, b. 31 Jul 1926

Children of Emma Cockey and Bruce H. Helfrich:
1. Robert Bruce Helfrich, b. 4 Aug 1916
2. Thomas Cockey Helfrich, b. 15 Jun 1918
3. Samuel Dalton Helfrich, b. 11 Jul 1924
4. Mary Thomas Warfield Helfrich, b. 14 Apr 1932

Deaths:
Sallie Anne Warfield, d. 10 Mar 1881
Dr. Evan W. Warfield, d. 17 Feb 1904

Susanna D. Cockey, d. 30 Jul 1897
Charles Thomas Cockey, d. 16 Jan 1917
Thomas Beal Cockey, d. 10 Oct 1925
Charles Thomas Cockey, d. 20 Jun 1936
Mary Thomas Warfield Cockey, d. 16 Jul 1943

Bruce Hook Helfrich, d. 21 Nov 1963
Emma Shepherd Cockey Helfrich, d. 13 Aug 1968

Matthew Fontaine Maury Werth, d. 10 Mar 1965
Sallie Ann Warfield Cockey Werth, d. -- May 1977

Eva Warfield Cockey Regester, d. 5 Nov 1967
Henry Slicer Register, d. 13 May 1970

MOSES PARLETT COE BIBLE

Bible published in 1872. Family data gleaned from a photocopy of the bible pages which were once in the possession of Mrs. Albert F. Maggioncalda (neé Robinson) of Kingsville, Baltimore County, MD who presented it to the Historical Society of Harford County in March, 1993. Moses Parlett Coe's wife Hannah Elizabeth Walker was a daughter of Jesse and Victorine Walker of Harford County.

Marriages:
Moses Parlett Coe, of Baltimore County, and Hannah Elizabeth Walker, of Harford County, m. 31 Oct 1865 at Epsom Church

James O. Townsley and Annie C. Coe m. 28 Jan 1886

Births:
Moses P. Coe, b. 13 May 1839
Lizzie H. Walker, b. 24 Jul 1846

[Children of Moses and Lizzie Coe]:
1. Annie Cecelia Coe, b. 24 Jul 1866

2. Nora Grace Coe, b. 2 May 1868
3. George Wilford Coe, b. 27 Mar 1870
4. Henry Elmer Coe, b. 12 Jan 1872
5. Alverdie Coe, b. 3 Jan 1874
6. Victorine Coe, b. 28 Feb 1876
7. Howard Emery Coe, b. 14 Aug 1878
8. Walter Coe, b. 4 Mar 1881
9. Laura V. Coe, b. 26 Mar 1885
10. Stella Coe, b. 10 Oct 1887

Deaths:
Stella Coe, d. 10 Feb 1892, scarlet fever
Moses P. Coe, d. 18 Apr 1920
Hannah E. Coe, d. 1 Feb 1929
H. Elmer Coe, d. 9 Feb 1933
George Wilford Coe, d. 27 Apr 1950
Walter Coe, d. 9 Dec 1966
Howard Emory Coe, d. 14 Jan 1967

Mora Grace Townsley, d. 12 Sep 1943
Annie Cecelia Townsley, d. 5 Nov 1947

Laura V. Isenock, d. 7 Dec 1921
Victorine Isenock, d. 10 Mar 1957

Alverta Robinson, d. 6 Jan 1964

JAMES C. COLE BIBLE

Bible published in 1851 by Alden, Beardsley & Company. Family data gleaned from a typescript of records copied by Jon Harlan Livezey in 1975.

Marriages:
James C. Cole and Mary A. Everist m. 7 Feb 1839
Benjamin N. Wells and Mary A. Cole m. 10 Sep 1854
William H. Arnold and Laura J. Cole m. 2 Apr 1867

Births:
James C. Cole, son of Ezikel and Sarah Cole, b. 2 Apr 1814
Mary A. Everist, dau. of Job and Kezia Everist, b. 1 Mar 1809

Children of James C. and Mary Ann Cole:
1. Sarah Kezia Cole, b. 12 Jan 1841
2. Larrow [Laura] Jane Cole, b. 23 Mar 1842
3. Frances Emily Cole, b. 25 Jan 1844
4. William Lewis Cole, b. 16 Nov 1845
5. James A Cole, b. 22 Dec 1847
6. John A. Chapman Cole, b. 17 May 1850

Ira Fielden Arnold, son of William H. and Laura J. Arnold, b. 9 Jan 1868

Deaths:
James C. Cole, d. 6 Jul 1851

Children of James C. and Mary A. Cole:
1. Sarah Kezia Cole, d. 5 Jul 1851
2. James Amos Cole, d. 17 Jul 1851
3. Frances Emily Cole, d. 17 Jul 1851
4. Laura J. Arnold, d. 24 Jun 1922
5. John A. Chapman Cole, d. 10 Apr 1927
6. William L. Cole, d. 13 Nov 1863, age 17 years, 11 months and 27 days

Joseph Wells, d. 29 Jul 1857
Mary A. Wells, d. 22 (28?) Nov 1898
Benjamin N. Wells, d. 6 Jun 1859
Avarilla Wells, consort of Benjamin N. Wells, d. 5 Mar 1853

Job Everist, d. 29 Aug 1857
Thomas C. Everist, d. 18 Jul 1861 in his 56th year

JOHN MARCHBORN COOLEY BIBLE

Bible published in 1869 by The American Bible Society in New York. On the flyleaf: "Jno. M. Cooley & Hattie L. Cooley." Family data gleaned from a typescript of records copied by Jon Harlan Livezey in 1977.

Marriages:
John M. Cooley and Hattie Lord m. 24 Jul 1866
Marvin Lord Cooley and Helen Esther Jones m. 26 Jan 1894
John Marvin Cooley and Lillian G. Robey m. 26 Jun 1918

Charles Marvin Cooley and Verneal Kincaid m. 26 Sep 1957

Births:
John Marchborn Cooley, b. 1 Mar 1827
Hattie (Lord) Cooley, b. 22 Jul 1842

Marvin L. Cooley, b. 22 Jul 1868
Helen E. (Jones) Cooley, b. 10 Oct 1869

John Marvin Cooley, son of Marvin L. and Helen E. Cooley, b. 24 Aug 1895
Lillian Grace (Robey) Cooley, wife of John Marvin Cooley, b. 9 Dec 1896

Children of John M. and Lillian G. Cooley:
1. Helen Leonore Cooley, b. 2 Oct 1921
2. Charles Marvin Cooley, b. 12 Jul 1924

Verneal (Kincaid) Cooley, wife of Charles Marvin Cooley, b. 5 Jan 1925
Susan Lynne Cooley and Margaret Anne Cooley, twin daughters of Charles and Verneal Cooley, b. 10 Jan 1961

Mary Dearborn Lord, mother of Hattie Lord Cooley, b. 17 Apr 1797, d. 22 Mar 1879

John Lord, father of H. L. Cooley, b. 22 Jan 1799, d. 29 Apr 1883

Deaths:
John M. Cooley, d. 13 Apr 1878
Hattie L. Cooley, his wife, d. 3 Jan 1907
Marvin Lord Cooley, their son, d. 17 Jun 1925
Helen E. Cooley, his wife, d. ---- [blank]
Lillian Grace Cooley, wife of John Marvin Cooley, d. 14 Mar 1963

JOSHUA COOPER BIBLE

Bible published in 1796 by Mark and Charles Kerr, His Majesty's Printers, Edinburgh. Family data gleaned from a typescript at the Maryland Historical Society. The bible was originally owned by Joshua Cooper of Peach Bottom Township, York County, PA, which adjoined Harford County, MD.

Joshua Cooper, b. 1785

Joshua Cooper was boearn in the Year of 1785 the 20 day of April. Now reder take Note this was rote in the year of 18096 and then I was 21 years old.

Hannah Cooper her Bible Bought from William Barclay ---- [illegible]

Hannah Lukens, dau. of Nicholas and Sarah Cooper, her bible 1824

Joshua Cooper his hand pen his Bible 1800/26
Joshua Cooper his book God gave him Grace to look
Priscilla Lukens, b. 10 Apr 1822
Priscilla Lukens, b. 10 Apr 1824/22

GEORGE CREVENSTEN BIBLE

Bible published in 1834 by McCarty & Davis, 171 Market Street, Philadelphia, PA, "Holy Bible, by Special Command of His Majesty King I of England." Family data gleaned from a typescript at the Maryland Historical Society.

Family Records:
George Crevensten and Martha Greenfield m. 21 Apr 1818
Mary Margaret Crevensten, b. 18 Apr 1819

GEORGE A. CREVENSTEN BIBLE

No publication information available. Family data gleaned from a typescript of records copied by Jon Harlan Livezey in 1975, noting that the bible had been "badly damaged by immersion in water."

Marriages:
George A. Crevensten and Sarah J. Welsh m. 1 Jul 1858
Robert Greenfield Crevensten and Mary Elizabeth Forsythe m. 27 Oct 1885(?)

Emily Isadore Crevensten and George Edwin Pritchard m. 3 Oct 1886(?)
Isaac Henry Crevensten and Altossa Biddle m. 5 Apr 1893
Addie Abercrombie Crevensten and William Linus Whiting m. 29 Jul 1896
Mary Altossa Crevensten and D. Allen Penick m. ---- [blank]

Births:
George A. Crevensten, son of George and Martha Crevensten, b. 17 Mar 1826

Sarah Jenness Welsh, dau. of Robert W. and Sarah Welsh, b. 26 Aug 1836

Children of George A. and Sarah J. Crevensten:
1. Mary Florence Reese Crevensten, b. 10 Apr 1859
2. Robert Greenfield Swan Crevensten, b. 17 -- 1861
3. Isaac Henry Whitfield Crevensten, b. 22 Jun 1863
4. Emily Isadore Crevensten, b. 24 Oct 1865
5. George Elliott Crevensten, b. 29 Jun 1868
6. Clyde Russell Crevensten, b. 9 Feb 1871
7. Clara Elizabeth Crevensten, b. 27 Jun 1874
8. Addie A. Crevensten, b. 6 Feb 1878

Children of George E. and Emily I. Pritchard:
1. Guy Edwin Pritchard, b. 23 May 1887
2. George Ray Pritchard, b. 8 Mar 1889
3. Austin Bernard Pritchard, b. 14 Jan 1893
4. Sadie Christiana Pritchard, b. 24 Feb 1895
5. Ross Elliott Pritchard, b. 23 Sep 1897
6. Clara Frances Pritchard, b. 25 Nov 1899
7. Ethel Estelle Pritchard, b. 20 Feb 1901
8. Mary Kathryn Pritchard, b. 7 Jun 1905

Children of Clyde Russell and Mary A. Crevensten:
1. Clyde George Crevensten, b. 27 Sep 1909(?), Chester, PA
2. Mary Altossa Crevensten, b. 19 Sep 1912, Tampa, FL

Deaths:
Robert W. Welsh, d. 6(?) Jul 1860 (1866?), age 70 years, 3 months and 1 day
Sarah Welsh, d. 15 Jun 1877, age 80 years and 6 months
Isaac P.(?) Welsh, d. 27 Feb 1864, age 26 years and 9 months

Clara Frances Pritchard, d. 1 Sep 1900, age 9 months and 6 days

Martha Crevensten, d. 7 Aug 1870, age 77
George Elliott Crevensten, d. 14 Feb 1888, age 19
George Alexander Crevensten, d. 29 Apr 1900, age 74
Sarah Jenness Crevensten, d. 3 Aug 1901, age 65

CROMPTON-DAVIS BIBLE

Bible published by Kimber & Sharpless, Philadelphia, PA (undated). Family data gleaned from a typescript at the Maryland Historical Society.

Marriages:
John G. Crompton and Ann C. Townsend m. 27 Aug 1843
Jesse W. Davis and Annie E. Crompton m. 9 Apr 1863
Jesse W. Davis and Hester McCarns m. 17 Mar 1868

Births:
John G. Crompton, b. 19 Apr 1822

Children of John G. and Ann Crompton:
1. Ann Elizar Crompton, b. 14 Jul 1844
2. Stephen John Oliver Crompton, b. 7 Mar 1847

Children of Jesse W. and Annie E. Davis:
1. Lena Leona Davis, b. 27 Nov 1863
2. Harry Russell Davis, b. 10 Aug 1867

Children of Jesse W. and Hettie Davis:
1. Alfonzo Davis, b. 3 Sep 1868
2. Meta May Davis, b. 21 Nov 1869
3. Hilda Herndon Davis, b. 4 Nov 1871
4. Jennie Theoba Davis, b. 4 Mar 1874
5. Mary E. Davis, b. 9 Apr 1876
6. John Harvey Davis, b. 15 Aug 1878
7. Wilton Howard Davis, b. 11 Sep 1881

Jesse W. Davis, b. 6 Jan 1842
Hester Davis, b. 26 Aug 1846

Deaths:
Stephen John Crompton, d. 4 Feb 1859, age 11 years and 11 months

Annie E. Davis, d. 20 Aug 1867, age 23 years, 1 month and 6 days
Hettie Davis, wife of Jesse W. Davis, d. 8 Nov 1910, age 68 years, 10 months and 3 days

Children of Jesse W. and Annie Davis:
1. Harry Russell Davis, d. 25 Sep 1867, age 7 weeks and 4 days
2. Lena Leona Ulrich, d. 3 Feb 1957, age 93 years, 2 months and 6 days

Children of Jesse W. and Hettie Davis:
1. Jennie T. Davis, d. 22 Sep 1950, age 76 years and 6 months
2. Mary E. Davis, d. 11 Jun 1933, age 77 years and 2 months
3. Alfonzo Davis, d. 14 Sep 1868, age 11 days
4. Meta May Davis, d. 28 Jun 1870, age 7 months and 7 days
5. John Harvey Davis, d. 11 Dec 1883
6. Hilda H. (Davis) McCrone, d. 2 Nov 1956, age 85 years and 18 days

BENJAMIN CRONIN BIBLE

No publication information available (title page missing). Family data gleaned from a typescript at the Maryland Historical Society.

Marriage:
Benjamin F. Cronin and Elizabeth ---- m. ---- [*Ed. Note:* Their marriage date was not recorded in the bible transcript, but Harford County records indicate Benjamin F. Cronin and Sarah Elizabeth Courtney obtained a marriage license on 4 Mar 1846].

Births:
Children of Benjamin and Elizabeth Cronin:
1. John Wesley Cronin, b. 29 Dec 1846
2. Franklin Cronin, b. 10 Aug 1848
3. Kate Cronin, b. 20 Mar 1850
4. Adla Augusta Cronin, b. 28 Jul 1852
5. Cyrus Cronin, b. 14 Oct 1854
6. Fanny Bell Cronin, b. 14 Oct 1856
7. Emily C. Cronin, b. 15 Oct 1858
8. William Hays Cronin, b. 13 Mar 1862

Deaths:
Children of Benjamin and Elizabeth Cronin:
1. Emily C. Cronin, d. 22 Nov 1941
2. Fannie B. Cronin, d. 15 Dec 1954

JOHN W. CRONIN BIBLE

Bible published in 1841 by Land & Sandfor. Inscribed: "J. W. & S. A. Cronin."
Family data gleaned from a typescript at the Maryland Historical Society.
Marriages:

John Wesley Cronin and Sarah Augusta Michener m. 13 Aug 1840
L. Wesley Ayars and Maggie R. Cronin m. 24 May 1866

Births:
Children of John W. and Sarah A. Cronin:
1. Margaret Rebecca Cronin, b. 20 Jul 1841
2. Mary Ellen Cronin, b. 18 Jan 1844
3. Sarah Wesley Cronin, b. 2 Sep 1845

Charles Cronin Ayars, son of L. W. and Maggie R. Ayars, b. 22 Aug 1867

Deaths:
Sarah A. Cronin, wife of Rev. J. W. Cronin, d. 22 May 1846, age 33

Sarah Wesley Cronin, dau. of J. W. and Sarah A. Cronin, b. 7 Feb 1857, age 10 years, 5 months and 5 days

FRANK DAVIS BIBLE

No publication information available (title page missing, but two appendices were dated 1872 and 1873). Family data gleaned from a typescript at the Maryland Historical Society. Bible originally owned by Frank and Ella Davis of Harford County, MD.

Marriage:
Frank Davis and Ella M. Spicer m. 24 Dec 1884 by Rev. John H. Marsh at Friendship M. E. Church. [*Ed. Note:* It is now known as Fallston United Methodist Church].

Births:
Frank Davis, son of James S. and Sarah Davis, b. at Mill Green, 24 Sep 1857

Ella Marian Spicer, dau. of James A. and Elizabeth Spicer, b. at Fallston, 12 Oct 1864

Children of Frank and Ella M. Davis (All were born at or near Mill Green):
1. Walter Hicks Davis, b. 31 Dec 1885
2. Sarah Sybella Davis, b. 2 Feb 1889
3. Frank Rudisill Davis, b. 15 Jul 1890
4. James Willard Davis, b. 3 Mar 1892
5. Thomas Smithson Davis, b. 3 Jul 1896

Deaths:
Frank Davis, d. 4 Oct 1928
Ella Marian (Spicer) Davis, d. 13 Apr 1943

Frank Rudisill Davis, d. 4 Apr 1955 [*Ed. Note:* He was a World War I veteran whose obituary and service record were inserted in the bible, but not abstracted herein. Bible also contained obituaries of Wilson Osborne, Elizabeth Spicer Gerlach, and J. Willard Davis, plus an article about him from "The Maryland Teacher"].

DILL-HUTTON BIBLE

No publication information available. Family data gleaned from a typescript in the *Notebook* (No. 3) of the Baltimore County Genealogical Society which was made available by Malcolm Dill of Lutherville, MD in 1980.

Marriages:
Alexander C. Dill and Jane Rowan m. 30 Oct 1838 at Centreville, IN
Jesse M. Hutton and Rebecca E. Shaw m. 4 Jan 1842 at Xenia, OH
Matthew H. Dill and Emily L. Hutton m. 23 Sep 1862 at Richmond, IN

Births:
Jesse M. Hutton, b. 30 Jan 1809 at New Market, MD
Rebecca Lathrop Shaw, b. 27 Sep 1821 at Waynesville, OH
Alexander C. Dill, b. 3 Jan 1812 in Green County, PA
Jane Rowan, b. 18 Sep 1819 in Hamilton County, OH
Matthew H. Dill, b. 5 Jan 1840 at Centreville, IN
Emily Lathrop Hutton, b. 29 Sep 1842 at Richmond, IN

Deaths:
Alexander C. Dill, d. 12 Nov 1862, age 51 years, 10 months and 9 days at Richmond, IN
Frank Eugene Dill, d. 1 Oct 1892 age 2 (21?) years and 5 months at Richmond, IN
Jane Dill, d. 10 Oct 1894, age 75 years and 22 days at Richmond, IN
Matthew H. Dill, d. 20 Jan 1906, age 66, at Pasadena, CA and bur. at Richmond, IN

Emily H. Dill, d. 21 Nov 1919, age 77, at Richmond, IN
Camilla W.(?) Dill, d. 1 Apr 1910, age 38, at Richmond, IN
Laura H. Dill, d. 17 Jan 1904, age 26, at Mudlania, IN and bur. at Richmond, IN
William R. Dill, d. 18 Nov 1927

Rebecca L. Hutton, d. 23 Feb 1885, age 63, at Richmond, IN
Jesse M. Hutton, d. 25 Mar 1886 at Richmond, IN

DORSEY-LEWIS BIBLE

Bible published in 1850 by Joseph Longking, Publisher, for George Lane and Levi Scott of the Methodist Episcopal Church at the Conference Office, 200 Mulberry Street, New York. This transcript was published in the *Maryland Genealogical Society Bulletin* (Vol. 26, No. 1) in Winter, 1985. It is inscribed "Elizabeth Dorsey's Book" and the information was copied in 1974.

Marriage:
Abner K. Lewis, of Boston, MA, and Miss Mary Ann Dorsey, of Marriottsville, Carroll County, MD, dau. of Nicholas Dorsey, Esq., m. 25 Feb 1847 in Baltimore by Rev. John McKein.

Births:
Abner K. Lewis, b. 10 Oct 1823
Mary Ann Dorsey, b. 3 Jul 1813
Henry Dorsey Lewis, b. 8 Jun 1848

Deaths:
Henry Dorsey Lewis, d. 21 Jun 1848
Abner K. Lewis, d. 30 Jun 1853
Mary Ann Lewis, d. 2 Feb 1863

Cassander Dorsey, d. 18 Feb 1853, age 77 years and 4 months
Nicholas Dorsey, d. 1 Apr 1853, age 81 years and 14 days
Joshua Dorsey, d. 12 Jan 1881, age 82 years
Elizabeth Dorsey, d. 2 Mar 1881, age 76 years, 7 months and 15 days

Family Record (Clipping in Bible):
Samuel T. Boss, of Washington, DC, and Miss Sadie Bingham, of this city, m. 4

Mar ---- by Rev. E. E. Shipley (undated *Morning Herald*).

WILLIAM DOSH BIBLE

Bible published in 1827 (name of publisher not given). Written on the flyleaf: "William Dosh, Baltimore, August 14, 1839." Family data gleaned from a typescript in the *Notebook* (No. 3) of the Baltimore County Genealogical Society which was made available by Mrs. Clifford LaMason of Baltimore, MD in 1980. The records had been sent to her by Betty Yeager Pastre who stated the bible had been waterlogged and some of the death dates given in parentheses were her own calculations.

Marriages:
George Goodlow Dosh and Anna Elizabeth Hofman m. ---- [no date]
Harry Kronenberg Dosh and Cora E. ---- m. ---- [no date]
Anna Elizabeth Dosh and ---- LaMason m. ---- [no date]

Births:
George Goodlow Dosh, b. 7 Dec 1837 at Baltimore, MD
Anna Elizabeth Hofman, his wife, b. 27 Aug 1843 at Carlisle, PA

Children of George G. and Anna E. Dosh:
(All were born in Carlisle, PA except Anna who was born in Lancaster)
1. George Philip Dosh, b. 30 Jan 1865
2. Charles Frederick Dosh, b. 10 Aug 1866
3. William Dosh, b. 18 Sep 1870
4. Edgar Dosh, b. 8 Apr 1873
5. Anna Elizabeth Dosh, b. 12 Nov 1875
6. Grant Dosh, b. 19 Nov 1879
7. Infant boy Dosh, b. ---- 1882
8. Harry Kronenberg Dosh, b. 3 Oct 1885
9. Mary Sheaffer Dosh, b. 9 Oct 1888

Cora E. Dosh, b. 24 Jun 1888
Charles Albert LaMason, b. 30 Oct 1901

Deaths:
George Goodlow Dosh, d. 12 Mar 1917 at Carlisle
Ann Elizabeth Dosh, his wife, d. 28 May 1913 at Carlisle
Cora E. Dosh, d. 7 Sep 1978, age 90 years, 2 months and 14 days; bur. in Old
    Graveyard by the Hoffman Funeral Home

Margarett H. Dosh, d. 7 Mar 1858, age 51 years, 2 months and 15 days (b. 23 Dec 1806)
William F. Dosh, d. 4 Apr 1844, age 35 years, 1 month and 4 days (b. 28 Feb 1809)
Rebecca Dosh, d. 16 Apr 1846, age 71 (b. 1775)
George G. Dosh, d. 15 Apr 1859, age about 49 (b. 1810)
Rosetta Dosh, d. 3 Jul 1851 in her 35th year (b. 1816)

Children of George G. and Anna E. Dosh:
1. George Philip Dosh, d. 1 Jan 1931 at Carlisle
2. Charles Frederick Dosh, d. 8 Feb 1869 at Carlisle
3. William Dosh, b. 16 Oct 1959 at Carlisle
4. Anna Elizabeth LaMason, d. 7 Nov 1953 at Lancaster
5. Grant Dosh, d. 27 Oct 1947 at Harrisburg
6. ---- (infant boy) Dosh, d. 21 Apr 1882 at Carlisle
7. Harry Kronenberg Dosh, d. 23 Jul 1962 at Carlisle, age 76 years, 9 months and 20 days
8. Mary Sheaffer Yeager, d. 29 Aug 1962 at Camden, NJ

George P. Hofman, d. 4 Jun 1881 (b. 1806)
Mrs. Elizabeth Brashears, wife of John Brashears and dau. of the late John M. Dosh of Baltimore, d. 20 Mar 1852 in her 47th year

Notebook Editor Notes:
1. John Michael Dosh, native of Germany, d. Thurs. evening 25 Jan 1816 in his 49th year; funeral from his late residence in Baltimore at 41 S. Charles Street (*Baltimore American*, 27 Jan 1816)

2. Rebecca Dosh of Berwick, Adams County, PA, wrote her will on 14 Oct 1844 and it was probated on 26 Oct 1846 in Baltimore County, MD. She was apparently the widow of John M. Dosh, Sr. (*Baltimore Sun*, 20 Apr 1846; Baltimore County Wills 21:292)

FREDERICK ELLENDER BIBLE

Bible printed in 1801 in New York by and for William Durell, Bookseller. Family data gleaned from a typescript in the *Notebook* (No. 23) of the Baltimore County Genealogical Society. [*Ed. Note:* Some of the dates of birth were entered in the bible at two different times and some of those dates do not match].

Births:
Frederick Ellender, b. 24 Feb 1740(?), a native of Germany

Children of Frederick and ---- Ellender:
1. Frederick Ellender, b. 12 Mar 1778
2. Charity Ellender(?), b. 12 Jun 178(?)
3. Elizabeth Ellender, b. 9 Aug 1783
4. Harriet Ellender, b. 25 Sep 1787
5. Richard(?) Ellender, b. 27 Oct 1789(?)

Casander Graham, dau. of John and Delia Graham, b. 4(?) Jul 1777

Charity ---- [wife of Frederick Ellender], b. 15 Jun 1781

Children of Frederick and Charity Ellender:
1. Sarah Ellender, b. 20 Feb 1801 (1804?)
2. Elizer [Eliza] Ellender, b. 9 Apr 1805
3. Delily [Delila] Ellender, b. 6 Feb 1807
4. Mary Ann Ellender, b. 26 Oct 1809
5. July Ann Ellender, b. 9 Aug 1810
6. July Ann [Julia] Ellender, b. 14 Oct 1811
7. Frederick Ellender, Jr., b. 4 Sep 1812 (13?)
8. Charity Ellender, b. 29 Jan 1815
9. George Ellender, b. 22 Oct 1817
10. Georgeann[a] Ellender, b. 4 Oct 1820
11. Mandy E. [Amanda] Ellender, b. 5 Mar 1822
12. George W. Ellender, b. 15 Sep 1824

[Children of ---- and Delila Bowen]:
1. Catherine Anne Bowen, b. 8(9?) Jan 1828
2. Frederick E. Bowen, Sr., b. 22 Dec 1830
3. Eliza Ann Bowen, 19 Sep 1832

Sarah Ann Laughlin [Lofflin], daughter of ---- and Charity Lofflin, b. 8 Feb 1844(?)

Deaths:
Frederick Ellender, d. 13 Jul 1841
Charity Ellender [his wife], d. 30 Dec 1861

Children of Frederick and Charity Ellender:
1. Sarah Ellender, d. 6 Oct 1876
2. Eliza Ellender, d. 18 Jan 1874
3. Delily (Ellender) Bowen, d. 22 Jan 1861(?)
4. Mary Ann Ellender, d. 26 Sep 1871
5. July Ann Ellender, d. 9 Aug 1811
6. July Ann Ellender, d. 8 Oct 1887 [*Ed. Note:* This is their second daughter by that name. She was listed as Julia Wilcocks when her father wrote his will on 10 Jul 1841]
7. Frederick Ellender, Jr., d. 6 Feb 1874
8. Charity Ellender, d. 15 Jun 1845
9. Georgeanna Ellender, d. 27 Oct 1820

Frederick E. Bowen, Sr., d. 11 Sep 1833(?)

JOHN HENRY EMMORD BIBLE

Bible published in 1879 by A. J. Holman & Co., 930 Arch Street, Philadelphia, PA. Family data gleaned from a typescript at the Maryland Historical Society.

Marriages:
J. Henry Emmord, of Perryman, and Laura E. Lantz, of Baltimore, m. 12 Mar 1878 at 144 Barre Street in Baltimore by Rev. Henry Scheib

Harry Oscar Emmord, of Perryman, and Eva Grace Forwood, of Forest Hill, m. 31 Jan 1911 at Perryman, Harford County, MD

Laura Winifred Emmord, of Perryman, and Maurice Julius Boeschel, of Oldenburg, IN, m. 10 Nov 1927 at Perryman, Harford County, MD

John George Lantz [of Germany] m. first to Lucy Imorde [no date] and second to Mary Margaret Elizabeth Rieger [no date].

Births:
Harry Oscar Emmord, b. at Perryman, 17 Jun 1879
Laura Winifred Emmord, b. at Perryman, 20 Sep 1882
John George Lantz, b. in Hessecastle, Germany, 14 Nov 1824
Mary Margaret Elizabeth Rieger, b. 21 Jan 1831

Deaths:
M. M. E. Lantz, d. 11 Mar 1887
George Lewis Lantz, d. 11 Sep 1889
John George Lantz, d. 25 Dec 1902
Edna A. Lantz, d. 2 Jan 1912
Bertha C. Lantz, d. 7 May 1915
Alfred L. Lantz, d. 6 Aug 1916
Mary (Mollie) C. Lantz, d. 5 Jun 1918
Emma C. Lantz, d. 31 Oct 1932
Charles H. Lantz, 1 Oct 1940
John George Lantz, d. 25 Dec 1902
[*Ed. Note:* Four children of John George Lantz and Lucy Imorde died in infancy, but no names or dates were given in this record].

Frederick William, d. 12 Sep 1907
Frederick William, Sr., d. 2 Apr 1908

Mary Margaret Elizabeth Rieger, d. 11 Mar 1887

FERGUSON-PRICE BIBLE

Bible published in 1840 by H. & E. Phinney, Cooperstown, NY. Family data gleaned from a typescript at the Maryland Historical Society.

Marriages:
John Ferguson and ---- [not named] m. 5 Dec 1864 [*Ed. Note:* No marriage record found in Harford County]

Henry Ferguson and ---- [not named] m. 12 Jul 1863 [*Ed. Note:* No marriage record found in Harford County]

Births:
Henry J. Ferguson, d. 14 Jan 1833
Hellen Fergerson, b. Sat., 22 Aug 1844, 11 a.m.
Charlotte A. Fergerson, b. 1 Jan 1848
John Fergerson, b. 23 Jul 1848
Louis Albridge(?) Ferguson, b. Thurs., 6 Sep 1866, 7 p.m.

Agnes Elizabeth Price, b. Sun., 10 Nov 1873, 9 p.m.

John F. Price, b. Mon., 18 Apr 1874, 3 a.m.
Harry Gilmore Price, b. Sat., 26 May 1866, 9 a.m.
Richard T. Opperman, b. 13 Feb 1868
Agnes E. Opperman, b. 10 Nov 1873
Hugo Frederick Opperman, b. 28 Nov 1894
Harry Lee Opperman, b. Wed., 16 Jun 1897, half past 2 o'clock p.m.
Lulu E. Opperman, b. 2 Jan 1900

Henry A. Price, b. 8 May 1849
Howard Lee Price, b. Mon., 31 May 1869, 12:25 o'clock
Routh Price, b. Tues., 4 Sep 1894
Raymond Wesley Price, b. Tues., 21 Apr 1896
Harry A. Price, b. 26 Nov 1919
Thelma Reese Price, dau. of Lulu and George Price, b. 25 Sep 1920
Albert Wesley Price, son of Raymond and Winnie Price, b. 14 Mar 1927

Jennie A. Roberson, b. Fri., 31 Jul 1847, 3 a.m.

Deaths:
Henry A. Price, d. 16 Nov 1941
Albert W. Price, d. 12 Jun 1950
Joseph A. Price, d. Sat. evening, 2 Nov 1912, age 75
John Ferguson Price, d. Wed., 12 Feb 1936, 4:30 p.m., bur. at Abingdon, MD
Harry G. Price, d. 8 Mar 1930 at San Francisco, CA and "buried out there"
Charlotte A. Price, d. Thurs., 6 Apr 1922, 8 p.m., age 74

Helen M. Ferguson, d. 29 Sep 1849
Mary E. Ferguson, d. 23 Nov 1862
John J. Ferguson, d. Fri., 10 Nov 1872
John J. Ferguson, Jr., d. 21 Aug 1921, 2:30 a.m., at St. Francis Hospital in San Francisco, CA; cremated Cypress Lawn Cemetery, 23 Aug 1921, San Mateo County, CA

Harry Lee Opperman, d. 24 Apr 1899
Frederick Hugo Opperman, d. Sun., 18 Aug 1896
Agnes E. Opperman, d. Wed., 25 Apr 1956 at 10 o'clock at Bon Secours Hospital in Baltimore

Great Grandmother - Mary E. Burton - Mary E. Ferguson - Ninar's Mother [no date]

Richard Opperman - Pop - b. 13 Feb 1868, d. Thurs., 24 Mar 1921 at Chester Station, PA

JAMES W. FORWOOD BIBLE

No publication information available. Family data gleaned from a typescript at the Maryland Historical Society.

Marriage:
James Worthington Forwood and Mary Rebecca Forwood m. 2 Apr 1897 at the Darlington Rectory [Harford County]

Births:
James Worthington Forwood, b. 16 Mar 1870
Mary Rebecca Forwood, b. 11 Dec 1875

Children of James W. and Mary R. Forwood:
1. Harry Maxwell Forwood, b. 28 Jul 1898
2. Helen Forwood, b. 26 Jul 1900
3. Robert Forwood, b. 10 Aug 1908
4. James Worthington Forwood, b. 16 Oct 1911

Deaths:
Henry Forwood, d. 31 Oct 1910
Robert Forwood, d. -- Jan ----
James W. Forwood, Sr., d. -- Jul ----

Blanche W. Shinnick, wife of O. W. Shinnick and dau. of Robert and Sarah Forwood, d. 1 Aug 1914 at her residence at 1408 1st Street in Brooklyn, Anne Arundel County, MD; buried at Mount Olivet Cemetery.

JOHN FORWOOD BIBLE

Bible published in 1814 by Mathew Carey, 121 Chestnut Street, Philadelphia, PA. Family data gleaned from a typescript at the Maryland Historical Society. Inscribed "John and Hannah Forwood's Book, 1815."

Marriages:
John and Hannah Forwood m. 8 Mar 1785
William Smithson and Juliann Forwood m. 2 Dec 1835

William Smithson and Sarah Ann Rigdon m. 2 Jan 1844

Julia Smithson and ---- m. 4 Oct 1863 [*Ed. Note:* Marriage license states she married Parker Lee Forwood]

Louisa Smithson and ---- m. 4 Jan 1866 [*Ed. Note:* Parenthetical entry in the bible states she married John Toy]

William Smithson, Jr. and Annie Cummins m. 8 Feb 1877
William Smithson, Jr. and Sophia Frank m. 15 Jan 1879 [*Ed. Note:* Parenthetical entry stated they were the parents of Julia Tucker and that Sophia Frank was adopted by the family of Nicholas A. McComas, a Baltimore gunsmith at 44 Pratt Street near Gay Street].

Births:
John Forwood, b. 1 Apr 1762
Hannah Forwood, wife of John, b. 6 Oct 1767

Children of John and Hannah Forwood:
1. Elizabeth and Leah Forwood, b. 8 Nov 1785
2. William Forwood, b. 30 Aug 1787
3. Sarah Forwood, b. 26 Sep 1789
4. George Forwood, b. 27 Nov 1791
5. Robert Forwood, b. 23 Aug 1793
6. Jacob Forwood, b. 6 Jun 1795
7. Parker Forwood, b. 17 May 1797
8. Samuel Forwood, b. 7 May 1799
9. John Clark Forwood, b. 23 Jun 1801
10. Mary Forwood, b. 29 Apr 1803
11. Julia Forwood, b. 24 Mar 1807
12. Amor Forwood, b. 25 Feb 1809
13. Jane Amelia Forwood, b. 8 Jan 1812

Children of William and Sophia Smithson:
1. Anna Louisa Smithson, b. 6 May 1880
2. Emma Julia Smithson, b. 25 Mar 1882
3. William Preston Smithson, b. 25 Mar 1884

George B. Rigdon, son of Benjamin, b. 7 Feb 1849

Deaths:
Leah Forwood, d. 8 Nov 1785
Sarah Forwood, d. 24 Apr 1791 (or 1793)
George Forwood, d. 13 Aug 1793
Jane Amelia Forwood, d. 22 Sep 1815
Elizabeth Forwood alias Johnson, d. 10 Mar 1820
Robert Forwood, d. 10 Aug 1826
Mary Forwood, d. 30 Jul 1828
Hannah Forwood, wife of John, d 4 May 1829
John Forwood, d. 22 May 1835
Amor S. Forwood, d. 31 Aug 1843
John C. Forwood, d. 28 Dec 1857
William Forwood, d. 12 Sep 1860
Jacob Forwood, d. -- Oct 1860 [*Ed. Note:* He actually died 19 Sep 1860]
Dr. Parker Forwood, d. 26 Jan 1866
Margaret Smithson, d. 30 Jun 1858
George Smithson, d. 30 Jun 1858
Franklin Smithson, d. 16 Nov 1850
Juliann Smithson, d. 2 Sep 1842 in 36th year
Mary Smithson, d. 20 Mar 1839
Sallie Ann Smithson, d. 11 Feb 1876
Annie Smithson, wife of William, d. 31 Jan 1878
William Smithson, d. 23 Jan 1877, age 70 years, 4 months and 16 days

Louisa Toy, d. 4 Aug 1866

Family Records:
Children of William and Margaret Smithson:
1. William Smithson, b. 18 Aug 1806
2. Elizabeth Smithson, b. 10 Apr 1808
3. Sarah Smithson, b. 20 Nov 1809
4. Mary Smithson, b. 25 May 1811
5. Henry Smithson, b. 30 Apr 1813
6. George W. Smithson, b. 1 Jul 1815
7. James Smithson, b. 14 Jun 1817
8. Franklin Smithson, b. 22 Nov 1819
9. Priscilla F. Smithson, b. 30 Oct 1821
10. Cassandra G. Smithson, b. 20 May 1824

Children of William and Juliann Smithson:
1. William Smithson, b. 12 Nov 1836
2. Mary Elizabeth Smithson, b. 20 Sep 1838
3. Louisa A. Smithson, b. 28 Jan 1840
4. Juliann Smithson, b. 1 Sep 1842

Children of Benjamin and Elizabeth Rigdon:
1. Thomas Baker Rigdon, b. 29 Jan 1789
2. Stephen Rigdon, b. 21 Oct 1790
3. Samuel Forwood Rigdon, b. 23 Sep 1792
4. Ely Rigdon, b. 4 Oct 1794
5. Alexander Rigdon, b. 5 Apr 1796
6. George Sankey Rigdon, b. 24 Mar 1798
7. John Forwood Rigdon, b. 22 Feb 1800
8. Hannah Rigdon, b. 10 Feb 1802
9. Lacy Rigdon, b. 17 Feb 1804
10. Benjamin Rigdon, b. 24 Jan 1806
11. Lillie Rigdon, b. 24 Nov 1807
12. Elizabeth Rigdon, b. 22 Dec 1808
13. Laomi Rigdon, b. 27 Oct 1810
14. Sarah Ann Rigdon, b. 23 Jun 1813

WILLIAM FORWOOD BIBLE

Bible published in 1851 by George Lane & Lewis Scott, 200 Mulberry Street, New York; Joseph Longking, printer. Family data gleaned from a typescript at the Maryland Historical Society. Bible originally owned by William and Sarah Forwood of Deer Creek in Harford County.

Marriages:
William and Sarah Forwood m. 12 Feb 1818
Lawrence Forwood and Jennie Forwood m. Wed., 30 Sep 1885, at Belmont, Peach
    Bottom, PA, by Rev. G. W. Crawford

Births:
William Forwood, b. 30 Aug 1787
Sarah Forwood, b. 19 Oct 1796

Children of William and Sarah Forwood:
1. Emily B. Forwood, b. 18 Dec 1818
2. George W. Forwood, b. 8 Feb 1821
3. Hannah Jane Forwood, b. 27 Jan 1823
4. Margaret E. Forwood, b. 19 Feb 1825
5. John Amor Forwood, b. 11 Feb 1826
6. Robert Forwood, b. 10 Dec 1828
7. James G. Forwood, b. 23 Jun 1831
8. Parker F. Forwood, b. 18 Oct 1833
9. Julia Ann Forwood, b. 20 Jul 1836
10. Samuel W. Forwood, b. 12 Sep 1838
11. Loammie Forwood, b. 27 Nov 1843

H. Jennie Forwood, b. 25 Nov 1867
Lawrence H. Forwood, b. 26 Jun 1859
Robert Raymond Forwood, b. 26 Aug 1886
Mary Isabel Forwood, b. 12 Jan 1890
Sarah Margaret Forwood, b. 4 Dec 1891
Walter Forwood, b. 15 May 1897

Robert H. Archer, b. 3 Sep 1882

Children of Robert H. and Mary I. Archer:
1. Robert Harris Archer, b. 28 Jun 1913
2. John Archer, b. 13 Mar 1915

Deaths:
William Forwood, d. at 12 o'clock p.m. on 11 Sep 1860, age 73 years and 12 days
Sarah Forwood, wife of William, d. 17 May 1888, age 91 years, 7 months and 28 days
Lawrence Forwood, d. 14 Mar 1917
Hannah Jane [Jennie] Forwood, d. 5 Jan 1954
Robert Raymond Forwood, d. 18 Nov 1957

Mary Isabel Forwood Archer, d. 15 Jan 1921
Major Robert H. Archer, husband of Mary Isabel Forwood, d. 31 Jul 1948

Children of William and Sarah Forwood:
1. George W. Forwood, d. 24 Oct 1890, age 69 years, 8 months and 16 days
2. John A. Forwood, d. 1 Mar 1907, age 81 years and 18 days
3. Robert Forwood, d. 15 Feb 1904, age 79 years, 2 months and 5 days

4. Samuel W. Forwood, d. 15 May 1870, age 32 years, 8 months and 3 days
5. James G. Forwood, d. 1 Jun 1881, age 49 years, 11 months and 8 days
6. Emily B. Watters, wife of Henry R. Watters, d. 29 Dec 1878, age 60 years and 11 days
7. Hannah J. Forwood, d. 4 Mar 1885, age 62 years, 1 month and 7 days
8. Julia A. Forwood, d. 8 Jul 1896, age 59 years, 11 months and 22 days

FULFORD-MITCHELL BIBLE

Bible published in 1802 by Mathew Carey, 113 Market Street, Philadelphia, PA. The Fulford and Mitchell family lived in Harford County, MD, and information from this bible was copied by the Maryland State DAR Chairperson of Genealogical Records just before it was sold at public auction on 2 Dec 1961. The purchaser of the bible was not indicated.

Marriage:
Henry Fulford, Jr. and Maria C. Mitchell m. ---- [*Ed. Note:* No marriage information was recorded in this bible transcript; however, Henry Fulford, Jr. married Maria C. Mitchell by 1839 and died on 1 Aug 1844. His death notice in the *Baltimore Sun* on 5 Aug 1844 stated he was the son-in-law of Alexander Mitchell].

Births:
Children of Henry Jr. and Maria Fulford:
1. William Fulford, b. 18 Jan 1840
2. Alexander Mitchell Fulford, b. 5 Dec 1841
3. Mary Patterson Fulford, b. 29 Feb 1844

Deaths:
Nathaniel W. S. Hays, d. at his residence near Bel Air, Harford County, on 20 Apr 1863

Henry Fulford, Jr., d. 1 Aug 1844 in his 28th year

Children of Henry Jr. and Maria Fulford:
1. William Fulford, d. Wed., 6 Jan 1841, age 11 months and 19 days
2. Mary Patterson Fulford, d. Fri. night at half past 11 o'clock, 31 Jan 1845, age 11 months and 1 day
3. Elizabeth Mitchell, beloved wife of Alexander, d. Tues. morning at half past 10 o'clock, 7 Nov 1848, age 70 years, 3 months and 27 days

4. Alexander Mitchell, d. Wed. afternoon at 5 o'clock on 20 Nov 1850, age 73 years and 11 months

Children of Alexander and Elizabeth Mitchell:
1. Stephen Walker Mitchell, d. in Philadelphia on Sun. morning, 6 Nov 1831, age 26 years and 8 months
2. George Torrance Mitchell, d. in the City of Piura about 40 miles in the interior from Payta, South America on the Pacific, on 25 Oct 1845, age 30 years and 5 days
3. Edmund Mitchell, d. Thurs. afternoon at 3 o'clock, 10 Oct 1850, age 32 years, 8 months and 10 days
4. William Maitland Mitchell, d. at his residence near Winchester, TN on Wed. at 12 o'clock, 1 Jan 1851, age 40 years, 1 month and 11 days
5. Patrick Henry Mitchell, d. Sun. morning at half past 1 o'clock, 30 Dec 1855, age 34 years, 6 months and 4 days

GALLOWAY-KNAUFF BIBLE

Bible published by Kimber and Sharpless (no date indicated) and sold at their store in Philadelphia at No. 50 North 4th Street. This transcript was published in the *Maryland Genealogical Society Bulletin* (Vol. 27, No. 4) in Fall, 1986, noting: "The first two pages of vital statistics are loose. The three other pages appear to have been bound into the bible. They are smaller in size than the bible pages and a deeper yellow."

Marriages:
Robert C. Galloway and Martha G. Galloway m. 5 May 1805
Mosses G. Galloway and Harriet Galloway m. 13 Mar ----
Thomas J. Lemmon and Mary G. D. Lemmon m. 15 Jun 1830
William Knauff and Mary E. Kinghorn m. 31 Dec 1849
William G. Knauff and Annie B. McElvain m. 24 Jul 1876
Charles A. Knauff and Aggie Nicol m. 23 Dec 1880
Edward E. Knauff and Ollie Pergoy m. 30 Aug ----
Edward E. Knauff and Mamie E. Klug m. 26 Nov 18-- (torn)
Edward R. Knauff and Irma Markley m. 21 Sep ----
Milton W. Knauff and Mildred Grace Fiedley m. 17 Aug 1940 [*Note:* Written in pencil: "Fiedler" (instead of "Fiedley")]

Births:
Mosses G. Galloway, b. 24 Feb 1806

Mary G. D. Galloway, b. 27 Jul 1808

[Children of Moses and Mary Galloway]:
1. Elizabeth T. Galloway, b. 6 Jan 1810
2. Thomas B. Galloway, b. 23 Jul 1813
3. ---n C. Galloway, b. 4 Oct 1817
4. R. C. Galloway, b. 11 Apr 1822

Bayla Smith, b. 17 Mar ----
Edward Steward, b. 1808
Mary E. Kinghorn, b. 19 Nov 1829

[Children of William and Mary Knauff]:
1. Elizabeth Deborah Knauff, b. 6 Feb 1841
2. Laura Virginia Knuaff, b. 5 Dec 1853
3. William G. Knauff, b. 7 Dec 1855
4. Charles Albert Knauff, b. 12 Jul 1858
5. Robert E. Knoff *[sic]*, b. 12 Apr 1861
6. Ella F. Knauff, b. 18 Nov 1865
7. Edward E. Knauff, b. 30 Aug 1868

Helene G. Knauff, b. 3 Jul 1890
Howard E. Knauff, b. 29 Jan 1892
Edna (Klug) Knauff, b. 9 Nov 1893
Edward R. Knauff, b. 21 Sep 1898
Milton M. Knauff, b. 21 May 1910
Howard E. Knauff, b. 25 Nov 1932
Bruce R. Knauff, b. 20 Aug 1943
Glen Galloway Knauff, b. 21 May 1947

Deaths:
C. Galloway, d. 1 Oct 1850 in his 28th year
Robert C. Galloway, d. 30 Jan 1844 in his 65th year. *Note:* Written in pencil: borne 1779
Martha G. Galloway, d. 16 Mar 1833 in her 49th year. *Note:* Written in pencil: borne 1784
Thomas B. Galloway, d. 23 May 1823 in his 10th year. *Note:* Written in pencil: borne 1800 [*Ed Note:* There is an apparent error in the transcript since his age and dates do not compute].

Elizabeth Deborah Knauff, d. 2(?) Aug ----, age 6 months
Robert E. Knauff, d. 1 Jul 1864, age 9 years, 3 months and 16 days
Mary E. Knauff, d. 8 Oct 1899, age 68
William Knauff, d. 17 Jan 1911, age 38 (sick 13 days)
William G. Knauff, d. 14 Aug 1939 in his 84th year
Laura Virginia Knauff, d. 13 Jan 1878 in her 25th year
Mamie E. Knauff, d. 12 Jan 1911
Edward E. Knauff, d. 6 Sep 1947
Edward Roston Knauff, d. 21 Jul 1945, age 47 [*Note:* Written in pencil: "Royston" (instead of "Roston")]

Ann Raven, d. ---- [blank]
Charles Brian, d. 7 Jul 1844 in his 30th year
Emory ---- [blank], drowned 19 Nov 1842 in his 21st year
Alexander Wanderford(?), d. 28 Jun 1858 in his 23rd year

Family Records:
Laura V. Knauff joined Caroline Street Church on 30 Sep 1877

HARRIET GALLOWAY BIBLE

Bible published in 1847 for Kimber & Sharpless by Jesper Harding in Philadelphia. This transcript was published in the *Maryland Genealogical Society Bulletin* (Vol. 29, No. 2) in Spring, 1988, noting that some information was written on sheets of paper inserted in the bible. Inscribed on the flyleaf: "Harriet Galloway's Book - Given her by her husband Moses G. Galloway, November, 1847."

Marriages:
Moses G. Galloway and Harriet McClellan m. 13 Mar 1828
Moses G. Galloway and Isabella Hulse m. 11 Dec 1851
William A. Galloway and Jemima Porter m. 29 May 1856
William M. Boon [Boone] and Harriet A. Galloway m. 22 Sep 1858
George Albert Boyden and Harriet Virginia Galloway, dau. of William Andrew
    Galloway and Jemima Porter, m. 16 Apr 1886 at 8 o'clock at bride's residence,
    134 South Eden Street, Baltimore, MD, by Rev. Roe
James Wilkinson and Mary E. Galloway ("Aunt Mary") m. 16 Nov 1854

Births:
[Children of Moses G. and Harriet Galloway]:
1. Robert C. Galloway, b. 1 Aug 1830

2. Marthy Presbury Galloway b. 30 Mar 1833 (twin)
3. Mary Eliza Galloway, b. 31 Mar 1833 (twin)
4. William Andrew Galloway, b. 15 Jul 1835
5. Harriet Ann Galloway, b. 14 Jan 1839
6. Gouldsmith Day Galloway, b. 29 Dec 1840
7. Ephemia Jeremiah Galloway, b. 23 May 1842
8. Moses George Galloway, b. 28 Jan 1844

[Children of Moses G. and Isabella Galloway]:
1. John Galloway, b. 7 Oct 1852
2. Henry Clay Galloway, b. 25 Sep 1854
Children of Harriet A. and William M. Boone:
1. Mary Ella Shreeves Boone, b. 13 Jul 1859
2. Clara Dew Boone, b. 25 Jan 1861
3. William Joseph Boone, b. 8 Dec 1862
4. Emma Boone, b. 13 Apr 1872
5. Mabury G. Boone, b. 6 Jan 1878

William E. E. Sparks, b. 10 Jan 1881

Harriet R. Bowen, b. 4 Apr 1886
Clara M. Bowen, b. 6 Sep 1891
J. Raymond Bowen, b. 29 Aug 1893

A. Lewis Martini, b. 9 (or 19) Apr 1910
Harriet L. Martini, b. 2 May 1915

Eleanor M. Hood, b. 26 May 1921

Nancy Ann Lenore Bowen, b. 13 Dec 1930

George Albert Boyden, b. at Altoona, PA, 18 Jul 1856, son of William Boyden and
    Sarah Jane Daugherty

James Wilkinson, b. 7 Apr 1829

[Children of James and Mary Wilkinson]:
1. Harriet Ann Wilkinson, b. 18 Sep 1856
2. Samuel George Wilkinson, b. 13 Jul 1858

3. Joseph Levey Wilkinson, b. 30 Jul 1860
4. Mary Alice Wilkinson, b. 12 Sep 1862

William A. Galloway ("Uncle Billy"), b. 15 Jul 1835
Jemima Galloway, b. 22 May 1837

Children of William and Jemima Galloway:
1. Harriet Virginia Galloway, b. 2 Oct 1857
2. Mary Elizabeth Galloway, b. 29 Jul 1860
3. William George Galloway, b. 22 Sep 1862
4. Henry Luther Galloway, b. 9 Aug 1864

Children of George A. and Harriet V. Boyden:
1. Beatrice Virginia Boyden, b. about 12:35 a.m., 25 Apr 1887 at 1928 Linden Avenue, Baltimore, MD
2. George Albert Boyden, b. about 6:25 p.m., 15 Dec 1888 at 134 S. Eden Street, Baltimore, MD
3. Donald Galloway Boyden, b. about 3:30 a.m., 19 Aug 1892 at 1031 Caroline Street, Baltimore, MD
4. John Calvin Boyden, b. about 7 a.m., 26 Apr 1895 at Second Cottage East from ---- Avenue, Washington Avenue, Mt. Washington, MD
5. George A. Boyden, b. 17 Feb 1907, Mt. Washington

Deaths:
Ephemia J. Galloway, stillborn 15 Apr 1829
Marthy P. Galloway, d. 8 Feb 1834, age 10 months and 8 days
Ephemia J. (Eeff Jeremiah) Galloway, d. 15 Sep 1845, age 3 years and 4 months
Harriet Galloway, d. 4 May 1848, age 45 years and 3 month [*Note:* The "3 month" was written in pencil]
Gouldsmith D. Galloway, d. 9 Sep 1851, age 10 years and 8 months
Robert C. Galloway, d. 27 Dec 1852, age 22 years, 4 months and 3 weeks
Moses G. Galloway, d. 20 Oct 1853, age 9 years and 9 months
Moses G. Galloway, d. 2 Jun 1855, age 49 years and 4 months
William A. Galloway, son of Moses G. and Harriet A. Galloway, d. 19 Jan ---- [blank]
Jemima Galloway (neé Porter), wife of William A. Galloway, d. 10 Dec 1914
Mary E. Jewell neé Decker neé Galloway, dau. of William A. and Jemima Galloway, d. 19 Jan ---- [blank]
Harriet Virginia Boyden (neé Galloway), dau. of William A. and Jemima Galloway, and wife of G. A. Boyden, d. 11 Dec 1915

Eliza Farrer, d. 1 Mar 1847, age 49
William M. Boone, d. 22 Sep 1914
Harriet Ann Boone, d. 16 Jul 1916
Clara Dew Sparks, d. 12 Jan 1943
Mary Ella Bowen, d. 24 Nov 1944
Emma Boone George, d. 29 Aug 1946
Mabury G. Lynch, d. 13 Feb 1964
J. Raymond Bowen, d. 22 Nov 1939
Harriet R. Bowen Martini, d. 12 Nov 1949
William Everett Edward Sparks, d. 21 Feb 1959
Clara M. Bowen Hood, d. 28 Feb 1971
A. Lewis Martini, d. -- Sep 1910
Harriet Ann Wilkinson, d. 11 Dec 1850, age 4 years and 2 months
James Wilkinson, d. 24 Dec 1889, age 60 years and 8 months

GEORGE W. GALLUP BIBLE

Bible published in 1852 by Jasper Harding, Philadelphia, PA. Family data gleaned from a typescript at the Maryland Historical Society. Bible originally owned by George W. Gallup of Perryman, Harford County, MD. [*Ed. Note:* Gallup historians indicate the family initially settled in Stonington, CT, later moved to Vermont and migrated to Newcastle, DE before settling in Harford County, MD].

Marriages:
Oliver Gallup and Perme Ann Holloway m. 14 Feb 1820
Oliver Gallup and Catherine Martin m. 15 Jan 1828
John Oliver Gallup and Annie Virginia Stevens m. 3 Nov 1859
George Alfonso Nelson and Annie Elizabeth Gallup m. 3 Jan 1860
Daniel Gallup and Annie E. Devoe m. 28 Apr 1864

Births:
Children of Oliver and Permelia Gallup:
1. Margarett Ann Gallup, b. 16 Mar 1822
2. William Henry Gallup, b. 13 Jul 1824

Children of Oliver and Catherine Gallup:
1. Ann Elizabeth Gallup, b. 19 Dec 1828
2. Daniel Gallup, b. 16 Dec 1830

3. John Oliver Gallup, b. 21 Aug 1833
4. Marry Louisa Gallup, b. 21 Oct 1835
5. Charles Thomas Gallup, b. 28 Aug 1837
6. Catherine Maria Gallup, b. 24 Dec 1839
7. Carline Preston Gallup, b. 28 Jan 1842
8. George Washington Gallup, b. 16 Jan 1845
9. Emily Williams Gallup, b. 10 Dec 1847
Oliver Stevens Gallup, son of John O. and Annie V. Gallup, b. 18 Oct 1866

Deaths:
Anna Elizabeth Martin, wife of John Martin, d. 28 Sep 1828
Mary E. Martin, dau. of John Martin, d. -- Jun 1839
John Martin, d. 26 Sep 1841

Charles T. Gallup, d. 17 Nov 1889
Catharine Martin Gallup, d. 3 Aug 1891
Oliver Gallup, d. 7 Dec 1861, age 62
Mary L. Gallup, d. 22 Apr 1865
John O. Gallup, d. 17 May 1873
Daniel Gallup, d. 28 Apr 1895
George W. Gallup, d. 21 Oct 1890
William H. Gallup, d. 4 Dec 1903

Margarett A. Holloway, d. 2 Nov 1864, age 42

Family Records (Clippings in Bible):
1. John Gallup, d. 17 May 1873 at his residence on Oxford Neck in Talbot County, MD, in his 40th year.

2. William Summerfield Bond, d. in the morning of 24 Apr ----, in his 22nd year, after a lingering illness; funeral from the residence of his aunt at 134 E. Monument Street [Baltimore City].

3. Mary L. Gallup, second dau. of the late Oliver and Catherine Gallup, d. near Perrymansvlle on 22 Apr ---- [1865].

4. Oliver Gallup, d. at his residence on Bush River Neck in Harford County, in his 62nd year [date not given]; "Cambridge, OH papers please copy."

GILLESPIE-HUGHES BIBLE

No publication information available. This transcript was published in the *Maryland Genealogical Society Bulletin* (Vol. 29, No. 4) in Fall, 1988, noting: "These Bible records are from the Orams Church Bible of 1831 which states it was located in Oella, Baltimore County, Maryland."

Marriages:
William A. Gillespie and Elizabeth Ann Hughes m. 3 Mar 1853
Edward J. Stansbury and Mary Elizabeth Gillespie m. 1 Jan 1873 [*Note:* In the 1873 date a "3" was written over a "2"]
Thomas Gillespie and Louisa Gillespie m. 16 Aug 1880
Thomas German and Florence Gillespie m. 4 Dec 1881

Births:
William A. Gillespie, b. 9 Jan 1829
William James Gillespie, b. 22 Mar 1828
Mary E. Gillespie, b. 9 Jan 1854
Laura Virginia Gillespie, b. 5 Jun 1856
Emma Jane Gillespie, b. 11 Mar 1858
Annie Louisa Gillespie, b. 23 Jan 1860
Nelly Florence Gillespie, b. 26 Dec 1862
Hatty Brown Gillespie, b. 2 Dec 1864
William Andrew Gillespie, b. 15 Apr 1872

Sophia Jane Hughes, b. 11 Jan 1830
Elizabeth Ann Hughes, b. 2 May 1833
William Henry Hughes, b. 10 Sep 1838
Elisha Harrison Hughes, b. 15 Apr 1840
Martha Ann Hughes, b. 22 Feb 1844
Frances Ann Hughes, b. 12 Mar 1849
Amanda Melvina Fritzelen Hughes, b. 7 Apr 1852

Bessie Alisha Evans, b. 4 May 1876
Annie Louisa Evans, b. 29 Jan 1878
Battie Blanche Evans, b. ---- [blank]

Emerson Eugene Stansbury, b. 25 Apr ----
Florence Vernon Stansbury, b. 19 Jun 1879

William Lerue Campbell, b. 1 Jun 1881 [*Ed. Note:* Name was first entered as "Willim Relau Campbell" and was then crossed out].

Deaths:
Henry Hughes, d. -- Sep 1856
Maggie Hughes, d. 3 Dec 1864
Elizabeth Hughes, d. 8 Feb 1865

Jonathan Gillespie, d. 8 Apr 1854(?)
Mary Ann Gillespie, d. 29 Dec 1863
William Andrew Gillespie, d. 12 Jun 1872, age 43 years, 5 months and 3 days
Elizabeth Ann Gillespie, d. 30 Jun 1884, age 51 years, 1 month and 28 days

Louisa Cook, d. 20 Jun 1864

Emma Jane Evans, d. 25 Feb 1878, age 22 years

Mary Elizabeth Stansbury, d. 8 Aug 1880, age 26 years and 7 months

Annie Louisa Campbell, d. 28 Jun 1880, age 21 years
William Relau Campbell, d. 18 Jul 1881, age 6 weeks and 4 days. [*Note:* See above; middle name probably "Larue"].

Family Records (Clippings in Bible):
1. Florence German, wife of Thomas C. German, d. on the 15th instant [no year given] in her 22nd year; funeral on Monday morning at 10 o'clock from her late residence, 463 East Chase Street; funeral service will be held at Baltimore Cemetery. [*Note:* Another entry in the bible stated she died in September, 1884, age 20].

2. Elizabeth Hughes, d. 5 Feb --- [no year given] in her 65th year; funeral tomorrow [place not indicated].

3. Louisa Cook, d. on the 23rd instant [no year given] in her 28th year, leaving a child one week old, a husband and large circle of friends ... at her residence, Woodbine Cottage, near Shrewsbury, York County (PA). [*Note:* Another entry in the bible stated she died 20 Jun 1864].

JOHN GRAPE BIBLE

Bible published in 1857 by E. H. Butler, Philadelphia. Inscribed on the clasp: "Presented to John Grape by his class, May 1st, 1859." Family data gleaned from a typescript at the Maryland Historical Society.

Marriages:
John Grape and Ann Maria Hindes m. 12 Feb 1839 by Rev. Charles B. Tibbett
John Grape and Mary Cline m. -- Feb ---- [date not given]

Births:
John Grape, b. 16 Sep 1801
Ann Maria Grape, b. ---- [blank]

Children of John and Ann Maria Grape:
1. John William Grape, b. 15 Dec 1839
2. Thomas Edward Grape, b. 1 Mar 1841
3. Samuel Grape, b. 10 Oct 1842
4. Joseph Grape, b. 29 Oct 1844
5. Mary Elizabeth Grape, b. 18 Oct 1848
6. Laura Janet Grape, b. 20 Jan 1850
7. Henry Evans Grape, b. 4 Sep 1851

Deaths:
Harry Allen Grape, d. ---- [blank]
Harry Winter Grape, d. 27 Jan 1871
John Grape, d. 21 Jul 1872
Ann M. Grape, d. 23 Dec 1891
John W. Grape, d. 12 Dec 1876
Thomas E. Grape, d. -- Aug 1885
Samuel Grape, d. -- Jun 1881
Mary E. Buck, d. 20 Apr 1901

MICAJAH GREENFIELD BIBLE

Bible published in 1747 by Thomas Baskett, printer to Oxford University, "Holy Bible, by His Majesty's Special Command, appointed to be read in the Churches." Family data gleaned from a typescript at the Maryland Historical Society.

Marriage:
Jacob Greenfield and Elizabeth Everist, dau. of Joseph Everist, m. 29 Sep 1791

Births:
---- Waltham [page torn], son of Thomas Waltham and ----a his wife, b. 13 Mar 1795, d. -- Sep 1798

--sas Waltham [page torn], son of Thomas and ---tha, b. 27 Nov 1798

Jacob Greenfield, son of Micajah and Martha his wife, b. 13 Dec 1762
My twin sons [Greenfield] b. 13 Jan and d. the third day after their birth in 1765

My dau. Mary [Greenfield] b. 7 Sep 1766

Martha Greenfield, dau. of Micajah and Mary his wife, b. 22 Jan 1772

Children of William and Mary Osborn:
1. Cordelia Osborn, b. 4 May 1768
2. Aberilla Osborn, b. 22 Feb 1770
3. Cyrus Osborn, b. 12 Jan 1773
4. Sarah Osborn, b. 7 Sep 1777
5. Frances Osborn, b. 17 Sep 1780

Children of Jacob and Elizabeth Greenfield:
1. Mary Greenfield, b. 3 Sep 1792
2. Joseph Greenfield, b. 1 Jan 1794
3. Martha Greenfield, b. 6 Oct 1795
4. Henry Austin Greenfield, b. 30 Oct 1797
5. Jacob Greenfield, b. 7 Sep 1799
6. Elizabeth Greenfield, b. 24 Sep 1801

Deaths:
"Mary Garrettson, wife of Aquila Garrettson and dau. of Micajah Greenfield and Martha his wife, d. 6 of March at about -- o'clock at night of a Tues. and was tacon sick on Sun. the 3 about the same our as above 17-7" *[sic]*

My wife Martha [Greenfield], d. 10 Apr 1768 in her 27th year

Micajah Greenfield, d. 25 Dec 1772, age 39 years on 17 Jul 1772

JOHN HENRY GRENINGER BIBLE

Pictorial Family Bible, The Light of the World, 1892. A photocopy and typescript of the bible records was submitted by the owner Carleton L. Weidemeyer of Clearwater, FL in 2002, noting that this family lived in the Second District of Baltimore County. He also researched and prepared the notes presented herein and listed the following chain of possession of the family bible: John Henry Greninger, Fannie Sutch Greninger, Nellie Catherine (Greninger) Weidemeyer, Carleton L. Weidemeyer.

Marriages:
John Henry Greninger and Fannie May Sutch m. 27 Jun 1894 at Hebbville, MD by Rev. B. F. Keller, Minister of the Gospel, in presence of Fannie E. Keller.

Esther Havilla Greninger and Walter Winfield Keck m. 12 Jun 1913

Births:
Henry Leslie Greninger, b. 6 Feb 1895 at Hebbville, MD, bapt. 14 Apr 1895 by Rev. H. N. Greninger

Esther Havilla Greninger, b. 18 Mar 1897 at Hebbville, MD, bapt. 4 Apr 1897 by Rev. M. A. Kennelly

Ruth Caroline Greninger, b. 18 Dec 1899 at Hebbville, MD, bapt. 19 Jan 1900 by Rev. M. A. Kennelly

Nellie Catherine Greninger, b. 11 Sep 1910 at Hebbville, MD, bapt. 16 Oct 1910 by Rev. H. N. Greninger

Deaths:
Henry Noah Greninger, d. 23 Feb 1916 at Hebbville, MD, bur. in Mt. Olive Cemetery

Susanna Graham Greninger, d. 4 Jun 1932 at Milford, bur. in Mt. Olive Cemetery

Leslie Greninger, d. 9 Nov 1938 by accident, bur. in Mt. Olive Cemetery

John Henry Greninger, d. 25 Apr 1944 at Randallstown, MD, bur. in Mt. Olive Cemetery

Fannie May Greninger (Mom), d. 22 Feb 1952 at home of Ruth Marriott in Rockdale, MD, bur. in Mt. Olive Cemetery

Family Records:
(Notes prepared by Carleton L. Weidemeyer)

1. Henry Leslie Greninger was a building contractor, residing on Rolling Road, Hebbville, MD, and married Lillian Zimmerman. Henry died as a result of an automobile accident on 9 Nov 1938 and is buried in Mt. Olive Cemetery, Randallstown, MD (*Baltimore Sun*, 10 Nov 1938).

2. Esther Haville Greninger married (1) Walter Winfield Keck who operated Keck's Barber Shop in Randallstown, MD. Walter died 21 Feb 1951 and is buried in an unmarked grave in Mt. Olive Cemetery. Esther married (2) Albert J. Carstens and they are both interred in Mt. Olive Cemetery.

3. Ruth Caroline Greninger married building contractor William Saum Marriott and lived in Rockdale, Baltimore County, MD until her death on 6 Jul 1992. She and her husband are interred at Mt. Olive Cemetery (*Baltimore Sun*, 9 Jul 1992).

4. Nellie Catherine Greninger was born at the Toll Gate House on Liberty Road in Randallstown, MD (the bible entry is erroneois as to place of birth). Her parents were keepers and operators of the toll gate at the time and later returned to Hebbville. She graduated from Randallstown High School in 1927, married Lloyd H. Weidemeyer, and died in Clearwater, Pinellas County, FL.

5. Rev. Henry Noah Greninger is the father of John Henry Greninger and paternal grandfather of Nellie Catherine and her siblings. Rev. H. N. Greninger was Pastor of Salem Evangelical Church at Hebbville, Baltimore County, MD.

STEPHEN B. HANNA BIBLE

Bible published by Samuel D. Burlock, Philadelphia, PA (date not indicated). Family data gleaned from a typescript at the Maryland Historical Society.

Marriages:
Stephen B. Hanna and Cassandra Griffin m. 26 Feb 1851 by Rev. George Hildt

Births:
Stephen B. Hanna, b. 17 Nov 1822
Cassandra Griffin, b. 27 Nov 1824

Children of Stephen B. and Cassandra Hanna:
1. Olivia Jane Hanna, b. 7 Dec 1851
2. George T. and John R. Hanna, b. 29 Mar 1853
3. Robert N. Hanna, b. 9 Feb 1855
4. J. Howard Hanna, b. 10 Dec 1856
5. Annie May Hanna, b. 12 Nov 1859
6. Lydia Cassandra Hanna, b. 1 Feb 1862

Deaths:
John R. Hanna, d. -- Jul 1853
Cassandra Hanna, d. -- May, 1876
Stephen B. Hanna, d. -- Feb 1897

HERMAN HANSON BIBLE

Bible published in 1875 by A. D. Holman & Co. Family data gleaned from a typescript at the Maryland Historical Society.

Marriage:
Herman Hanson and Emilie Emmord m. 4 Oct 1881 by Rev. S. C. Lettner with George Emmord and Lucy Lantz as witnesses. [*Note:* Their marriage certificate was written in German].

Births:
Thomas Hanson, b. 22 Dec 1820
Sophia Hanson, b. 6 Jun 1820
Herman Hanson, b. 30 Jan 1850
Emelia Hanson, b. 15 Mar 1860

Children of Herman and Emelia Hanson:
1. ---- Hanson, infant son, b. & d. 1 Dec 1882
2. Amelie Sophia Hanson, b. 16 Mar 1885
3. Ada Louise Hanson, b. 13 Jun 1887
4. Mary Irene Hanson, b. 10 Mar 1889
5. Ruth Hanson, b. 28 Feb 1891
6. Emmord Hanson, b. 6 Jan 1893
7. Herman William Hanson, b. 8 Oct 1894
8. Herman Hanson, b. 18 Sep 1896
9. Thomas Earl Hanson, b. 23 Aug 1898
10. Naomi Hanson, b. 13 Sep 1900

Deaths:
Thomas Hanson, d. 20 Nov 1887
Sophia Hanson, d. 26 Feb 1895
Herman Hanson, d. 28 Dec 1938
Emelia Hanson, d. 23 Apr 1903
Herman William Hanson, d. 21 Mar 1896
Herman Hanson, d. 19 Sep 1896

HENRY E. HARKINS BIBLE

Published in 1891 by the Bible Publishing House in Syracuse, NY. Family data gleaned from a typescript at the Maryland Historical Society.

Marriages:
Henry Edgar Harkins and Sallie Ann Monks m. 8 Oct 1890
Lester Winfield Tucker and Beatrice Harkins m. 2 Nov 1912
Lester Winfield Tucker, Jr. and Nancy Louise Wagner m. 24 Aug 1940
Don A. Brennan and Beatrice Louise Tucker m. 9 May 1942

Births:
Beatrice Harkins, b. 1 Sep 1891
Marguerite Eileen Harkins, b. 14 Nov 1895

Lester Winfield Tucker, Jr., b. 3 Mar 1915
Beatrice Louise Tucker, b. 8 Mar 1918
Lester Winfield Tucker III, b. 30 May 1946
Edward Buckley Tucker, b. 14 Feb 1950
James Wagner Tucker, b. 4 Mar 1955

Donna Leslie Brennan, b. 13 Mar 1945

Deaths:
Edward T. Monks, d. -- Sep 1924
Ellen Treadway Monks, d. 21 Aug 1879

Marguerite Elline Harkins, d. 31 Mar 1910
Harry E. Harkins, d. 24 May 1929

Sallie M. Harkins, d. 2 Jan 1942

Lester Winfield Tucker, d. 1 Jul 1953

HARKINS-ROBINSON BIBLE

Bible published by Whilt & Yost, 805 Market Street, Philadelphia (no date given). Family data gleaned from a typescript at the Maryland Historical Society. Some of the information was written on pieces of paper inserted in the bible.

Marriage:
Joseph A. Harkins and Miss Lourenna S. Robinson m. 21 Dec 1865 at Deer Creek Chapel

Thomas Robinson and Elizabeth Grafton m. 19 Nov 1835

Births:
Children of Joseph and Lourenna Harkins:
1. Henry Edgar Harkins, b. 12 Oct 1866
2. Maurice Stevenson Harkins, b. 15 Jul 1869
3. Thomas Livingston Harkins, b. 17 May 1872
4. Jessie L. Harkins, b. 14 Sep 1874
5. Edwin Wilson Harkins, b. 1 Oct 1876
6. Joseph Robinson Harkins, b. 11 Oct 1878
7. Charles Littleton Harkins, b. 2 Nov 1881

Thomas Robinson, b. 23 Jun 1811
Elizabeth Grafton, b. 6 Mar 1817

Children of Thomas and Elizabeth Robinson:
1. Hester Jane Robinson, b. Fri., 19 Sep 1836
2. Christine Robinson, b. 30 Jan 1838
3. Lorena Robinson, b. 30 Mar 1840
4. Sarah Elizabeth Robinson, b. 19 Dec 1841
5. Margaret Lucinda Robinson, b. 19 Sep 1843
6. Thomas Jefferson Robinson, b. 11 May 1846
7. Mary Ann Robinson, b. 30 Oct 1848
8. Rebecca Adelia Robinson, b. 3 Jan 1852
9. Emma Jannette Robinson, b. 27 Apr 1854

10. Charles Littleton Robinson, b. 28 Sep 1857
11. John Cameron Robinson, b. 28 Jun 1859

Deaths:
Joseph A. Harkins, d. Mon., 17 Aug 1914 at 8 a.m.
Lorena S. Harkins, d. 26 Nov 1917
John H. Harkins, d. 25 Oct 1917 at 8 o'clock
Mrs. Lorena S. Harkins, widow of the deceased Capt. Joseph A. Harkins and dau. of Thomas and Elizabeth Robinson, d. 26 Nov 1917 [*Ed. Note:* However, another entry in the bible stated she died Mon., 25 Nov 1918 at 5 p.m.]

Thomas Robinson, d. 4 Jan 1900
Elizabeth Robinson, d. 6 Apr 1892
Hester Jane Robinson, d. 2 Aug 1842

Family Records:
(Deaths)
Aunt Sallie 1840
Aunt Margaret 1850
Grandfather 1852
Uncle George 1854
Aunt Eliza 1858
Grandmother 1888
Aunt Hannah 1904
Uncle John 1915
Samuel Scarf 1873

HASTINGS-RICHARDSON BIBLE

Bible published in 1834 by the American Bible Society in New York. Family data gleaned from a typescript at the Maryland Historical Society. [*Ed. Note:* It contains records of the Hastings and Richardson families of Shelby County, KY, of which three members married and founded families in Harford County, MD].

Marriages:
John D. Hastings and Frances B. Lloyd m. 10 Mar 1828
John M. Richardson and Elizabeth J. Hastings m. 15 Feb 1844
Charles E. Blumer and Eurith C. Hastings m. 12 Feb 1859
John T. Hastings and Mary E. Lancaster m. 20 Jun 1880

Births:
John D. Hastings, b. ---- [no date]
Frances B. Hastings b. 13 Mar 1808

Children of John D. and Frances B. Hastings:
1. Elizabeth Jane Hastings, b. 10 Dec 1828
2. Eurith C. Hastings, b. 28 Sep 1832
3. John T. H. Hastings, b. 7 Apr 1839

John M. Richardson, son of William and Matilda Richardson, b. 2 Aug 1818

Children of John M. and Elizabeth Richardson:
1. Frances M. Richardson, b. 22 Jun 1846
2. John W. Richardson, b. 21 Nov 1848
3. George J. T. Richardson, b. 17 Mar 1851
4. Lizzie Judson Richardson, b. 16 Sep 1854
5. Mary Thomas Richardson, b. 25 Nov 1857
6. Eurith B. Richardson, b. 12 Mar 1859
7. Minnie Belle Richardson, b. 24 Apr 1862

Deaths:
---- [blank] Richardson, d. 7 Mar 1845
Eurith B. Richardson, d. 30 Jun 1853
George J. Richardson, d. 6 Nov 1864

NATHANIEL W. S. HAYS BIBLE

Bible published in 1830 by McCarty & Davis, 171 Market Street, Philadelphia, PA (printed by I. Ashmead & Company). The Hays family lived in Harford County, MD. Information from the bible was copied by the Maryland State DAR Chairperson of Genealogical Records just before the bible was sold at public auction on 2 Dec 1961. The purchaser of the bible was not indicated.

Marriages:
Nathaniel W. S. Hays, son of Archer and Hannah Hays, m. Mary Fulford, dau. of William and Mary Fulford, on Tues. evening, 28 Jan 1834, by Rev. William Finney

Nathaniel W. S. Hays and Mrs. Maria C. Fulford, dau. of Alexander and Elizabeth Torrance Mitchell of the City of Baltimore, on Tues. morning, 13 Apr 1858, at the hour of 6 o'clock, by Rev. Joseph F. Smith

Births:
William Hays, b. Thurs. night, 18 Oct 1838
Archer Hays, son of Nathaniel and Mary Hays, b. Sun. morning, 11 Jan 1855

Deaths:
William Fulford, d. Tues. morning, 24 Apr 1838, age 60 years and 15 days

William Hays, d. Wed. night, 27 Mar 1839, age 5 months and 9 days

Mary L. Hays, wife of Nathaniel W. S. Hays and dau. of the late William Fulford, d. at Mont Albo farm near Belleair [Bel Air] on Mon. morning, 12 May 1856, at the hour of 7 o'clock, age 49 years and 2 months

Archer Hays, d. at Prospect Mill, Harford County, on 7 Jul 1827 at 3 o'clock in the afternoon, age ---- [not indicated]

Nathaniel W. S. Hays, d. at Mont Albo farm, his residence near Bel Air, MD, on Mon. evening, 20 Apr 1863, at 20 minutes of 7 o'clock

Dr. Archer Hays, son of N. W. S. and Mary Lorman Hays, d. Sun., 25 Sep 1870

HARRY DAVID HANWAY BIBLE

Bible published in 1891 by the American Bible Society in New York. Family data gleaned from a typescript at the Maryland Historical Society.

Marriages:
Lillian Hanway and Harry Lee Thompson m. 20 Apr 1910
Sarah Grace Hanway and Charles W. Michael, Jr. m. 14 Dec 1910
Margaret W. Finney and Edwin H. W. Harlan m. 23 Nov 1911

[*Ed. Note:* Although not recorded in the bible, the marriage certificate of Harry David Hanway and Lidie R. Divers states they married on 21 May 1883. Family records also state he married second to Hazel S. ----; however, no marriage record was found in Harford County].

Births:
Children of Harry D. and Lidie R. Hanway:
1. C. Clifford Hanway, b. 22 Feb 1884

2. Sarah Grace Hanway, b. 12 May 1886
3. Lillian B. Hanway, b. 14 Mar 1888
4. Margaret W. Hanway, b. 1 Jan 1890
5. Lida Hanway, b. -- Feb 1891

Harry D. Hanway, Jr., son of Harry David and Hazel E. Hanway, b. 4 Sep 1909

Children of Harry L. and Lillian H. Thompson:
1. Lillian Hanway Thompson, b. 11 Sep 1911
2. Harry Lee Thompson, Jr., b. 23 Apr 1913

Children of Charles W. and Grace H. Michael:
1. Charles W. Michael, b. 11 Mar 1913
2. Sarah Elizabeth Michael, b. 25 Jul 1919

Edwin H. W. Harlan, Jr., son of Edwin H. W. and Margaret H. Harlan, b. 21 Apr 1921

Deaths:
Lida R. Hanway, d. 16 Dec 1891, age 26
Lida R. Hanway, Jr., d. 17 Nov 1892, age 21 months
Harry D. Hanway, Jr., son of Harry D. and Hazel W. Hanway, d. 6 Sep 1909
Lillian (Hanway) Thompson, wife of Harry Lee Thompson, d. 13 May 1916
Harry D. Hanway, husband of Hazel Hanway, d. 19 Mar 1925
Hazel E. Hanway, d. 9 Aug 1935

Margaret H. Harlan, wife of Edwin Harlan, d. 13 Jan 1936
Edwin H. W. Harlan, husband of Margaret H. Harlan, d. 7 Aug 1939

Charles W. Michael, husband of Grace H. Michael, d. 8 Oct 1952

HENRY HERRING BIBLE

Bible published in 1812 by Mathew Carey, No. 122 Market Street, Philadelphia. A transcript was published in the *Maryland Genealogical Society Bulletin* (Vol. 32, No. 2) in Spring, 1991.

Marriages:
Henry Herring and Miss Eliza Poe, both of Baltimore City, m. Thurs., 17 Nov ----

[blank] at 20 minutes past 6 o'clock by Rev. John Glendy at Mr. David Poe's house. Attendants: Mr. Benjamin Robinson & Miss Susan Guthrie and Mr. George Herring & Miss Jane Buchanan. Witnesses: Mr. Ludwig Herring, Mrs. Elizabeth Herring, Sr., Mr. David Poe, Mrs. Elizabeth Poe, Mr. William Clemm, Mrs. Harriet Clemm, Mrs. Bridget Poe, Mr. Jacob Poe, Miss Sarah Thompson, Miss Maria Poe, Mrs. Marcy Kennedy, and in 15 minutes after, the Party removed to the Herring's house in Queen Street and spent the evening very agreeably. Signed: H. Herring [*Ed. Note:* Their marriage notice appeared in the *Baltimore American* on 22 Nov 1814].

Henry Herring, of Baltimore, and Louisa Lowry, eldest dau. of Louis and Mary Lowry of Philadelphia, m. at Philadelphia on Thurs., 24 Mar 1825 by Rev. Samuel Helfenstein.

Births:
Children of Henry and Eliza Herring:
1. Elizabeth Rebecca Herring, b. 18 Oct 1815, bapt. 23 Jan 1816 by Rev. Mr. Wyatt
2. Lewis David Herring, b. 30 Jan 1817, bapt. 20 Oct 1817 by Rev. Mr. Wyatt
3. Henry Herring, b. 11 Oct 1818, bapt. about 10 Jan 1819 by Rev. Dr. Wyatt
4. George Augustus Herring, b. 7 Oct 1820, bapt. 9 Mar 1821 by Rev. Dr. Wyatt in Christ Church
5. Emily Virginia Herring, b. 10 Aug 1822, bapt. 11 Nov 1822 by Rt. Revd. Bishop Kemp

Children of Henry and Louisa Herring:
1. Mary Esther Herring, b. Sat. evening, 7 Jan 1826 at half past 7 o'clock, bapt. 20 Aug 1827 by Rev. William W. Wyatt
2. Louisa Lowry Herring, b. Fri., 20 July at 10 o'clock in the morning, bapt. by Rev. William E. Wyatt on 20 Aug 1827 and died the same day at half past 4 o'clock, being one month old
3. Ann Louisa Herring, b. Mon., 6 Oct 1828 at half past 8 o'clock a.m.
4. Sophia DeHaven Herring, b. Tues., 31 Aug 1830 at 3 o'clock a.m.
5. Caroline Lowry Herring, b. Tues., 15 Jul 1834 at half past 11 o'clock p.m.
6. Howard McKenzie Herring, b. Sun., 28 Nov 1847 at 20 minutes past 1 o'clock
7. Mildred Tutts(?) Herring, b. Sun. night, 17 Sep 1837 at 20 minutes before 11 o'clock
8. Henrietta Herring, b. Mon. morning, 16 Sep 1839 at a quarter before 5 o'clock
9. Malcolm Lowry Herring, b. Sun., Christmas Day, 25 Dec 1842 at half past 3 o'clock a.m.
10. Clifford Herring, b. 2 Apr 1845 at a quarter past 11 o'clock p.m.

Death:
Eliza Herring, wife of Henry Herring, d. Sun. evening, 8 Dec 1822 of a pulmonary disease, age 29 years, 2 months and 9 days, leaving a husband and 5 small children: Elizabeth, Rebecca, Louis David, Henry, George Augustus, and Emily Virginia.

GEORGE HESS FAMILY BIBLE

No publication information available (title page missing). Family data gleaned from a typescript at the Maryland Historical Society. The bible was originally the property of someone in Harry Hess Nagle's mother's family in Baltimore. There were no birth records in the bible and the marriages had no dates. It was noted that the persons were addressed as "brother" and "sister" and they were probably members of the Good Will Evangelical (now E.M.B.) Church in Harford County or Grace Church in Baltimore, of the same denomination, where Mr. Nagle's mother was a member. In the front and back of the bible were pasted newspaper clippings, mostly obituary notices from a church newspaper, some of them printed in German (which were not abstracted here).

Marriages:
John Edward Hess m. Cora Edna Preston
Thomas E. Stifler m. Clara Irene Hess
Robert D. Sewell m. Mamie Hess
Chester C. Johnson m. Bertha Elnora Hess
Ralph Kurtz m. Carrie L. Hess
Selda E. Hess m. John W. Middendorf
James Bunyan Hess m. Curtha Emily Van Zant
Charles B. Hess m. Bessie Chenworth
Benjamin G. Hess m. May Base

[*Ed. Note:* It was not part of this bible record, but Harford County marriage records indicate Henry Hess and Margaret Gross obtained a license to marry on 17 Apr 1842, and the marriage of George Hess and Annie C. Peppler on 28 Oct 1873 appeared in the *Baltimore Sun* on 31 Oct 1873].

Death:
Mrs. Lilly A. Northamer, d. ----

Family Records (Clippings in Bible):
1. George Hess, son of Henry and Margaret, d. near Good Will, Harford County,

11 Apr 1876, age 26 years, 2 months and 17 days. He was sick but a short time. His remains were taken to Baltimore from which place he removed a few months ago.

2. George Gross, of Stemmers Run, d. 4 Nov 1877 in his 56th year. Born in Province of Alsace in the vicinity of Bloomort, came to U.S. with his father at age 8. Gross family settled in Jarrettsville. Deceased left a widow, 7 children, and brothers and sisters. He was buried at Mt. Carmel Cemetery near Baltimore.

3. George Hess, husband of Annie Hess, d. 11 Apr ---- [in 1876; see above]. Born 25 Jan 1850. Funeral from home of his father-in-law Alexander Peppler on Pennsylvania Avenue [Baltimore City].

4. Lillie A. Northamer (neé Hess), wife of W. T. Northamer, d. 5 May 1917 in Baltimore. Born 27 Feb 1877 in Harford County, dau. of Jacob Hess of Goodwill. Member of Grace Church in Baltimore. Leaves a husband, daughter, father, stepmother, brother and three sisters.

5. William Engel, son of William and Margaret Engel, d. 19 Oct 1877 at Alberton, Baltimore County, age about 15. Survived by parents, three brothers and four sisters.

6. Maggie Engle, dau. of William and Margaret Engle, d. 23 Jun 1878 of consumption at Elysville, Howard County, IN, age 20 years, 2 months and 11 days.

7. Margaret Horn, wife of William Horn, d. 25 Jun 1877 near Jarrettsville, age 51 years, 7 months and 11 days. Born in York County, PA.

THEODORE J. HETRICK BIBLE

Bible published by Jones Brothers & Company, Cincinnati, OH (date not given). Inscribed: "Presented by his mother on his 21st birthday, Jan 7th, 1878." Family data gleaned from a typescript at the Maryland Historical Society. Bible originally owned by Theodore J. Hetrick of Darlington, MD.

Marriage:
Theodore J. Hetrick of Darlington, MD, and Mary Virginia Walker of Havre de Grace, MD, m. 9 Jan 1889 at Wesleyan Church by Rev. J. W. Charlton. Witnessed by one hundred friends.

Deaths:
Adam Hetrick, d. 10 Jan 1902, age 80

Catherine W. Hetrick, d. 20 Oct 1918, age 92
Janie E. Hetrick, d. 19 Feb 1932, age 76
Clara Hetrick, d. 8 Jul 1932, age 86
Mary Virginia Walker Hetrick, d. 23 Apr 1934, age 69
Theodore Jacob Hetrick, d. 1 Jan 1936, age 78

Christian H. Walker, d. 22 Sep 1912, age 84
Cornelia A. Walker, d. -- Aug 1913, age 76
Winfield S. Walker, d. 24 May 1929, age 68

Annie L. Keen, d. 27 Jun 1913, age 51
William J. Keen, d. 12 Jan 1913, age 54

Annie S. Hopkins, d. 8 Jul 1932, age 72

Catherine W. Bailey, d 5 Mar 1949, age 86

HIGGINS-GUEST BIBLE

Bible cover page states "Baltimore: A. C. Thomas, 15 Post Office Avenue" [no date given]. Inscribed in the bible: "Presented to Lizzie A. Guest on her tenth birthday by John W. Guest (her father), November 28th, 1886." This transcript was published in the *Maryland Genealogical Society Bulletin* (Vol. 30, No. 3) in Summer, 1989. The information was submitted by the owner, Ormond Donald Higgins of Timonium, Baltimore County, MD, who noted the following: "This bible was inherited by my Aunt Marie Agnes (Coyne) Higgins upon the death of Elizabeth A. Higgins. Upon the death of Marie, the bible passed to Mrs. Marlene Lufriu of Littlestown, PA (Marie's niece). Marlene presented the bible to me in October, 1988. I will be eternally grateful for this gift."

Marriages:
Elizabeth A. Guest and James A Higgins m. 17 Feb 1898 at Baltimore in the presence of Mrs. O. C. Roth and Mrs. Ida Royer (minister's name not signed). [*Ed. Note:* Another entry in the bible stated they were married on 18 Feb 1898].
John W. Guest and M. M. Kirby m. 16 Jun 1856

Births:
Mary M. Guest, b. 18 Aug 1839
John W. Guest, b. 3 Jul 1835

[Children of John and Mary Guest]:
1. George Guest, b. 6 Sep 1859
2. John E. Guest, b. 12 Dec 1863
3. Lizzie Alexandra Guest, b. 28 Mar 1875

James Albert Higgins, b. -- May 1876

[Children of James and Elizabeth Higgins]:
1. Albert Sherman Higgins, b. 28 Sep 1904
2. Robert Elwood Higgins, b. 16 Jan 1907
3. Ormond Graham Higgins, b. 26 Mar 1910

Deaths:
George Guest, d. 23 Nov 1864
John E. Guest, d. 20 Jan 1864, age 6 weeks
John W. Guest, d. 3 Jul 1904, age 70
Mary M. Guest, d. 22 Jun 1909

Albert Sherman Higgins, d. 4 Nov 1905

GEORGE W. HOPKINS BIBLE

Bible published in 1839 by Thomas Mason and George Lane for the Methodist Episcopal Church at the Conference Office, 200 Mulberry Street, New York; James Collard, printer. Inscribed: "This bible belongs to George W. Hopkins and his wife Sophia Hopkins." Family data gleaned from a typescript at the Maryland Historical Society. The bible also included pages from a small notebook.

Marriages:
Hannah Eliza Hopkins and Charles Willey m. ---- [*Ed. Note:* Harford County marriage license issued to Charles Willey and Eliza Hopkins on 12 Jan 1821].

Charlotte M. Hopkins and James Stephenson m. ---- [*Ed. Note:* Harford County marriage license issued to James Stephenson and Charlotter Hopkins on 26 Jul 1831].

Caroline G. Hopkins and Thomas Smith m. ---- [*Ed. Note:* Harford County marriage license issued to Nathaniel Smith and Caroline Hopkins on 16 Nov 1836].

Louisa S. Hopkins and Thomas Cord m. ---- [*Ed. Note:* Harford County marriage license issued to Thomas Cord and Louisa J. Hopkins on 5 Feb 1840].

William Edward Hopkins and Mary Parker m. ---- [*Ed. Note:* No marriage license found in Harford County].

George W. Hopkins and Sophia Spencer m. 22 Feb 1842 [*Ed. Note:* Harford County marriage license issued to them on 21 Feb 1842].

Sarah Ann Hopkins, dau. of George W. and Sophia H. Hopkins, and George W. Walker m. 26 Nov 1868

Margaret P. Hopkins and John N. Hoopman m. 16 Dec 1878

Carrie G. Hopkins and George T. Hanna m. 3 Apr 1878

John E. Hopkins and Etta Hopkins m. 12 Jan 1881

Samuel G. Hopkins and Ann S. Hetrick m. 15 Feb 1882

Lurenna E. Hopkins and John Newton Hoopman m. 28 Jan 1892

Mary Rebecca Hopkins and Robert James Walker m. 26 Apr 1905

Hannah Eliza Hopkins and John Reese Walker m. 8 Jul 1906 in Chester, PA

Births:
Samuel G. Hopkins, son of Samuel, b. 13 Dec 1774

Mary Mitchell, wife of Samuel G. Hopkins and dau. of William Mitchell, b. -- Oct 1782

Children of Samuel G. and Mary Hopkins:
1. Hannah Eliza Hopkins, b. -- Oct 1802, m. Charles Willey
2. Charlotte M. Hopkins, b. 27 Jun 1805, m. James Stephenson
3. Sarah Ann Hopkins, b. 9 Nov 1807
4. Caroline G. Hopkins, b. 22 Jul 1810, m. Thomas Smith
5. Louisa S. Hopkins, b. 27 Mar 1813, m. Thomas Cord
6. George W. Hopkins, b. 29 Feb 1816, m. Sophia Spencer, b. 10 Nov 1819

7. William Edward Hopkins, b. 20 Jul 1822, m. Mary Parker
8. Samuel Parker Hopkins, b. ---- [date not given]

Children of George W. and Sophia Hopkins:
1. Mary R. Hopkins, b. 20 Feb 1843
2. Hannah E. Hopkins, b. 1 Sep 1844
3. Sarah A. and Luranna E. Hopkins, b. 4 May 1846
4. Margaret P. Hopkins, b. 26 Aug 1848
5. Caroline C. Hopkins, b. 26 Apr 1850
6. John E. Hopkins, b. 16 Jan 1852
7. Samuel G. Hopkins, b. 9 Mar 1853
8. Sophia E. Hopkins, b. 19 Aug 1854

Deaths:
George W. Hopkins, d. 16 Jun 1878, age 62 years, 3 months and 15 days

Ella S. Hopkins, d. 2 Oct 1881, age 27 years, 1 month and 13 days

John E. Hopkins, d. 6 Oct 1886, age 33 years, 8 months and 22 days

Margaret P. Hoopman, d. 15 Oct 1887, age 39 years, 1 month and 18 days

Sophia Spencer Hopkins, wife of George W. Hopkins, d. 3 Nov 1900, age 80 years, 10 months and 21 days

Mary Rebecca Hopkins Walker, widow of the late Robert J. Walker, d. 2 Apr 1916

Family Records:
John E. Hopkins, d. Wed., Oct 6th, 1886 at 25 minutes past 12 o'clock, was brought to the residence of his mother Sophia Hopkins and bur. on Fri., Oct 8th at Rock Run. Pallbearers were his cousins William Stephenson, Hermon Spencer, Augustus Smith, Silas Bailey, George Bailey, Otha Smith and Fred Hopkins.

Etta Hopkins was taken sick Oct 20th, 1886 on Wed. just two weeks from the death of her husband, John E. Hopkins. She gave birth to a daughter; Dr. Finney, attending physician.

Cassandra Hanna, d. in Havre de Grace Hospital, Tues., Apr 26th, 1927, bur. April 29th, 1927 in Rock Run.

Robert Hanna, d. suddenly Apr 23rd, 1927 at his home near Rock Run Church on Sat. evening and bur. Tues. the 26th, Rock Run Cemetery. Pallbearers: William Craig, Livingstone Smith, Theodore Hetrick, Will Sheridan, Ed N. Baldwin and Wade Lee.

Lurenna E. Hopkins Hoopman, 2nd wife of John N. Hoopman, d. feb 21st, 1923 at her home 717 Madison Street in Chester, PA. Services at Rock Run Methodist Episcopal Church.

Ruth A. Briney, widow of Jacob Briney, d. 13 Apr 1908 at 2:30 a.m., survived by 3 daughters, Mrs. Richard Sheridan, Mrs. E. A. Gorrell and Mrs. William Sheridan, and 2 sons, Howard Briney and William Briney.

Rev. William R. Gwinn, d. 18 Jun 1878, survived by his widow (Mrs. Sarah M. Gwinn) and 3 children, Mrs. George Moore, Mr. William Gwinn and Mr. Hugh Gwinn.

Susan G. Wilson, bur. from her residence on Thurs., 28 Sep 1893 at 10:30 a.m. in Rock Run Cemetery.

J. B. Gallion, bur. Thurs., 22 Mar 1894 at 10 a.m. in Rock Run Church Cemetery.

Mrs. Priscilla Stephenson, bur. from her late residence on 20 Feb 1861 at 10 a.m.

William B. Stephenson, bur. from his residence near Rock Run on Sat. 16 Feb 1884 at 11 a.m.
Mrs. Sophia Hopkins, bur. from her late residence on Mon. 5 Nov 1900 at 1 p.m. in Rock Run.

Ann P. Stephenson, bur. from the residence of William Stephenson on Fri., 12 Feb 1892 at 11 a.m.
William Stephenson, bur. 28 Sep 1895

Austin Hopkins, d. 29 Dec 1885
Ethel C. Hopkins, d. 18 Sep 1902
S. Gover Hopkins, d. -- Oct 1904

Mrs. Carrie G. Hanna, wife of George T. Hanna, d. 8 Nov 1904, bur. 10 Nov 1904.

Lydia Hopkins Cronin, d. suddenly 8 Jun 1929 and bur. 10 Jun 1929 at Abingdon Cemetery.

William T. Spencer, 90th birthday, 16 Jun 1921

Mrs. Sarah S. Walker, wife of Robert J. Walker and dau. of the late John W. and Rebecca K. Spencer, bur. 30 Mar 1904.

Robert J. Walker, d. 9 Mar 1913 at his home in Harford County; Mary R. Hopkins, his wife.

J. Reese Walker, d. 29 Apr 1915

Mary R. Walker, widow of Robert J. Walker, d. 2 Apr 1916

John Earnshaw, d. 6 Mar ----, age 82

Ettie Rogers, d. 16 May 1920 at 2 o'clock a.m.

John Herman, son of Samuel and Mary, d. 21 Oct 1824, age 3 months and 23 days

Hannah Eliza ---- [Willey], d. 18 Apr 1827, age 23 years and 6 months

Sarah Ann ---- [Hopkins], d. -- May 1829, age 21 years and 6 months

Charlotte Mitchell, d. -- Jan 1829, age 29

JOSEPH R. HOPKINS BIBLE

Bible published by Jones Brothers (date and place not indicated). Family data gleaned from a typescript at the Maryland Historical Society.

Marriages:
Joseph Reese Hopkins and Maria McCausland, both of Harford County, m. 5 Jan 1865 at Baltimore by Rev. Samuel Spranklin. Witnesses: B. J. Spranklin and James Small.

Murray J. Hopkins and Mamie Burkins m. 3 May 1898

Births:
Joseph Reese Hopkins, b. 17 Dec 1835

Children of Joseph R. and Maria Hopkins:
1. Annie McCausland Hopkins, b. 26 Apr 1866
2. Murray Lindley Hopkins, b. 6 May 1873

Children of Murray L. and Mamie Hopkins:
1. Mary McCausland Hopkins, b. 31 Jul 1899
2. Murray Lindley Hopkins, Jr., b. 30 Sep 1902

Deaths:
Ann (Higginbotham) McCausland, mother of Maria Hopkins, d. -- Feb 1860

Leetta (Miller) Hopkins, mother of Joseph R. Hopkins, d. 11 Dec 1871
Joseph Reese Hopkins, d. 13 Feb 1907

Family Records (Clippings in Bible):

1. Elizabeth (Hopkins) Small, age 82, widow of James Small, farmer in Harford County, d. at residence of dau.-in-law Mrs. Joseph Small, 205 W. 25th Street [Baltimore]; bur. Rockland Church, Harford County; she was b. in Harford County and for 61 years a Methodist Episcopalian; had 6 sons: John Small (west), Noah Small (Bel Air), James and Frederick Small (Baltimore), and Harry and Sylvester Small (Baltimore County).

2. J. W. McCausland, age 42, d. in Denver 19th Jan instant [no year given]; horseman, native of Greensboro, PA.

3. Dora K. (Davis) Bramble, age 22, dau. of Jeff D. and Sarah M. Davis, and wife of Fulton C. Bramble, d. 14 Feb 1910, bur. at Mt. Zion Cemetery; funeral from residence of her father-in-law William E. Bramble, 939 N. Broadway [Baltimore].

4. Hattie G. Bramble, eldest dau. of William E. Bramble, 939 N. Broadway [Baltimore], m. Forrest Bramble, a distant relation, at Madison Square M. E. Church by Rev. Dr. E. L. Hubbard [no date given]; brother W. Edward Bramble, sister Fannie Bramble, best man Alfred Gawthrop.

5. Florence H---ton(?) Pipino m. Levin Feaster Anderson, son of Charles E. Anderson [no date given], at their future home, gift of groom's father, 1302 Tatnall St. [Baltimore], by Rev. W. Lightburne of Wesley M. E. Church, Dover, formerly pastor of Epworth Church; sister Hattie G. Pipino.

6. Edward Hopkins, age 67, farmer near Darlington [Harford County], found drowned in Deer Creek at Dukes Lock [no date given]; brother of the late Dr. Ephraim Hopkins; father of Mr. Kent Hopkins.

7. John McCausland, g---? of paint (?) industry, Port Deposit, MD [no date given].

WILLIAM HOPKINS BIBLE

No publication information available. Family data gleaned from a typescript at the Maryland Historical Society.

Marriages:
William Hopkins of J. and Ellen Morris m. at residence of Bennett Hopkins on 8 Jan 1852 by Rev. C. Reed

William H. Hanna and Rose E. Hopkins m. 3 Feb 1881 by Rev. W. L. Keiffer
William J. Hopkins and Ida E. Forsythe m. 9 Jun 1881 by Rev. J. W. Steel

Wakeman H. Scott and Florida Hopkins m. 10 Jul 1884 by Rev. J. W. Smith

James O. Gorrell and Angie V. Hopkins m. 14 Feb 1888 by Rev. J. R. Schultz

T. Kenton Hopkins and Bessie A. McCommons m. 31 Oct 1907 by Rev. J. H. Lane

T. Kenton Hopkins and Florence B. Price Harvey m. 27 Jan 1915 by Rev. J. H. Lane

Births:
William Hopkins, son of Joseph Reese and Laetta Hopkins, b. 17 Oct 1827
Ellen Morris, dau. of Rebecca and Lloyd Morris, b. 27 Oct 1824(6?)
Children of William and Ellen Hopkins:
1. Ann Jane Hopkins, b. 26 Jan 1853
2. Angelina Virginia Hopkins, b. 9 Nov 1854
3. Rose Ellen Hopkins, b. 14 Jan 1856
4. William Joseph Hopkins, b. 4 Nov 1857
5. Lloyd Hopkins, b. 29 May 1860
6. Florida Hopkins, b. 18 Apr 1862

James Oliver Gorrell, son of James Lee and Sarah A. Gorrell, b. 21 Dec 1860

Rose Lyle Gorrell, dau. of James O. and Angie V. Gorrell, b. 25 Jan 1894

Deaths:
William J. Hopkins, d. 9 Jun 1916
Bessie A. Hopkins, d. 22 Dec 1912
Florence B. Hopkins, d. 1 Feb 1953

Children of William and Ellen Hopkins:
1. Ann Jane Hopkins, d. 15 Mar 1858
2. Lloyd Hopkins, d. 9 Jan 1863

Rebecca Morris, wife of Lloyd Morris, d. 16 Mar 1882

William Hopkins, son of Joseph Reese Hopkins and Laetta Hopkins, d. 5 Feb 1889, age 61 years, 3 months and 19 days

Ellen Hopkins, wife of William Hopkins of Joseph, and dau. of Rebecca and Lloyd Morris, d. 30 Jul 1860, age 63 years, 9 months and 3 days

---- Gorrell, infant son of James O. and Angie V. Gorrell, b. and d. 13 Apr 1890

Rose Lyle Gorrell, "beloved and only child" of James O. and Angie V. Gorrell, d. 15 Mar 1895 at 8 p.m., age 1 year, 1 month and 18 days

Henry Presbery Morris, son of Rebecca and Lloyd Morris, d. 28 Oct 1884

Family Records (Clippings in Bible):
1. Shure's Landing: At Churchville Presbyterian Church, 3 Feb [1881] William Hanna of Fountain Green and Rose Hopkins, dau. of William Hopkins of this neighborhood, were married by W. T. L. Kieffer.

2. Funeral of William Hopkins of Joseph took place on the 7th [exact date not indicated]; interred at Darlington Cemetery; fatally injured by being caught in circular saw at Gover & Hopkins saw mill at Deer Creek; a good man and fine citizen. [*Ed. Note:* Another entry in Bible states he was "58/59 years old in 1886"].

MATTHEW HOWLETT BIBLE

No publication information available. Family data gleaned from a typescript at the Maryland Historical Society.

Marriages:
Matthew Howlett and Eliza Mitchell m. 3 Jan 1815 [*Note Written on Typescript in 1989:* "Elizabeth Mitchell, dau. of Ezekiel and Mary Mitchell of Havre de Grace. See his Harford County Will, Liber TSB-6-folio 101"].

William Howlett and Elizabeth Teaney m. 25 Nov 1849 [*Note Written on Typescript in 1989:* "She was Elizabeth Taney (ca.1830-1919), dau. of Samuel and Catherine Taney of Pennsylvania"].

Richard T. Howlett and Mrs. Ann Wiligon m. 6 Jan 1858
Matthew Howlett and Frances Louise Barratt m. 19 Dec 1861

Births:
Matthew Howlett, b. 17 Aug 1791
Eliza Howlett, his wife, b. 20 Jan 1798

Children of Matthew and Eliza Howlett:
1. William Howlett, b. 18 Aug 1815
2. Mary Howlett, b. 11 May 1817
3. James Howlett, b. 14 Feb 1819
4. Catherine Howlett, b. 6 Aug 1820
5. John Howlett, b. 18 Apr 1822
6. Ezekiel Howlett, b. 5 Feb 1824
7. Ambrose Howlett, b. 5 Sep 1825
8. Eliza Ann Howlett, b. 27 Apr 1827
9. Richard Thomas Howlett, b. 21 Dec 1829
10. Matthew Howlett, b. 13 Apr 1831
11. Martha Caroline Howlett, b. 13 Mar 1833
12. Benjamin Franklin Howlett, b. 15 Aug 1835
13. Frances Maria Howlett, b. 9 Mar 1838

Children of James and Catherine Howlett:
1. Martha Howlett, b. 12 Nov 1764
2. John Howlett, b. 21 Oct 1770
3. Mary Howlett, b. 23 Sep 1781
4. Nancy Howlett, b. 7 May 1783
5. Catherine Howlett, b. 23 Jun 1785
6. James Howlett, b. 7 Feb 1788
7. Matthew Howlett, b. 17 Aug 1791

Matthew Howlett, b. 15 Apr 1831
Fannie Howlett [his wife], b. 29 Dec 1840

Children of Matthew and Fannie Howlett:
1. Harry M. Howlett, b. 19 Dec 1862
2. ---- Howlett, second son, b. 19 Dec 1864
3. Clara-bell Howlett, b. 29 Dec 1865
4. ---- Howlett, second dau., b. 27 May 1867
5. ---- Howlett, third son, b. 3 Feb 1869
6. William W. Howlett, b. 31 Jan 1871

John Thomas Adams, son of William and Martha Caroline Adams, b. 11 Mar 1855

Deaths:
James Howlett, d. 14 Mar 1819
Catherine Howlett, his wife, d. 26 Dec 1826
Matthew Howlett, d. 18 Feb 1881
Fannie Howlett [his wife], d. 15 Aug 1878

Children of Matthew and Eliza Howlett:
1. James Howlett, d. 9 Oct 1819
2. Ambrose Howlett, d. 15 Aug 1831
3. Benjamin Franklin Howlett, b. 15 Aug 1840
4. Frances Maria Howlett, b. 5 Sep 1840
5. John R. Howlett, d. 7 Feb 1848
6. Matthew Howlett, b. 17 Sep 1862

Mrs. Martha Lee, d. 27 Nov 1858

Hannah Howlett, wife of William Howlett, d. 15 Aug 1865

William Adams, son of William and Martha C. Adams, d. 15 Aug 1865

Martha C. Adams, d. 18 Aug 1865

Family Records:
Note written on this bible typescript in 1989: "Stephen John Howlett (1860-1898), son of William Howlett and Elizabeth Taney, married Mary Ann Knight (1860-1951), dau. of William Knight and Jane Ann Scott. Elizabeth Taney Howlett remar

to Samuel Forsythe at Cecil County in 1886."

JOHN M. HUFF BIBLE

Bible published in 1882 by A. J. Holman & Co., 1222 Arch Street, Philadelphia, PA. Family data gleaned from a typescript at the Maryland Historical Society. Bible originally owned by John Michael Huff of Mill Green, Harford County, MD.

Marriages:
John M. Huff and Casander D. Pyle m. 7 Mar 1883
Lester Huff and Mable M. Johnson m. 9 Jan 1915
Ellsworth Huff and Helen C. Brotherton m. 5 Jun 1918
Edgar W. Pyle and Edna Huff m. 14 Aug 1920
Earl L. Linaburg and Grace E. Huff m. 7 Jul 1945

Births:
John M. Huff, oldest son of John S. and Elizabeth Huff, b. 3 Nov 1847

Casander D. (Pyle) Huff, youngest dau. of Ely and Casander Pyle, b. 12 Nov 1858

Children of John M. and Casander Huff:
1. Della Huff, b. 22 Jan 1885
2. Ellsworth Huff, b. 19 Aug 1886
3. Lester Huff, b. 1 Apr 1889
4. Edna Huff, b. 27 Dec 1897

Children of Lester and Mabel M. Huff:
1. Ethel May Huff, b. 20 May 1920
2. Grace E. Huff, b. 19 Apr 1925

Deaths:
Della Huff, dau. of John M. and Casander D. Huff, d. 21 Mar 1885
John M. Huff, son of John S. and Elizabeth Huff, d. 23 Dec 1918
Cassie D. Huff, youngest dau. of Ely and Casander Pyle, d. 25 Jan 1920
Lester Huff, son of J. M. and Cassie D. Huff, d. 14 Apr 1927

JOHN HUGHES BIBLE

Bible published in 1822 by H. C. Carey and I. Lea, 126 Chestnut Street, Philadelphia, PA. Family data gleaned from a typescript at the Maryland Historical Society.

Marriages:
John Hughes and Charlott ---- m. 27 Dec 1796

Amos H. Hughes, age 29, son of John and Charlott Hughes, and Hannah C. Adams, dau. of William and Cathrine Adams, m. 25 Feb 1841

George B. Silver, son of Samuel and Sarah Silver, and Charlott C. Hughes, dau. of Amos and Hannah Hughes, m. 28 Nov 1865
Robert P. Mitchell, son of John and Eliza Mitchell, and Mary Hughes, dau. of Amos and Hannah Hughes, m. 15 Jan 1867

Ambrose Cooley, son of Daniel and Harriet Cooley, and Caroline A. Hughes, dau. of Amos H. and Hannah Hughes, m. 25 May 1871

Births:
John Hughes, son of John Haul Hughes, b. 21 Aug 1772
Charlott Hughes, dau. of William and Clemency Mitchell, wife of John Hughes, b. 25 Mar 1772

[Children of John and Charlott Hughes]:
1. Mary Hughes, b. 26 May 1798
2. John Haul Hughes, b. 29 May 1800
3. Clemency Hughes, b. 17 Feb 1803
4. Kent Hughes, b. -- Sep 1806
5. Ann Hughes, b. 15 Apr 1809
6. Amos H. Hughes, b. 25 Feb 1812
7. Sarah Hughes, b. 29 Mar 1815 (twin)
8. Charlott Hughes, b. 29 Mar 1815 (twin)

George Hughes, son of Clemency, b. 19 Aug 1822
Susanna E. Hughes, dau. of Clemency, b. 24 Jan 1828

Amos Jarvis, b. 13 Oct 1838

Mary E. Hopkins, dau. of Henry and Ann Hopkins, b. 15 May 1832
John H. Hopkins, b. 15 Nov 1834

James A Knight, son of Thomas A. Knight, b. 4 Nov 1838
Gover H. Knight, b. 21 Mar 1841
Sarah Ann Knight, b. 20 Apr 1844
Sharlott F. Knight, b. 8 Sep 1846

Deaths:
Kent Hughes, d. 17 Aug 1820
John Haul Hughes, d. 3 May 1824
John Hughes, d. 26 Mar 1853, age 82
Charlott Hughes, wife of John Hughes, d. 18 Jul 1846
Mary C. Hughes, wife of Robert P. Mitchell, d. 16 Apr 1901

Children of John and Charlott Hughes:
1. Amos Hollis Hughes, d. 4 Oct 1892
2. Clemency Hughes Jarvis, d. 10 Jun 1890
3. Anne Hughes Knight, d. 14 Jun 1898
4. Sarah Hughes Waltham, d. 2 Oct 1889
5. Charlott Hughes Cole, d. 30 Nov 1878

Mary Chesney, dau. of John and Charlott Hughes and consort of William Chesney, d. 26 Nov 1871

George Bartol Silver, husband of Charlott Hughes, d. 12 Dec 1902

JOHN S. HUTCHINS BIBLE

Bible published by The National Publishing Company and Jones Brothers and Company in the 1870s. The year of publication is shown as "187-" (the last digit was not printed). Written inside the front cover: "This book was purchased by John Slade Hutchins from a book agent" [no date given]. Family data gleaned from a typescript at the Maryland Historical Society by William Hollifield III in 1974.

Marriages:
"This certifies that the rite of Holy Matrimony was celebrated between John Slade Hutchins of William Hutchins and Mary Rampley and Mary Jane Hawkins of John Hawkins and Susan Thompson in 1845."

Martha J. Hutchins and William Hutchins m. ---- [no date]
Annie R. Hutchins and Joshua Hutchins Cockey m. 5 Dec 1873
Mary Susan Hutchins and Charles Streett m. ---- [no date]

Laura Hutchins and Nicholas Hutchins m. 17 Jan 1884 "first marriage"
Gertrude Hutchins and John Cole Bosley m. 21 Oct 1885
William Beauregard Hutchins and Laura May Bosley m. 6 Dec 1885
Laura Hutchins and William Herbert Hutchins m. 7 Jan 1891 "second marriage"
Estelle Hutchins and Harry Thornton Pearce m. 15 Jun 1892
Maude Hutchins and John Myers Pearce m. 29 Oct 1897
Charles Lee Hutchins and Frances Loryma Quinby m. 19 Jun 1901 at Suffolk, VA

Births:
[Children of John S. and Mary R. Hutchins]:
1. Martha Jane Hutchins, b. 4 Mar 1848
2. Mary Susan Hutchins, b. 11 Jan 1850
3. Annie Rebecca Hutchins, b. 7 Feb 1852
4. Amanda Zena Hutchins, b. 12 Jan 1854
5. Laura Hutchins, b. 12 Dec 1855
6. Alverda Hutchins, b. 29 Apr 1858
7. William Beauregard Hutchins, b. 18 Nov 1862
8. Gertrude Hutchins, b. 31 Jul 1865
9. Charles Lee Hutchins, b. 6 Jan 1868
10. Estelle Hutchins and Maud Hutchins, b. 6 Dec 1870

John Hawkins, b. 1805 "May he rest in peace. Grandfather of Mary Jane Hawkins Hutchins."

Mary Jane Hutchins, b. 16 Feb 1828

Mary Susan Hawkins, b. 14 Feb 1808 "Grandmother of Mary J. Hawkins Hutchins children"

Charles Quinby Hutchins, son of C. Lee Hutchins, Sr., b. 18 Sep 1902, 11:15 p.m., Thurs.

Deaths:
Alverda Hutchins, d. Sun., 4 Aug 1878, dau. of John and Mary Hutchins

John Slade Hutchins, d. Sat., 18 Jun 1881, father of above Alverda and son of William Hutchins and Mary Ramply

Mary Susan Hawkins, d. Sun., 7 Mar 1886

Alfred Garrison, d. ---- [blank]
Mary A. Hutchins Garrison, d. ---- [blank]

John Hawkins, d. 8 Jan 1884, Mary Jane Hawkins Hutchins father

Thomas Hawkins, d. ---- [no date] at New Orleans, LA, brother of Mary Jane Hawkins Hutchins

William B. Hutchins, d. 12 Nov 19-- [last two digits not given] at "The Oaks," son of John S. and Mary J. Hawkins Hutchins of Allanta Hall, Harford County
Edward Hawkins, d. ---- [no date]
Alverda Hawkins Birmingham, d. ---- [no date]
Rebecca Hawkins Scarff "died in travail" [no date]

[Children of John S. and Mary R. Hutchins]:
1. William Beauregard Hutchins, d. 12 Nov ---- [blank]
2. Martha Jane Hutchins Hutchins, d. 29 Oct 1923 at 10 a.m.
3. Annie Rebecca Hutchins Cockey, d. 1 Dec 1927 at 8 p.m.
4. Mary Susan Hutchins Streett, d. 20 Mar 1931 at 10 a.m.
5. Gertrude Hutchins Bosley, d. 11 Oct 1933
6. Laura Hutchins Hutchins, d. 18 Oct 1937 at 1 p.m.
7. Charles Lee Hutchins, d. 22 Sep 1949 at 3 p.m.
8. Maude Hutchins Pearce, d. 17 Aug 1951 at 11 a.m.
9. Estelle Hutchins Pearce, d. Sun, 5 Feb 1956 at 11:30 a.m.

ANNA D. HUTSON BIBLE

No publication information available. "Presented to Anna D. Hutson by her grandmother Ann Peregoy Read. She has found Peace with God at ----- [blank] meeting in the year 18-- [blank]." Family data from Bible was published by the St. Mary's County Genealogical Society Inc. in its newsletter *The Generator* (Vol. 19, No. 10, July-August, 1996).

Marriages:
Frederick L. Deets and Alice Wolfe m. 8 -- 1884
Joseph Emory Hutson and Mary Horst m. 6 Feb 1887
William H. Smiley and Anna D. Hutson m. 13 Jun 1893

Samuel T. Hutson and Helen Sherman m. -- May 1871 [*Ed. Note:* Their marriage notice in the *Baltimore Sun* on 3 May 1871 stated Samuel T. Hutson and Miss Helen C. Sherman married on 1 May 1871]

Katherine Elizabeth Hutson and Harry Edwin Jones m. 9 Nov 1909
---- [blank] Hutson and Ruth Singleton m. ---- [no date]

Births:
Children of Joseph Emory and Mary Hutson:
1. Kate Elizabeth Hutson, b. 26 Oct 1889
2. Anna Mary Hutson, b. 2 Apr 1892
3. Walter Emory Hutson, b. 4 Aug 1894

Children of Samuel and Catharine Hutson:
1. Anna Deborah Hutson, b. 24 Jun 1858(?)
2. James Thomas Hutson, b. 3 Mar 1860
3. Emory Hutson, b. 27 Jun 1863

Frederick L. Deets, b. 19 May 1861
Alice V. Wolfe, b. 12 Apr 1864
William H. Smiley, b. 4 Sep 1864
Ruth Singleton Hutson, b. 2 -- 1910

Deaths:
James Thomas Hutson, d. 20 Mar 1863(?), age 1 year and 20 days
Samuel Thomas Hutson, d. 31 Oct 1883 in his 56th year
Helen C. Hutson, wife of the late S. T. Hutson, d. 11 Nov ----

MICHAEL HUTSON BIBLE

Bible published in 1816 by T. Kinnersley, Acton Place, Kingsland Road, London. Family data was published by the St. Mary's County Genealogical Society Inc. in its newsletter *The Generator* (Vol. 19, No. 10, July-August, 1996), noting that the Hutson family lived in Baltimore City and County and subsequently migrated to Howard County, MD.

Marriages:
Michael Hutson and Deborah Plummer m. 9 Jan 1812
James D. Hutson and Sarah Stevens m. 9 Jan 1821
Eliza Hutson and Fayet Plummer m. 26 Dec 1831

Elis Rachael Elizabeth Hutson and Jess Smith m. 1 Feb 1838
Mary Melvina Hutson and Elias Joseph Read m. 10 Dec 1844
Samuel Thomas Hutson and Catharine Read m. 23 Feb 1855
Sophia Hutson and William Henry Westaway m. 4 Feb 1858
---- [blank] Hutson and Washington Ridgely m. 4 Feb 1873
Samuel Thomas Hutson and Hellen C. Sherman m. 1 May 1871
Ellen Hutson and Washington Ridgely m. 5 Feb 1873
Joseph Emory Hutson and Mary Horst m. 6 Feb 1887 by Rev. L. C. Burke

Katherine Elizabeth Hutson and Harry Edwin Jones m. 9 Nov 1909 by Rev. D. T. Neely assisted by Rev. Simpson Standfield and Rev. Vernon N. Ridgely

Anna Mary Hutson and Richers Watkins m. 22 Jun 1915 by Rev. James M. Wallace

Walter Emory Hudson and Sarah Spencer Atwell m. 21 Feb 1919 by Rev. Vernon N. Ridgely

Births:
Michael Hutson, b. 22 May 1784
Deborah Plummer, b. 15 Sep 1791

Children of Michael and Deborah Plummer:
1. Eliza Hutson, b. 7 Nov 1812
2. Rachael Elizabeth Hutson, b. 28 Mar 1816
3. Samuel Hutson, b. 6 Mar 1818
4. Michael Hutson, b. 22 Sep 1820
5. Sarah Ann Hutson, b. 16 Sep 1822
6. James Henry Hutson, b. 5 Feb 1825
7. Mary Melviney Hutson, b. 26 Jan 1827
8. Samuel Thomas Hutson, b. 26 Jun 1829
9. Edward Hutson, b. 8 Aug 1831
10. Sophia Hutson, b. 11 Feb 1833
11. Frances D. Hutson, b. 1 Mar 1836
12. Ellen Hutson, b. 15 Jun 1840

Children of Fayet (Fayite) and Eliza Plummer:
1. Edward C. Plummer, b. 17 Nov 1832
2. George Plummer, b. 26 Oct 1834(?)
3. Annalizer Plummer, b. 16 Jan 1852(?)

Anna Deborah Hutson, dau. of Samuel Thomas and Catharine Hutson, b. 24 Jun 1836

Joseph Emory Hutson, b. 27 Jun 1863

Children of Joseph Emory and Mary Hutson:
1. Katherine Elizabeth Hutson, b. 26 Oct 1889
2. Anna Mary Hutson, b. 2 Apr 1892
3. Walter Emory Hutson, b. 4 Aug 1894

Children of Anna and H. Richers Watkins:
1. Charles Bryan Watkins, b. 8 Nov 1918
2. Katharine Elizabeth Watkins, b. 20 Aug 1920

Dorothy Anna Jones, dau. of Katherine E. and Harry Jones, b. 23 Mar 1916

Mary Horst, dau. of Christian and Elizabeth Horst, b. 13 Jul 1867

Walter Emory Hutson, Jr., son of Walter and Sarah A. Hutson, b. 21 Mar 1920

Children of Samuel T. and Catharine Hutson:
1. James Thomas Hutson, b. 3 Mar 1860
2. Joseph Emory Hutson, b. 27 Jun 1863
3. Bertrand Sherman Hutson, b. 10 Jun 1875

Deaths:
James D. Hutson, d. 10 Dec 1827
Deborah Hutson, widow of Michael Hutson, d. 27 Mar 1869, age 77
Catherine Hutson, d. 16 Apr 1868 in her 55th year
Samuel Thomas Hutson, d. 31 Oct 1883 in his 55th year
James Thomas Hutson, d. 30 Mar 1861, age 1 year and 27 days
Mary Hutson, wife of Joseph Emory Hutson, d. 13 May 1932
Joseph Emory Hutson, d. 6 Dec 1943, age 80
Walter Emory Hutson, son of Mary and Joseph, d. 18 Dec 1971, age 77

Children of Michael and Deborah Hutson:
1. Samuel Hutson, d. 14 Mar 1816
2. Michael Hutson, d. 18 Aug 1821
3. James H. Hutson, d. 9 Feb 1829
4. Sarah Ann Hutson, d. 13 May 1827

5. Edward Hutson, d. 11 Mar 1832
6. Frances D. Hutson, d. 23 Aug 1836
7. Eliza (Hutson) Plummer, d. 29 Jan 1852

Family Records (Clippings in Bible):

Death notices from the *Baltimore Sun* on 11 Sep 1858 and 28 Mar 1869, each indicating "Eastern Shore papers please copy" as follows:
Michael Hutson, d. 10 Sep 1858 in his 75th year
Deborah Hutson, d. 27 Mar 1869 in her 77th year

BENJAMIN JEFFERS BIBLE

Bible published in 1856 by Jesper Harding, Philadelphia. Family data was gleaned from bible records which were supplemented with handwritten pages inserted therein. An undated note by the late Grace C. J. Currier of Harford County, MD stated, in part, "The first two sheets of this Benjamin Jeffers Bible record are in color. Richard gave them to me and I think the copies have been painted. They are very beautiful." Photocopies were submitted by C. Jeffers Schmidt, Jr., of Lancaster, VA in 2002. Bible was originally owned by Benjamin Jeffers who moved from Queen Anne's County to Harford County by 1843 and acquired land on Gunpowder Neck.

Marriages:
Benjamin Jeffers and Henrietta ---- m. ---- [*Ed. Note:* The children of this marriage were recorded in the family bible, but the date of marriage was not. Records in Queen Anne's County, MD indicate Benjamin Jeffers and Mary Henrietta Rouch were married 27 Sep 1826 by Rev. William T. Reed].

Benjamin Jeffers and Sarah A. Stapleford m. 25 Sep 1855 by Rev. Reace [i.e., Rev. Reese in Harford County]

William W. Jeffers and Martha R. Evans m. 24 Feb 1897
William L. Jeffers and Sarah Wiley m. 7 Apr 1906
William L. Jeffers and Ida A. Moxley m. 11 Jun 1914
James Jeffers and Lena Guttermuth m. 12 Sep 1906 [*Ed. Note:* She was noted as being his second wife; his first wife was not mentioned].

[Undated marriages mentioned in bible]:
John Calvin Jeffers and Helen Carroll
Joseph Jeffers and Anne ----

Bassel Jeffers and Nellie ----
George Jeffers and Mary Rembold

Births:
Children of Benjamin and Henrietta Jeffers:
1. Mary Elizabeth Jeffers, b. ---- 1828
2. Margaret Ann Jeffers, b. 19 Jul 1830
3. Johanathan Jeffers, b. 5 Jan 1834
4. Henrietta Jeffers, b. 30 Oct 1836
5. Benjamin Jeffers, b. 20 Nov 1838
6. Sarah Jane Jeffers, b. 4 Aug 1842
7. Bassel Jeffers, b. 14 Feb 1846

Children of Benjamin and Sarah Jeffers:
1. William Wesley Jeffers, b. 20 Sep 1856
2. Laura Jeffers, b. 26 Apr 1858
3. James Jeffers, b. 23 Sep 1859
4. George Jeffers, b. 16 Mar 1861
5. Joseph Jeffers, b. 5 May 1863

Children of James and Lena Jeffers:
1. Lena(?) Marie Jeffers, b. 16 Jun 1907
2. James Jeffers, Jr., b. 28 Feb 1909 [*Ed. Note:* One entry listed his name as James Jeffers, Jr. while another listed him as James B. Jeffers].
3. Elwood C. Jeffers, b. 24 Oct 1911
4. Norman(?) Jeffers, b. 7 Nov 1913
5. Joseph Lee Jeffers, b. 17 Dec 1917

Children of George and Mary Jeffers:
1. Florence Lillian Jeffers, b. 17 Jun ----
2. Blanche Irene Jeffers, b. 24 Jun ----
3. George Linwood Jeffers, b. 25 Feb ----

Anne Jeffers, b. 18 Jun 1863
Mary A. Jeffers, wife of George Jeffers, b. 12 Apr 1864
Sarah Rebecca Jeffers, dau. of Benjamin and Rebecca Jeffers, b. 19 Nov 1872
William L. Jeffers, b. 24 Jun 1884
John Calvin Jeffers, b. 22 Mar 1888
Arthur Jeffers, b. 11 Mar 1889

Bertha Elizabeth Jeffers, b. 9 Mar 1892
Clifton Jeffers, b. 10 May 1893
Grace Jeffers, b. 30 Nov 1895
Mary Helen Jeffers, b. 19 Apr 1898
Sarah May Jeffers, dau. of William and Martha Jeffers, b. 31 May 1898
Grace Carroll Jeffers, b. 20 Jan 1911
William Joseph Jeffers, b. 20 Aug 1911
Marian(?) Lee Jeffers, b. 25 Jun 1913

Deaths:
Laura Jeffers, dau. of Benjamin and Sally Jeffers, d. 29 Dec 1861, age 3 years, 8 months and 3 days
Benjamin Jeffers, d. 4 May 1865
Arthur Jeffers, d. 30 Jul 1889
Howard Jeffers, son of Joseph and Anne Jeffers, d. 6 Mar 1893
Bertha Elizabeth Jeffers, d. 27 Jul 1893
Grace Jeffers, d. 11 Jan 1896
Annie Jeffers, d. 31 Jan 1896
Mary A. Jeffers, wife of George Jeffers, d. 28 Oct 1897 at Manchester, VA, age 33 years, 6 months and 16 days
Sarah A. Jeffers, d. 6 May 1900, age 74 years, 9 months and 11 days
Sarah Wiley Jeffers, wife of William L. Jeffers, d. 7 Sep 1906
Clifton Jeffers, d. 21 Sep 1908
William Joseph Jeffers, d. 20 Aug 1911
Benjamin Jeffers, d. 8 Aug 1915, age 77
John Calvin Jeffers, d. 10 Feb 1917
Nellie Jeffers, wife of Bassel Jeffers, d. 17 Jun 1922, age 79
Joseph Jeffers, d. 28 Mar 1926
James Jeffers, d. 6 Oct 1928
George Jeffers, d. 27 Jan 1929
Anne Jeffers, d. 26 Feb 1932
Lena Jeffers, wife of James Jeffers, d. 5 Jul 1947(?)
Children of James and Lena Jeffers:
1. James Jeffers, Jr., d. 6 Feb 1965
2. Norman(?) Jeffers, d. 31 May 1956
3. Joseph Lee Jeffers, d. 12 Mar 1923

Lizzie Jeffers Archer, d. 28 Feb 1911
Sallie Casey, d. 26 Aug 1916, age 76
Mary Godwin, d. 30 Jul 1916, age 86

Henrietta Jeffers Shaw Leaverton, d. 31 Mar 1927

Family Records (Clippings in Bible):
1. William W. Jeffers, husband of Martha Jeffers (neé Evans), d. 12 Aug 1934 at his late residence on Harford Road and Gunpowder Falls. Funeral services at the above residence on Tues., Aug. 14, at 11 a.m. Interment in Fork M. E. Cemetery.
2. A special communication of Highland Lodge No. 184, A. F. and A. M., will be held Tues., Aug. 14, at 9:30 a.m. to attend the funeral of our late brother William H. Jeffers. Signed: E. Merriman Brooks, W. F.

ELISHA JOHNSON BIBLE

Bible published by The American Bible Society of New York in 1857. Family data gleaned from a typescript at the Maryland Historical Society.

Marriages:
Elisha Johnson and Ann E. Harkins m. 6 Feb 1862
Emory E. Johnson and Susie E. Pyle m. 23 Nov 1887
S. W. Gorrell and Ela May Johnson m. 31 Oct 1897
Elmer Johnson and Florence R. Johnson m. 24 Dec 1891

Births:
Emory Elsworth Johnson, b. 30 Dec 1862
William Elmer Johnson, b. 26 Mar 1870
Ela May Johnson, b. 27 Nov 1873
Deaths:
Ann Eliza Johnson, d. 6 Feb 1916
Elisha Johnson, d. 13 Feb 1916
W. Elmer Johnson, d. 17 Mar 1941
Chester C. Johnson, d. ---- [no date]

EMORY JOHNSON BIBLE

Bible published by A. J. Holman & Company, No. 1222 Arah St., Philadelphia, PA, in 1887. Family data gleaned from a typescript at the Maryland Historical Society.

Marriages:
"This is to certify that Emory E. Johnson and Susie E. Pyle were united by me in Holy Matrimony at Jarrettsville, Md. on the 23rd day of November, 1887, in the presence of Elisha Johnson and E. R. Pyle. Signed: T. E. Peters, Minister of the Gospel."
F. Heisse Johnson and Ethel Harlan Spencer m. 16 May 1914
Mabel M. Johnson and Lester Huff m. 9 Jan 1915
J. Raymond Johnson and Frances E. Wilson m. 7 Feb 1917
Melvin P. Johnson and Winifred Hawkins m. 11 Jun 1921
C. Ellsworth Johnson and Miriam Milhiser m. 20 Jun 1922

Births:
Emory Ellsworth Johnson, son of Elisha and Ann E. Johnson, b. 31 Dec 1862
Susie E. Johnson, dau. of Joshua H. and Gulielma E. Pyle, b. 7 Oct 1866

Children of Emory and Susie E. Johnson:
1. Fred Heisse Johnson, b. 16 Jan 1889
2. Mabel May Johnson, b. 7 Feb 1891
3. John Raymond Johnson, b. 1 Jul 1894
4. Carl Ellsworth Johnson, b. 28 Jun 1897
5. Melvin P. Johnson, b. 12 Aug 1899

Deaths:
Ann Eliza Johnson, d. 6 Feb 1916
Elisha Johnson, d. 13 Feb 1916
Emory E. Johnson, d. 29 Jun 1935
Susie E. Johnson, d. 27 Nov 1938

JOHNSTON-JOHNSON BIBLE

Bible published and sold by Kimber & Sharpless, 8 South 4th Street, Philadelphia, PA (no date given). Family data gleaned from a typescript at the Maryland Historical Society.

Marriages:
John Johnston and Charlotte Michael m. 15 Feb 1816 by Rev. William Stevens

James Taylor and Mary Ann Taylor m. 6 Oct 1829

James W. Johnson and Lidia A. Stockham m. 24 Feb 1853 by Rev. Mr. Brooks

William Barrow and Ann M. Johnson m. 8 May 1854 by Rev. Mr. Green

James A. Mount and Laura B. Johnson m. 7 Aug 1884 by Rev. J. Eckels

James Taylor and Mary Ann Canon m. -- Oct 1829 [*Ed. Note:* This entry appears to be in error because James Taylor married Mary Ann Taylor on 6 Oct 1829 as noted above. There was a James Taylor who married Mary Cannon on 7 Apr 1814 in Harford County]

Grafton B. Day and Sarah E. Johnson m. 15 May 1856

James W. Johnson and Hannah Michael m. 28 Jan ---- [date not given]

George J. Johnson and Cornelia E. Barrow m. 10 Jan 1859 by Rev. Mr. Monroe

James F. Ford and Marion Johnson m. 21 Feb 1883 by Rev. Mr. Marsh

Births:
Mary Ann Canon, b. 27 May 1810

Julian Hopkins, b. 25 Feb 1860

Clarence Jackson Mount, son of James A. and Laura Mount, b. 15 Dec 1884

Children of James and Maryan Taylor:
1. Frances Belck Taylor, b. 5 Nov 1830
2. Catherine A. Taylor, b. 5 Nov 1830
3. Mary Manda Taylor, b. 16 Dec 1833

Children of James and Naomi Michael:
1. Hannah Michael, b. 17 Aug 1790
2. Charlotte Michael, b. 27 Jan 1799
3. Miranda Michael, b. 10 Mar 1801
4. William Michael, b. 16 Aug 1804
5. Susannah Michael, b. 16 Sep 1807
6. Ann Matilda Michael, b. 25 Nov 1810

Children of George J. and Cornelia Johnson:
1. Marian Johnson, b. 16 Nov 1859
2. George Monroe Johnson, b. 22 Jul 1862
3. Laura B. Johnson, b. 8 Oct 1865

Children of John and Charlotte Johnston:
1. Ann Eliza Johnston, b. 9 May 1816
2. John Henry Johnston, b. 28 Dec 1817
3. Mary Ann Johnston, b. 25 Mar 1820
4. Thomas Frisby Johnston, b. 17 Aug 1822
5. James William Johnston, b. 4 Feb 1824
6. George Jackson Johnston, b. 24 Nov 1827
7. Ann Matilda Johnston, b. 30 Nov 1831
8. Charlotte Johnston, b. 20 Dec 1832
9. Sarah Elizabeth Johnston, b. 25 Sep 1834

Deaths:
Catherine Taylor, d. 4 Feb 1831
Mary Amanda Taylor, d. 16 Mar 1834

Lydia Johnson, wife of James Johnson, d. 7 Jan 1854 in her 24th year

Charlotte Johnson, wife of John Johnson, d. 2 May 1857 in her 57th year

John Johnson, d. -- Jan 1849 in his 83rd year

Frisby Johnson, d. 20 Jan ---- in his 77th year

Children of John and Charlotte Johnston:
1. Eliza Johnston, d. 7 Apr 1824 in her 8th year
2. Miranda Johnston, d. 11 Aug 1820 in her 6th month
3. Charlotte Johnston, d. 26 Oct 1833 in her 9th month
4. Thomas Frisby Johnston, d. 23 Apr 1834 in his 12th year

JOHN FLETCHER JONES BIBLE

Bible published in 1853 by Jesper Harding in Philadelphia, PA. Family data gleaned from a typescript of records copied by Jon Harlan Livezey in 1977.

Marriages:
John F. Jones and Helen M. Creswell m. 25 Apr 1850

Edwin Hopkins and Jessie M. Cooley m. 15 Apr 1905
J. F. Hopkins and Ella Hollis m. 28 Aug 1907
Carroll C. Hopkins and Laura Baldwin m. 1 Jan 1914
Roland Hopkins and Ann Seymour Jones m. -- Jun ---- [blank]
Samuel W. Hopkins and Lucy M. Jones m. 14 Mar 1875
J. Amos Jones and Mary M. Ross m. 28 Feb 1888 (1890 crossed out)
Marvin Lord Cooley and Helen Esther Jones m. 26 Jan 1894
John Marvin Cooley and Lillian Grace Robey m. 26 Jun 1918
J. Robert Thomas and Lucy M. Jones m. 27 Oct 1918
Harold Amos Jones and L. Allie Thomas m. 22 Nov 1919
Helen Marr Hopkins and C. Braddock Jones m. 26 Nov 1920
Helen Marr Hopkins and John Cross m. 13 Nov 1943

Births:
Children of John F. and Helen M. Jones:
1. Lucinda M. Jones, b. 5 Oct 1851
2. Esther Ann Jones, b. 14 Nov 1852
3. John Amos Jones, b. 11 Aug 1859
4. Marvin Lord Cooley, b. 22 Jul 1868
5. Helen Esther Jones, b. 10 Oct 1869 (year changed to 1870)

Clara Lord Cram, b. 13 Apr 1853

Deaths:
Esther A. Jones, d. 15 Feb 1853
John Fletcher Jones, d. 23 Jun 1890
Helen Marr Jones, d. 18 Sep 1905
J. Amos Jones, d. 26 Oct 1913
Lucinda M. Jones, d. 17 Jan 1934
Mary M. Jones, d. 13 Apr 1943

Hattie Lord Cooley, d. 3 Jan 1907
Marvin Lord Cooley, d. 17 Jun 1925 (July written in pencil), age 57, at Maryland
    General Hospital

Clara Lord Cram Prigg, d. 3 Dec 1931
Robert E. Prigg, d. 16 Oct 1939

Ella Hollis Hopkins, d. -- Dec 1948

Alan L. Hopkins, d. 24 May 1925 at Maryland General Hospital

Col. Samuel Roland Hopkins, d. 25 Nov 1949, age 65, at Alachua General Hospital in Gainesville, FL; interment in Arlington National Cemetery on 28 Nov 1949

Mary E. (Mollie) Troutner, d. 24 Apr 1933

JOHN A. KECK BIBLE

No publication information available. A typescript of the bible records was submitted by Carleton L. Weidemeyer of Clearwater, FL in 2002, noting that this family resided at Randallstown in Baltimore County. He also prepared the notes presented herein and listed the following chain of possession of the family bible: John A. Keck, Walter Winfield Keck, Esther Greninger Keck, Winifred Keck Snyder, and Ronald Francis Snyder of Palmetto, FL.

Births:
John A. Keck, b. 5 Mar 1868
Clementine Addie Lay, b. 16 Jul 1868

[Children of John and Clementine Keck]:
1. Lulu Lavanna Keck, b. 13 May 1890
2. Walter Winfield Keck, b. 27 Feb 1893
3. John Alfred Keck, b. 6 Dec 1895
4. Ruth Elizabeth Keck, b. 8 Jul 1900

Summerfield Childs, b. 8 Mar 1842
Susanna C. Younger, b. 6 Aug 1844

[Children of Summerfield and Susanna Childs]:
1. Harry E. Childs, b. 8 May 1862
2. Maria E. Childs, b. 1 Oct 1865
3. Lulu M. Childs, b. 30 Jun 1871
4. Emma L. Childs, b. 2 Apr 1874
5. Lemuel Levi Childs, b. 5 Apr 1877

Marion Whitmore, b. 6 Jan 1886

Leona Mary Childs, b. 11 Nov 1905

Deaths:
Clementine Addie Lay Keck, d. 28 Sep 1911

Lulu Lavanna Keck, d. 24 Sep 1890

Family Records:
(Notes prepared by Carleton L. Weidemeyer)

1. Keck Family Bible in possession of Ronald F. Snyder, of Palmetto, FL in 2002.

2. Walter Winfield Keck owned and operated Keck's Barber Shop at the point of Greene's Lane and Liberty Road, Randallstown, Baltimore County, MD until his death on 12 Feb 1951. He is buried in Mt. Olive Cemetery, Randallstown, MD in an unmarked grave.

EMANUEL KENT BIBLE

Bible printed in London in 1783 (publisher not indicated). Family data gleaned from a handwritten copy of the bible records placed in Filing Case A at the Maryland Historical Society in 1956 by W. Hand Browne, Jr., who noted the following: "The sheet containing several references to the Kent family was lifted from an old Bible, printed in London in 1783. It was found among my father's books, and undoubtedly was left to him by his father, William Browne, who moved to Baltimore early in the 1800s and joined the firm of his maternal uncle, Emanuel Kent, possibly the son of the Emanuel referred to in the above record."

Marriages:
Emanuel Kent and Ellen ---- m. 19 Jun 1788 at 9 o'clock in evening
Elizabeth Middleton and William Kilty m. -- Aug 1790
Mary Ashbury Alkin and Rubin Gilder m. 5 Oct 1790
Mary Ashbury Gilder and John Chalmers, Jr. m. 2 Jul 1797

Deaths:
Ann Kent, d. 7 Aug 1795

Joseph Spiaght "that old saint and servant of God, died 18 May 1791 in the 72nd year of his age, as a shock of corn fully ripe he was gathered into the graner."

GEORGE A. KIMBLE BIBLE

Bible published by National Publishing Company (date and place not stated) and presented to George A. and Phebe E. Kimble on 13 Jul 1882 (donor not indicated). Family data gleaned from a typescript at the Maryland Historical Society.

Marriages:
George A. Kimble, son of Alfred W. and Harriet Kimble, and Phebe E. Baldwin, dau. of Samuel T. and Frances Baldwin, m. 24 Dec 1873 by Rev. J. C. Hagey at the bride's home in the presence of E. N. Baldwin and A. W. Kimble.

Mary Frances Kimble and Matthew Sullivan m. 23 Feb 1905
Samuel Alfred Kimble and Gertie Thomas m. 8 Feb 1908
Harriet Semelia Kimble and William H. Sewell m. 4 Aug 1903
Lillian Pearl Kimble and Harry Lee m. 6 Nov 1924
Phoebe Loflin Kimble and Earl Lentz m. 17 Feb 1914
George Finney Kimble and Myrtle Martin m. 6 Apr 1912
Samuel T. Baldwin and Frances Loflin m. 11 Sep 1835

Births:
George A. Kimble, son of Alfred W. and Harriet Kimble, b. 16 Jul 1845
Phebe E. Baldwin, dau. of Samuel T. and Frances Baldwin, b. 12 Jun 1853

S. T. Baldwin, son of Tyler and Sarah Baldwin, b. 20 May 1818

Frances Loflin, dau. of Thomas and Matilda Loflin, b. 7 Jul 1817

Children of George A. and Phebe Kimble:
1. Mary Frances Kimble, b. 15 Dec 1874
2. Samuel Alfred Kimble, b. 10 Sep 1876
3. Harry Kirk Kimble, b. 16 Feb 1879
4. Hattie Semelia Kimble, b. 19 Jun 1882
5. Lillian Pearl Kimble, b. 20 Mar 1884
6. Phebe Loflin Kimble, b. 7 Jun 1886
7. George Finney Kimble, b. 15 Dec 1889

Deaths:
George A. Kimble, d. 28 Jun 1894

Phebe E. Kimble, widow of George A. Kimble, d. 25 Nov 1913, age 60 years, 5 months and 16 days; funeral from residence near Abingdon; interment at Calvary
Robert E. Kimble, son of the late Alfred and Ann Kimble, d. 24 Sep 1926; funeral from home of niece Mrs. William H. Sewell in Abingdon; interment at Calvary
William D. Kimble, son of Alfred W. and Harriet Kimble, d. 5 Feb 1926

Samuel A. Kimble, d. 30 Nov 1944

Mary Frances Sullivan, d. 28 Dec 1923

Lillian Pearl Lee, wife of Harry H. Lee, d. 7 Mar 1933; funeral from home of sister Mrs. William H. Sewell in Abingdon; interment at Calvary

Phebe Loflin Lentz, d. 23 Feb 1938

S. T. Baldwin, d. 9 Jun 1884
Frances Baldwin, d. 18 Mar 1888

Mrs. John P. Heard, d. 14 Jun 1943 at her home in Weatherford, OK; interment in Greenwood Cemetery

Harry Kirk, d. -- Jan 1935
John Kirk, husband of the late Sarah M. Kirk (neé Baldwin), d. 16 May 1924 at his home in Darlington; interment in Darlington Cemetery

Family Records:

Children of William H. and Hattie S. Sewell:
1. Nena Semelia Sewell, b. 12 Jul 1904
2. William Kimble Sewell, b. 9 Nov 1905
3. Lillian Phebe Sewell, b. 16 May 1908
4. Charles Smith Sewell, b. 8 May 1910

Children and grandchildren:

Phebe Evaline Kimble (Mrs. Lester Storms)
    1 son - Ronald Emmett Sisco [sic]

Katherine Elizabeth Kimble (Mrs. Robert Pickert)
    2 sons, 1 deceased, 2 daughters:
    Robert Wellington Pickert, Jr.
    Sally Lynn Pickert
    Bruce Gordon Pickert (drowned 1952, about 8 years old)
    Richard Martin Pickert

Virginia Martin Kimble (Mrs. Edward Carter)
    2 sons, 1 daughter:
    Dale Sandra Carter
    Edward Blair Carter
    Peter Turner Carter

George Finnie Kimble, Jr. (m. Jewell C. Kidd)
    2 sons, 4 daughters:
    Thomas Francis Morris (stepson)
    Diana Lynn Kimble
    Donna Lee Kimble
    George Finnie Kimble III (twin)
    Jennie Sue Kimble (twin)
    Cynthia Lou Kimble

Robert Sheldon Kimble (m. Adeline B. Ballister)
    1 son, 1 daughter:
    Robert Sheldon Kimble, Jr.
    Patrick Mary Kimble

Children of Rev. and Mrs. Hastings ("Mrs. Charles Henry Hastings' card, Dover, DE"):
1. Mary Elizabeth Hastings, 6 years, 14 May 1919
2. Thelma Louisa Hastings, 4 years, 26 Apr 1919
3. Mabel Linda Hastings, 1 year, 27 Feb 1919

ABRAM (ABRAHAM) KING BIBLE

Bible printed and sold by Isaac Collins of Trenton, NJ in 1791. Written on the first page: "Abram and Elizabeth King 1791." Family data gleaned from a typescript at the Maryland Historical Society.

Marriages:
Mary Elisa King and S. H. Wilson m. 1 Sep 1869
Rebecca A. King, dau. of David and Elisa King, and Cooper Reves, of Philadelphia, m. 1 Sep 1869

Births:
Elizabeth King, b. 8 Sep 1770
John King, b. 1 Mar 1790
George King, b. 13 Oct 1791

David King, b. 1 Jun 1799
Elizabeth Ann King, b. 29 Jun 1806 at 6 o'clock in the afternoon

Deaths:
David Taylor, d. 12 Sep 1795, age 13
John Taylor, d. 26 Jan 1811, age 68
Jane Taylor, d. 25 Feb 1813, age 73
Elizabeth Taylor, mother of Elizabeth King, d. 21 Nov 1814
William King, d. 3 May 1786
George King, d. 5 Dec 1782
Catherine King, d. 21 Jul 1804, age 72
John King, son of Abram and Elizabeth King, d. 28 Dec 1824 at 7 o'clock in the evening near Natches in the State of Mississippi, age 34 years, 8 months and 27 days
Jane King, dau. of William King, d. 7 Dec 1833 about half past 1 o'clock in the morning, supposed to be 47 years old
Elizabeth King, wife of Abraham King, d. 19 Nov 1853 at half past 6 o'clock in the evening, in her 84th year
George King, son of Abraham and Elizabeth King, d. 5 Jun 1869 in his 79th year
David King, son of Abraham and Elizabeth King, d. 18 Jan 1874 in his 75th year

Family Records (Clippings in Bible):
1. Abraham King, d. at Kingsville in Baltimore County on Sun., 11 Dec 1836 in his 77th year; a native of Pennsylvania, he immigrated to this State about 20 years ago and located in Baltimore County. [*Baltimore Chronicle*, 14 Dec 1836]

2. Hon. John C. King, ex-judge and well known jurist, d. at his home at 534 N. Fulton Avenue [in Baltimore City] on Fri. at 10:30 o'clock, age 85 [no date was given]; born in 1824 in Kingsville in Baltimore County, son of the late Mr. and Mrs. Joshua King who were natives of England; interment in Loudoun Park Cemetery; his nearest relatives are four cousins: Mr. Rufus King, Mrs. J. Holmes Smith of Baltimore, Mrs. J. E. Wilson of Bradshaw (Baltimore County), and Mrs. Elizabeth T. Watson of Fallston (Harford County). [*Ed. Note:* The name and exact date of this 1909 newspaper were not given].

PIERSON D. KLAIR BIBLE

Bible published in 1867 by the American Bible Society in New York. Family data was submitted in 2002 by Mrs. Roberta Kimball of Havre de Grace, Harford County, MD, noting the Klair family came to Harford County from Chester County,

PA in 1843. Pierson D. Klair was born in Dublin, MD and later resided in Havre de Grace, MD.

Marriage:
[*Ed. Note:* The marriage page is missing from the bible; however, records in Harford County document the Klair-Baldwin marriage as follows]:

Pearson D. Klair, age 21, farmer, and Vesty Baldwin, age 26, mantua maker, both of Harford County, m. 6 Feb 1866 at the residence of James Baldwin by S. M. Bayless, Minister of the Gospel in the Pres. Church [i.e., Deer Creek Harmony Presbyterian Church].

Births:
Pierson D. Klair, son of Hiram and Ann D. Klair, b. 11 Jun 1845
Vesta B. Baldwin, dau. of James and Sarah Baldwin, b. 18 Nov 1839

Children of Pierson and Vesta Klair:
1. Howard O. Klair, b. 17 Jan 1867 at 9 o'clock morning
2. Lewis H. Klair, b. 25 Sep 1870
3. Jesse B. Klair, b. 22 Oct 1872
4. Biard M. Klair and Magie A. Klair, b. 15 Mar 1874 9 o'clock evening [*Note:* Written in pencil over his first name is "Bayard" and "Maggie" is spelled with just one "g"]
5. Hiram Goldsg. Blair, b. 23 Dec 1876
6. Kenton D. Klair, b. 26 Jun 1884 at 6? [o'clock]

Deaths:
Biard M. Klair, d. 3 Jan 1875 about 5 o'clock sabbath morning
Kenton D. Klair, d. 30 Aug 1884

WILLIAM KNIGHT BIBLE

No publication information available. Family data gleaned from a typescript at the Maryland Historical Society which noted that Jane Ann Scott (who married William Knight) came to America from Ireland in 1850 with her sister Elizabeth Scott (who married William Kennedy). The old Knight family farm was located at what is now the interchange of Interstate 95 and Route 155 between Earlton and Havre de Grace in Harford County, MD.

Marriage:
William Knight and Jane Ann Scott m. ---- [*Ed. Note:* Their marriage was not

recorded in this bible transcript, but a marriage license was issued to William Knight and Jane Scott in Harford County on 17 Oct 1851].

Births:
Children of William and Jane Ann Knight:
1. William T. Knight, b. 11 Sep 1854
2. Maggie Knight, b. 17 Jun 1856
3. John W. Knight, b. 4 Sep 1858
4. Mary A. Knight, b. 14 Oct 1860
5. Robert H. L. Knight, b. 23 Mar 1863
6. George A. B. Knight, b. 19 Apr 1865

Deaths:
Mrs. Jane Knight, wife of William Knight, d. 17 Jan 1898
Mr. William Knight, husband of Jane Knight, d. 1 Apr 1898
G. Leon Knight, older son of John W. Knight, d. 16 Apr 1925
John W. Knight, d. suddenly 27 May 1928

Mary Jane Howlett Hopkins, youngest dau. of Mary A. Knight and John Howlett, d. 9 Feb 1928, age 33 years.

Family Records:
Children of John and Mary Eleanor (Nora) Knight:
1. Lola Estelle Knight, b. 10 Mar 1889
2. George Leon Knight, b. 16 Aug 1890
3. Jeanette M. Knight, b. 16 Feb 1893
4. James Harry Knight, b. 21 May 1895

JOHN S. LAGAN BIBLE

Bible published by P. J. Kennedy (a Ducay version), but no date was given. Family data gleaned from a typescript at the Maryland Historical Society. Bible originally owned by John S. Lagan of Harford County, MD.

Marriage:
John S. Lagan and Sarah A. Terry m. 8 Oct 1890

Births:
Children of John S. and Sarah A. Lagan:

1. Mary Lagan, b. 8 Jul 1891
2. Catharine Elizabeth Lagan, b. 10 Aug 1892
3. Margaret Mary Lagan, b. 23 Mar 1894
4. Sarah Ann Lagan, b. 18 May 1895
5. John Lagan, b. 22 Nov 1896
6. John Ralph Lagan, b. 6 Apr 1900

Deaths:
Mary Lagan, d. 9 Jul 1891
John Lagan, d. 8 Jan 1897, age 6 weeks and 5 days
John Steven Lagan, d. 15 Mar 1946, age 79
Sarah A. (Terry) Lagan, d. 1 Dec 1937

LAMDIN-FOX-HUGG BIBLE

No publication information available (title page missing). Family data gleaned from a photocopy of the bible filed in Filing Case A at the Maryland Historical Society.

Marriages:
Robert P. Lamdin and Fanny P. Dungan m. 18 Oct 1855
Charles J. Fox and Thomasine M. Lamdin m. 7 Oct 1885 at 2 p.m. [*Ed. Note:* An unidentified newspaper clipping in the bible stated they were both of Baltimore and were married by Rev. C. E. Felton]

Borneman Lancaster and Miss Sinclare m. ----
Sinclare Lancaster, son of Borneman, m. ----
Elizabeth Lancaster, dau. of Sinclare, m. Jacob H. Hugg ---- [*Ed. Note:* No date was given, but their first child was born 4 Nov 1780]

Ella Hugg and Thomas Litton m. ----
Eliza Hugg and John Green, Quaker of Philadelphia, m. ----
Jacob Hugg and Margaret Strobel m. ----
Nancy Hugg and Nicholas Lamdin, parents of Robert P. Lamdin, m. 29 Jun 1815

Eliza Green, dau. of Marie, and Hugh Davey, son of Capt. and Mrs. Hugh Davey, m. ----

John Fox and Harriett Danby m. 22 May 1845

Henry William Fox and Mary Ella Gressitt m. 4 Nov 1885

Births:
Children of Jacob and Elizabeth Hugg:
1. Jacob Hugg, b. 4 Nov 1780
2. William Hugg, b. 24 Nov 1782
3. Sinclare Lancaster Hugg, b. 5 Feb 1784
4. Ella Hugg, b. 17 Jan 1788
5. Joseph Hugg, b. 14 May 1790
6. Elizah Hugg, b. 29 Nov 1792
7. Nancy Hugg, b. 8 May 1795
8. John Hugg, b. 22 Sep 1797
9. Betsy Hugg, b. 9 May 1799
10. Jacob Washington Hugg, b. 19 Feb 1801

Children of Nicholas and Nancy Lamdin:
1. Thomas Jacob Lamdin, b. 7 Apr 1816
2. Elizabeth Jane Lamdin, b. 21 Jul 1818
3. Nicholas Martin Lamdin, b. 20 Oct 1820
4. Ann Marie Lamdin, b. 3 Mar 1823
5. John Hugg Lamdin, b. 3 Apr 1825
6. Robert Philip Lamdin, b. 17 Aug 1827
7. Amanda Susannah Lamdin, b. 18 Apr 1830

Children of Robert and Fanny Lamdin:
1. Abe Dungan Lamdin, b. 2 Dec 1857
2. Elizabeth Virginia Lamdin, b. 22 Dec 1859
3. Thomasine Morris Lamdin, b. 2 Sep 1861

John Fox, b. 14 Apr 1824
Charles J. Fox, b. 16 Aug 1858 at 5? p.m.
J. Sydney Fox, son of Henry W. Fox, b. 1887

Children of Charles and Thomasine Fox:
1. Fanny Dungan Fox, b. 4 Aug 1886 at 7:45 a.m.
2. Edgar Burrough Fox, b. 27 Jul 1889 at 9:10 p.m.
3. Hazel Annabel Fox, b. 1 Jul 1892 at 2 a.m.
4. John Morris Fox, b. 9 Jul 1894 at 8:55 a.m.

5. Marbury Brewer Fox, b. 25 Aug 1896

Children of John and Harriett Fox:
1. Henry William Fox, b. 3 Sep 1851 at 2? p.m.
2. John Sydney Fox, b. 19 Feb 1855 at 4 p.m.
3. Charles James Fox, b. 15 Aug 1858 at 5? p.m.

Harriett Danby, b. 28 May 1826
Mary Ella Gressitt, b. 27 Dec 1857
Fanny P. Dungan, dau. of Abel P. and Jane Dungan, b. 19 Oct 1831

Deaths:
Children of Jacob and Elizabeth Hugg:
1. Jacob Hugg, d. 7 Aug 1800
2. Sinclare Hugg, d. 28 Sep 1797
3. Sinclare Lancaster Hugg, d. 30 Aug 1800
4. Betsy Hugg, d. 31 Aug 1800
5. Maria Hugg, d. 27 Jun 1803

Robert P. Lamdin, d. 11 Oct 1897, age 71
Fannie P. Lamdin, wife of Robert P. Lamdin, d. 19 Dec 1891, age 60
John Sydney Fox, d. 11 Sep 1871 at 7? p.m.
Harriett Fox, d. 30 Jun 1874 suddenly about 12 p.m.
John Fox, d. 16 Jan 1888 at 4 p.m.
Edgar Burrough Fox, d. 10 Jul 1890, age 11 months and 4 days
J. Sydney Fox, son of Henry W. Fox, d. 11 Jul 1930, b. 1887
Charles J. Fox, d. 5 Apr 1940 at 12:45 a.m., age 81 years and 8 months
Thomasine M. Fox, d. 2 Nov 1941 ay 6:50 a.m., age 80 years and 2 months
Mary Ella Fox, d. 9 Jul 1944 at 12:50 a.m., age 86 years, 6 months and 18 days

Family Record (Clipping in Bible):
John Fox, a well known builder in Baltimore, was born in Birmingham on 14 Apr 1824 and came to Baltimore around 1846. He built Homestead on the Harford Road and developed land in Waverly. He built houses in Anacostia near Washington, DC, and the Hoen Building and private residences in Baltimore. His last project was building row homes at Eutaw Place. He was married twice and his second wife and two sons survive him, one of them being H. W. Fox of the Baltimore bar. John Fox died at his residence of bright's disease. [*Ed. Note:* The foregoing obituary was paraphrased since the undated photocopy was difficult to read].

BENEDICT LEE BIBLE

Bible published by Jesper Harding of Philadelphia, PA (no date given). Family data gleaned from a typescript at the Maryland Historical Society.

Marriages:
Benedict Lee and Catharine ---- m. ---- [*Ed. Note:* Their marriage was not recorded in this bible transcript, but the register of the First Methodist Episcopal Church in Baltimore City records the marriage of Benedict Lee and Catharine Wayman on 23 Apr 1818 by Rev. Christopher Frye].

Andrew French and Rebecca Lee m. 9 Nov 1854
Alice French and J. W. Bauer m. 12 Jan 1886
Elizabeth Hackney and J. W. Bauer m. 22 Sep 1915

Births:
Benedict Lee, son of George and Mary Lee, b. 6 Oct 1794
Catharine Wayman, dau. of Hezekiah and Elizabeth Wayman, b. 9 Nov 1800

Children of Benedict and Catharine Lee:
1. Elizabeth Lee, b. 7 Feb 1819
2. Enoch George Lee, b. 27 Apr 1820
3. Martha Lee, b. 26 Jul 1821
4. Amanda Mehynie(?) Lee, b. 29 Dec 1822
5. William Lee, b. 20 (26?) Mar 1825
6. Catharine Lee, b. 26 Jan 1828
7. Hezekiah Lee, b. 11 May 1829
8. John Thomas Lee, b. 19 Sep 1830
9. Joseph Lee, b. 28 Feb 1832
10. Edmond Lee, b. 27 Aug 1833
11. Rebecca Lee, b. 22 Feb 1835

Children of Lawless and Mary Austin:
1. Thomas Steuart Austin, b. 17 Feb 1816
2. David Lawless Austin, b. 6 Oct 1819

Children of Thomas Steuart and Elizabeth Austin:
1. Mary Catharine Austin, b. 15 Mar 1838
2. Elizabeth Austin, b. 29 Jan 1840

3. Thomas Hart Benton Austin, b. 4 Jan 1842
4. Martha Ann Austin, b. 15 Nov 1843
5. Georgeanna Mifflin Dallas Austin, b. 25 Jan 1845
6. James Knox Polk Austin, b. 25 Jan 1848
7. Mary Catharine Austin, b. 11 Feb 1849
8. Martha Rebecca Austin, b. 16 Jun 1852

Alice French, b. 15 Aug 1855
Catharan French, b. 10 May 1858
William A. French, b. 5 Mar 1863
Edmond Lee French, b. 12 Apr 1867

Elwood Lee Anderson, b. 21 Mar 1879
J. W. Bauer, b. 15 Oct 1862
Mrs. Elizabeth Hackney, b. 4 Oct 1862
Children of J. W. and Alice French Bauer:
1. Lawrence Edward Bauer, b. 23 Sep 1888
2. John Wilton Bauer, b. 15 Mar 1890
3. Rebecca May Bauer, b. 30 Jul 1892
4. Howard Andrew Bauer, b. 27 Feb 1894
5. Linwood French Bauer, b. 19 Sep 1896
6. Arthur Lee Clayton Bauer, b. 5 May 1900

Deaths:
Enoch Lee, d. 20 Apr 1881, age 61
Alice French Bauer, d. 1 Nov 1911, age 56
Clayton Bauer, d. 3 Aug 1945, age 45
Linwood French Bauer, d. 2 Jul 1901, age 4 years and 10 months

EDMOND LEE BIBLE

Bible published in 1868 by William W. Harding, No. 326 Chestnut Street, Philadelphia, PA. Family data gleaned from a typescript at the Maryland Historical Society. This Lee and Jones family were residents of Baltimore City and Harford County.

Marriages:
Edmond Lee and Mary V. Jones m. 5 Jan 1861
John Amos Ward and Isabelar Jones m. 22 Feb 1872

Births:
Edmond Lee, b. 27 Aug 1833
Mary V. Jones, b. 13 Dec 1841
Alice Cordalia ---- [blank], b. 7 Dec 1872

Deaths:
Alice Jones, d. 21 Mar 1858
Cordalia M. Jones, d. 10 Mar 1860
Isabelar Ward, d. 8 Apr 1873
Catherine Lee, d. 17 Nov 1874

ISAAC I. LEITHISER BIBLE

No publication information available. Family data gleaned from a typescript at the Maryland Historical Society.

Marriages:
Isaac I. Leithiser and Catharine A. Bayard m. 10 Feb 1874
Richard H. Leithiser and Rebecca Foster m. 11 Mar 1903

Births:
Thomas C. Bayard, b. 12 Nov 1819
Hartman Leithiser, b. 29 Mar 1826
Salome Ruby, b. 25 Mar 1826

Children of Thomas and Catharine Bayard:
1. Lewis H. Bayard, b. 15 Apr 1851
2. Samuel T. Bayard, b. 18 Jan 1853
3. Catherine A. Bayard, b. 22 Aug 1857

Children of Isaac and Catharine Leithiser:
1. Claudia Louis Liethiser, b. 30 Apr 1875
2. Richard Henry Leithiser, b. 19 Mar 1877
3. Annie W. Leithiser, b. 20 Mar 1879
4. Emma Oneida Leithiser, b. 12 Nov 1880
5. Lawrence Brett Leithiser, b. 6 Sep 1884
6. Bayard Leithiser, b. 8 Jul 1886
7. Myrtle Ruby Leithiser, b. 7 Apr 1889
8. Samuel Lyell Leithiser, b. 28 Mar 1893

9. Helen May Leithiser, b. 12 Dec 1894
10. Charles Austin Leithiser, b. 9 Apr 1899
11. Harry Eugene Leithiser, b. 8 Jan 1902
Children of Richard H. and Rebecca Leithiser:
1. Eldon Foster Leithiser, b. 19 Jul 1904
2. Ada Louise Leithiser, b. 10 Jul 1908

Richard Eldon Leithiser, son of Eldon Leithiser, b. 24 Jul 1929

Children of Richard Eldon Leithiser:
1. Richard Eldon Leithiser, b. 6 Jul 1951
2. William David Leithiser, b. 12 Jun 1954

Eleanora Leithiser Jarrell, dau. of Ada Lou and Joseph Jarrell, b. 18 Aug 1930

Deaths:
Thomas C. Bayard, d. 12 Jun 1858
Catharine Bayard, d. 26 Jan 1910
Lewis H. Bayard, d. 15 Jan 1865
Samuel T. Bayard, d. 15 Mar 1873
Catherine A. Bayard, d. 9 Apr 1918
Salome Ruby Leithiser, d. 28 Oct 1866

JAMES NEWTON LITTLE BIBLE

No publication information available. "Yost Bible, Philadelphia" was written on a transcript of the bible at the Maryland Historical Society.

Marriages:
James Newton Little and Eleanor Jane Jackson m. 22 Dec 1870
William Adam Little and Georgianna Founds m. 25 Oct 1892
Alexander Jackson Little and Elizabeth Moore m. 4 Apr 1900
Mary Elizabeth Little and John Bernard Dawson m. 17 Jun 1903
Harriett Connard Little and Thomas Morgan Owens m. 10 Oct 1900
Eleanor Chatman Little and Elmore Hazlett Owens m. 16 Oct 1901
James Burke Little and Bessie Craig m. ---- 1907
John Edward Little and Ethel Walker m. 11 Mar 1913

Births:
James Newton Little, b. 18 Aug 1832
Eleanor Jane Jackson, b. 5 Oct 1846

Children of James N. and Eleanor Jane Little:
1. William Adam Little, b. 27 Nov 1871
2. Alexander Jackson Little, b. 21 Feb 1873
3. Mary Elizabeth Little, b. 16 Feb 1875
4. Harriett Connard Little, b. 19 Feb 1878
5. Eleanor Chatman Little, b. 19 Apr 1881
6. James Burke Little, b. 14 Feb 1883
7. John Edward Little and Edward John Little, b. 21 Apr 1887

Deaths:
James Newton Little, d. 12 Apr 1914
Eleanor Jane Jackson Little, d. 3 Mar 1936

Children of James N. and Eleanor Jane Little:
1. Eleanor Chatman Little, d. 18 Jun 1941
2. James Burke Little, d. 7 Dec 1926
3. Edward John Little, d. 21 Apr 1887

ROBERT S. LIVEZEY BIBLE

Bible printed in 1892 (name of publisher not given). Family data gleaned from a typescript at the Maryland Historical Society.

Marriages:
Robert S. Livezey, son of Jacob Livezey, and Mary S. Swartz, dau. of James Swartz, m. 24 Jun 1884 at Churchville by Rev. Calvin D. Wilson. Witnesses were Florence O. Swartz and Jacob Livezey.

James E. Archer and Mary J. Livezey m. 20 Feb 1912
Jacob O. Livezey and Florence L. Everett m. -- Apr 1912
James S. Livezey and Frances B. Livezey m. -- Apr 1918
George M. Bailey and T. Priscilla Livezey m. 1 Mar 1919
Jacob O. Livezey and Maude M. Archer m. 19 Mar 1919
Clarence Morgan and A. Elizabeth Livezey m. 24 Nov 1925
Webster H. Livezey and Elizabeth E. Livezey m. ---- [*Ed. Note:* Their marriage certificate states Webster Livezey and Elizabeth E. Livezey were married on 29 Apr 1920]

Births:
Robert S. Livezey, b. 15 Aug 1854
Mary Ann Swartz, b. 3 Aug 1863

Children of Robert S. and Mary Ann Livezey:
1. Jacob O. Livezey, b. 7 Aug 1885
2. Robert H. Livezey, b. 23 Dec 1886
3. Mary J. Livezey, b. 16 Aug 1888
4. James S. Livezey, b. 21 Aug 1890
5. Webster H. Livezey, b. 1 May 1892
6. Clement S. Livezey, b. 30 Apr 1893
7. T. Priscilla Livezey, b. 3 Dec 1896
8. Pearl H. Livezey, b. 14 Sep 1898
9. A. Elizabeth Livezey, b. 18 Mar 1902

Deaths:
Clement Sewell Livezey, d. 30 Nov 1898
Robert S. Livezey, d. 16 Sep 1927
Florence Livezey, d. 2 Nov 1917
Mary Ann Livezey, d. 11 Jul 1939
Vernon E. Archer, d. -- Mar 1922

Family Records (Clippings in Bible):
1. Florence Swartz Mitchell, wife of Edward W. Mitchell, Sr., d. 12 Dec 1935, age 67; interment at Calvary.

2. Mrs. James E. Archer, of Carsins Run [Harford County], d. Wed., 17 Aug ---- [*Ed. Note:* Year was not given in Bible]; survived by husband, daughters Mrs. Anna Bishop, of Churchville, and Mrs. Rhoda Cosner, sons Harold and James Archer (at home), and grandchildren [not named]; interment at Mt. Carmel; pallbearers were nephews James Livezey, Robert Livezey, Wilbur Livezey, Charles Livezey, Winfield Archer, and Melvin Bailey.

3. Robert S. Livezey, an extensive farmer of old Quaker stock, d. at his residence near Bel Air on Fri., 16 Sep ---- [*Ed. Note:* Year was not given in Bible, but it was 1927]; survived by widow Mary Ann Livezey and 8 children: Robert Livezey, Jacob Livezey, James S. Livezey, Webster Livezey, Pearl Livezey, Mrs. James Archer, Mrs. George Bailey, and Mrs. Clarence Morgan; interment at Friends Cemetery in Fallston.

4. James H. Archer, age 74, son of the late John and Hannah Archer of Wilna [Harford County] and husband of Maggie A. Archer, d. at his residence in Bel Air on Fri., 16 Oct ---- after 2 years' illness; member of Mt. Carmel Church and a prominent farmer in Harford County all his life; survived by his widow Maggie, three daughters Mrs. Walter E. Boone, Mrs. Jacob O. Livezey, and Mrs. Earl White, one son F. Traynor Archer ("there was another son James E. Archer"), and two brothers Joseph W. Archer and George Archer; interment at Mt. Carmel; pallbearers were nephews Louis Archer, John Archer, Theodore Archer, Joseph F. Archer, Charles Archer, and Traynor Archer. [*Ed. Note:* The year of death was not given in the bible, but it was 1925].

THOMAS N. LIVEZEY BIBLE

No publication information available. Family data gleaned from a typescript at the Maryland Historical Society.

Marriage:
Thomas Livezey and Sylvania Stewart m. 19 Aug 1868

Births:
Thomas N. Livezey, b. 10 Sep 1839
Sylvania Stewart, b. 14 Mar 1849

Children of Thomas and Sylvania Livezey:
1. Florence Livezey, b. 12 Nov 1869
2. Kate E. S. Livezey, b. 9 Jan 1871
3. John S. Livezey, b. 9 Aug 1873
4. George K. Livezey, b. 20 Sep 1876
5. Thomas N. Livezey, b. 25 Nov 1880
6. Harry K. Livezey, b. 24 Apr 1883
7. Anna M. C. Livezey, b. 6 Jan 1887

Margaret E. Livezey, b. 24 Oct 1909
Paul Victor Livezey, b. 10 Nov 1911

Deaths:
Harry K. Livezey, d. 26 Sep 1883

Anna M. C. Livezey, d. 25 Feb 1887
John S. Livezey, d. 21 Jan 1888
Sylvania S. Livezey, d. 7 Sep 1924

JOSEPH LOBACH (LOBAUGH) BIBLE

Bible published and sold by Kimber and Sharpless, Philadelphia, PA (no date given). Family data gleaned from a typescript at the Maryland Historical Society. Bible originally owned by Joseph Lobach in 1849 ("his Bible") and by Jane Mary Kuhns in 1869 ("her Bible"). The last known owner of the bible was The Antique Shop at Carsins Run in Harford County, MD.

Marriages:
Joseph Lobach and Eliza Taylor m. 7 Apr 1835
Joseph Lobach and Ann R. Hughes m. 28 Jan 1856
John T. Lobach and Elizabeth Snyder m. 11 Mar 1858
Alfred T. Lobaugh and Elizabeth Pilkey m. 9 Jun 1861
Philip U. Kuhns and Jennie M. Lobaugh m. 8 Mar 1864 by Rev. Samuel Phillips

Births:
Joseph Lobach, b. 1 Jan 1806
Eliza Taylor, b. 10 Aug 1813

Children of Joseph and Eliza Lobach:
1. John Taylor Lobach, b. 3 Apr 1836 in Carlisle, PA
2. Alfred Theodore Lobach, b. 8 Nov 1838
3. Jane Mary Lobach, b. 10 May 1841
4. Emma Elizabeth Lobach, b. 29 Aug 1843
5. Andrew Jackson Lobach, b. 27 Apr 1845
6. Florrance Anna Lobach, b. 12 Oct 1847
7. Eliza Ann Lobach, b. 4 Sep 1849
8. Josephene Laura Lobach, b. 17 Mar 185-?
9. Rachael Catharine Lobach, b. 13 Oct 1858

Philip Uhler Kuhns, b. 10 Jun 1839

Children of Philip U. and Jennie M. Kuhns:
1. ---- Kuhns, infant dau., b. 31 Oct 1864
2. Harvey Eugene Kuhns, b. 2 Dec 1867 in Newton Township, Cumberland County, PA

3. John Theodore Kuhns, b. 21 Jun 1870 in Carlisle
4. Florence Maria Kuhns, b. 15 Dec 1871 in Carlisle
5. Milton Lobaugh Kuhns, b. 26 Dec 1873 in Carlisle
6. Lillian Gertrude Kuhns, b. 10 Apr 1876 in Carlisle
7. Grace Edith Kuhns, b. 15 Jan 1879 in Carlisle

Mary Janet Natcher, b. 6 Jul 1903

Deaths:
Florrance Anna Lobach, d. 7 Nov 1848
Eliza Lobach, wife of Joseph Lobach, d. 10 Sep 1849, age 36 years and 1 month
Eliza Ann Lobach, d. 13 May 1850
John T. Lobach, d. 7 Nov 1907, age 71

---- Kuhns, infant dau. of Philip U. and Jennie M. Kuhns, d. 31 Oct 1864
John Theodore Kuhns, d. 20 May 1871, age 11 months
Grace Edith Kuhns, d. 24 Oct 1882, age 3 years, 9 months and 9 days
Jane Mary Kuhns, wife of Philip U. Kuhns, d. 7 Jul 1916, age 75 years, 1 month and 27 days
Philip Uhler Kuhns, d. 1 Nov 1916, age 77 years, 4 months and 2 days

Mary Janet Natcher, d. 9 Feb 1911, age 7 years, 6 months and 23 days

WILLIAM C. LOCKARD BIBLE

No publication information available. Family data gleaned from a typescript at the Maryland Historical Society.

Marriage:
William C. Lockard and Miss Mary Eliza Bull, second child of Bennett L. and Charity Bull, m. 14 Apr 1853

Births:
William C. Lockard, b. 4 Aug 1828
Mary Eliza Lockard, b. Sun., 17 Sep 1826

Children of William C. and Mary E. Lockard:
1. James Thomas Lockard, b. Sun., 24 Jun 1855

2. John Amos Lockard, b. 5 Jan 1857
3. Samuel Lee Lockard, b. 22 Sep 1858
4. Mary Jane Lockard, b. 6 Sep 1860
5. Martha Eliza Lockard, b. 11 Dec 1861
6. William Henry Lockard, b. 24 Jan 1870

ALBERT R. MAGNESS BIBLE

Bible published in 1875 by Harding, Philadelphia. Family data gleaned from a typescript at the Maryland Historical Society.

Marriage:
Albert R. Magness and Amanda F. DeMoss m. 1 Jan 1861

Births:
Albert R. Magness, b. 25 Mar 1830
Amanda [DeMoss] Magness, b. 11 Aug 1844

[Children of Albert and Amanda Magness]:
1. Frank Magness, b. 10 Nov 1861
2. Ida Mae Magness, b. 1 Jan 1863
3. Clara Magness, b. 3 Jun 1865 (or 64)
4. Ramsy Lee Magness, b. 10 Mar 1867 (or 66)
5. Lizzie Magness, b. ---- [blank] 1869
6. Nora Jane Magness, b. -- Jan 1872
7. Walter Pinkney Magness, b. 15 Apr 1874
8. Albert Stanley Magness, b. 15 Jun 1876
9. William Henry Magness, b. 20 Oct 1878
10. Lillie Bell Magness, b. 16 Jun 1881
11. Bertha Mae Magness, b. 17 Jun 1885

Milton Bosley, b. 29 May 1918
Velma Bosley, b. 2 Sep 1914
Geraldine Bosley, b. 8 Jul 1923

Deaths:
Albert R. Magness, d. 14 Aug 1902 in his 73rd year
Walter P. Magness, d. 11 Jul 1920

THOMAS MAGNESS BIBLE

Bible published in 1823 by A. Paul, New York. Family data gleaned from a typescript at the Maryland Historical Society in 1988, noting that "the Bible is in very poor condition; copy very difficult to read."

Marriages:
Thomas Magness and Jemima Rockhold m. 22 Dec 1803
Thomas Tredway and Elizabeth Magness m. 27 Mar 1828
Harriet Ann Magness and John M. James m. 3 Nov 1821 [1829?]
Charles E. Magness and Mary Jane Whiteford m. 15 Oct 1847
Daniel Hains(?) and Mary Ann Rockhold m. 4 Jul 1833(?) [*Ed. Note:* Harford County marriage records state that Samuel Haines and Mary Ann Rockhold obtained a license on 11 Jul 1833].

Births:
Florance Virginia Watters, b. 5 Jul 1854
Charles Edward Watters, b. 7 Jun 1856

Harriet E. Magness, b. 23 Apr 1849
Charles Henry Magness, b. 9 Jul 1850

[Children of Thomas and Jemima Magness]:
1. Thomas Henry Magness, b. 5 Aug 1812
2. Ellen Magness, b. 24 Jul 1816
3. Charles Edward Magness, b. 4 Jan 1820
4. Nathaniel Parker Magness, b. 16 Mar 1823
5. William Parker (Magness) ---- [*Typescript Note:* "No date beside this name. Wm. Parker Magness is listed in the 1850 census, age 27, making his date of birth ca. 1823"].

Charles Howard Watters, b. 11 Dec 1851

Marietta E. James, b. -- Dec 1830(?)

[Children of Thomas and Elizabeth Tredway]:
1. John Edward Tredway, b. 2 Feb 1828 [1829?]
2. Thomas Magness Tredway, b. 16 Sep 1831
3. Ellen Cornelia Tredway, b. 8 Feb 1834

[Children of John and Harriet James]:
1. William Shewell James, b. 6 Aug 1830(?)
2. Sarah S. James, b. 19 Nov 1832
3. Mary E. James, b. 1 Dec 18--
4. Ellen Jane James, b. 1 Oct 18--

Charles E. Magness, b. -- Jan 1820

Mary Jain Whiteford, b. 1 Oct 1824

[Children of Charles and Mary Magness]:
1. Harriet Edward Magness, b. 23 Apr 1849
2. Charles H. Magness, b. 9 Jul 1850
3. John R. Magness, b. 15 Oct 1855
4. Arthur Courtney Magness, b. 17 Apr 1866

Jemima Rockhold, wife of Thomas Magness, b. 6 Aug 1786

[Children of Thomas and Jemima Magness]:
1. Elizabeth Magness, b. 23 Sep 1804
2. Harriett Magness, b. 14 Feb 1807(?)
3. John Rockhold Magness, b. 1 Sep 1809

Deaths:
Thomas M. Magness, d. 12 May 1854
William Parker Magness, d. 15 Jul 1853
Harriet E. Magness, d. 25 Nov 1935

Charles Howard Watters, d. 9 Aug 1859
Florance Virginia Watters, d. 13 Feb 1947

THOMAS H. MAGNESS BIBLE

No publication information available. Family data gleaned from a typescript at the Maryland Historical Society in 1989.

Marriages:
Thomas Magness and Susan Martin m. 2 Apr 1841
Abraham Martin and Mary Magness m. 26 Sep 1816

Births:
Thomas H. Magness, b. 5 Aug 1812
Susan A. Martin, b. 3 Mar 1819

Children of Thomas and Susan Magness:
1. Mary Jane Magness, b. 10 Feb 1842
2. Jarret Thomas Magness, b. 9 Apr 1845
3. Henry Farnandis Magness, b. 29 Nov 1849 at 9 p.m.

Children of Henry F. Magness and Laura A. Myers:
1. Rhea Sylva Magness, b. Sat., 14 Nov 1874, 7 a.m.
2. Thomas N. Magness, b. Fri., 13 Jun 1879, 4 p.m.
3. Leonidas M. Magness, b. Thurs., 13 Nov 1881, 9 p.m.
4. Lawrence Farnandis Magness, b. Tues., 21 Aug 1888, 11 p.m

Abram Martin, b. 8 Apr 1788
Mary Martin, his wife, b. 3 Nov 1793

[Children of Abram and Mary Martin]:
1. S. J. (Jane) Martin, b. 20 Aug 1817
2. S. A. (Susan Anne) Martin, b. 3 Mar 1819
3. Clara (Clarissa) Martin, b. 20 May 1821
4. Mary Martin, b. 20 Jun 1823

Deaths:
Mary Martin, wife of Abram, d. 17 Feb 1842
Clara Martin, d. 13 Aug 1864

Jarret Thomas Magness, d. 16 Jan 1849, age 3 years, 9 months and 7 days

MARTIN-SLEE BIBLE

No publication information available. A transcript from photocopies of the bible pages were placed in Filing Case A at the Library of the Maryland Historical Society in Baltimore by Jon Harlan Livezey in 1974.

Marriages:
Henry Martin and Susannah Hollis m. 12 Feb 1839 by Rev. Dulany
Henry Martin and Jane L. Smith m. 7 Oct 1847 by Rev. Hildt
Cicero C. Slee and Annie L. Martin m. 3 Apr 1873 by Rev. J. C. Sedwick

Births:
Sons of William and Mary Slee:
1. Cicero Columbus Slee, b. 21 Sep 1846
2. Coleman Slee, b. 18 Nov (1847) *[sic]*

Children of Cicero C. and Annie L. Slee:
1. Annie Mary Slee, b. 11 Jan 1874
2. John Bay Slee, b. 16 Jun 1875
3. Susie Frost Slee, b. 21 May 1877[?]
4. Harold Martin Slee, b. 23 Nov 1879
5. George Henry Slee, b. 3 May 1881
6. ---- Slee (daughter), b. 20 Jul 1884
7. Letitia Slee, b. 20 Jul 1884 *[sic]*
8. Warren Hudson Slee, b. 2 Apr 1886

Children of Henry and Susannah Martin:
1. Mary Martha Martin, b. 29 Nov 1839
2. Susannah E. J. Martin, b. 9 Jan 1842
3. Anna Latty Martin, b. 26 Jul 1848

Deaths:
Susannah Martin, wife of Henry Martin, d. 22 Feb 1842 in her 24th year
Henry Martin, husband of the lare Susannah Martin and of Jane L. Martin, d. 21 May 1855 in his 47th year
Eliza Jane Martin, d. 4 Jun 1915 in her 75th year

Isabella Wellener, wife of Thomas Wellener, d. 28 Aug 1868 in her 75th year
Elizabeth Wellener, wife of Basil S. Wellener, d. 30 Aug 1869 (1868?) in her 42nd year

Ann Smith, wife of Basil L. Smith, d. 23 May 1854 in her 83rd year
Jane L. Sank, wife of James H. Sank, d. 30 Apr 1869 in her 55th year
Coleman Slee, d. 9 Aug 1892 in his 44th year

McCOMAS-GILBERT BIBLE

No publication information available. Family data gleaned from a typescript of the bible at the Maryland Historical Society. The McComas and Gilbert families lived in Harford County.

Marriages:
W. Gilbert and Mary Ann Michael m. 29 Jan 1837 [*Ed. Note:* Harford County marriage records indicate William H. Gilbert and Mary Ann Michael obtained a license on 29 Jan 1839].

"Three lines written in pencil - illegible" *[sic]*

George ---- and Ellen ---- m. 17 Oct 1839(?) [*Ed. Note:* Harford County marriage records indicate George Gilbert and Ellen McComas obtained a license on 16 Oct 1839].

Amos ---- and Mary Carsins m. 16 Jan 1--5(?) [*Ed. Note:* Harford County marriage records indicate Amos Gilbert and Mary Carsins obtained a license on 16 Jan 1845].

Bennett and Martha S. Gilbert m. 3 Jan 1834 [*Ed. Note:* Harford County marriage records indicate Bennett Gilbert and Martha S. McComas obtained a license on 3 Jun 1834].

Births (On Paper Inserted in Bible):
Preston McComas, b. 1787
Hannah E.(?) McComas, b. 1790
Ellen B. McComas, b. 21 May 1816
Harry G. McComas, b. 29 Aug 1818
---- [name illegible], b. 3 -(?)- 1841
Alexander McComas, b. 27 Feb 1821
Daniel Preston McComas, b. 3 Jun 182-(?)
Nicholas A. McComas, b. 4 Mar 1827
James P. L. McComas, b. 8 May(?) 1830
Bennett Gilbert, b. 28 Feb 1806
Martha Susan Gilbert, b. 16 Nov 1813
Harry D. Gough, b. 9 Aug 1792

Deaths (On Paper inserted in Bible):
Preston McComas, d. 24 Aug 1837
Dan Preston McComas, d. 10 Jun 1842
James P. L. McComas, d. 15 Aug 1853
Hannah G.(?) McComas, d. 11 Jul 183-(?)
Harry D. Gough, d. 2 Dec 1867

etsy Mitchell, d. 21 Feb 1809

Ellen Gilbert, wife of George Gilbert, d. 11 Jul 1869, age 53 years, 4 months and 22 days (written on inside back cover of bible)

EDWARD DAWES McCONKY BIBLE

Bible printed at the University Press, Oxford, 1860. Sold by E. Gardner and Son, Oxford Bible Warehouse, Paternoster Row, London. "Family Register of Edward D. & Annie S. McConky." Family data gleaned from a photocopy of the bible records in Filing Case A at the Maryland Historical Society.

Marriage:
Edward D. McConky and Annie S. Cockey m. 16 Oct 1866 at Arlington in Baltimore County, MD

Births:
Edward Dawes McConky, b. 4 Jan 1843, Baltimore City

Annie Stansbury Cockey, b. 16 Apr 1843 at Arlington in Baltimore County

Mary Grafton McConky, their first child, b. 16 Aug 1867 at Arlington in Baltimore County

Edward Dawes McConky, Jr., their second child, b. Fri., 11 May 1877 at 4 p.m. at their residence in Baltimore City, No. 28 Madison Avenue; bapt. Sun., 1 Jun 1879 at 6 p.m. at Memorial P. E. Church by Rev. W. M. Dame, Rector.

SARAH ANN McMULLEN BIBLE

Bible published in 1839 by Robinson & Franklin, New York. "Sarah Ann McMullen" is stamped on the cover. Family data gleaned from a typescript at the Maryland Historical Society in 1973, noting that "the entries are in many hands, the original in quite ornate printing." It also indicated that another McMullen Bible, presumably of an earlier generation, was destroyed by fire.

Marriages:
Joseph McMullen, Jr. and Sarah Ann Owens m. 2 Jul 1839
Clarence S. McMullin and Tressa May Wilgus m. 4 Oct 1908

Births:
Joseph McMullin, Sr., b. 10 Jan 1783
[Children of Joseph and Sarah Ann McMullin]:
1. Haslet O. McMullin, b. 17 Apr 1840
2. Amelia A. McMullin, b. 25 Nov 1841
3. William Andrew McMullin, b. 1 Oct (1843)
4. Joseph Francis McMullin, b. 20 Jul 1845
5. Mary E. McMullin, b. 31 [sic] Apr 1837
6. Sarah Agness McMullin, b. 20 Oct 1849
7. Lewis James McMullin, b. 8 Jan 1851
8. Philip Raftringe(?) McMullin, b. 8 May 1853

Clarance S. McMullin, b. 25 Feb 1880
Oscar M. McMullin, b. 3 Oct 1882
Ivan M. McMullin, b. 28 May 1906
Oscar M. McMullin, Jr., b. 13 Jun 1907

[Children of Clarence and Tressa McMullin]:
1. Clarence S. McMullin, Jr., b. 11 Apr 1910
2. Curtis E. McMullin, b. 11 Nov 1913

Tressa May [Wilgus] McMullen, b. 6 Jun 1887

Deaths:
William Barrett, d. 8 Jan 1823 in his 64th year

Joseph McMullin, Sr., d. Sat., 5 Oct 1844
Mary McMullin, d. 1 Oct 1845
Elizabeth McMullen, d. 8 Feb 1899 at 7:50 p.m.
Lewis James McMullen, d. 19 Jun 1908 at 7:10 a.m.
Oscar M. McMullin, Jr., d. 15 Oct 1907, age 4 months and 2 days
James McMullin, d. Good Friday morning, 3 Apr ---- in his 58th year [*Ed. Note:* This information was gleaned from an undated and unnamed newspaper clipping].
Sarah A. McMullin, d. 1859
Joseph McMullin, d. 1859
Sarah A. McMullin, d. 9 Mar 1850
Sarah Agness McMullen, Sr., d. 20 Oct 1848(?)
Andrew McMullin, Sr., d. 20 Apr 1863
James McMullen, d. 3 Apr 1874 in his 58th year

melia A. McMullin, d. 3 Mar 1878 in her 36th year

HENRY C. MICHAEL BIBLE

Bible published by John E. Potter & Co., 614 & 617 Sansom Street, Philadelphia, PA (no date given). Family data gleaned from a typescript at the Maryland Historical Society.

Marriages:
Cyrus Courtney and Avarilla Bailey m. 22 Dec 1812
Henry C. Michael and Cornelia F. Courtney m. 18 Jan 1853
Frank M. Irwin and Ava E. Michael m. 31 Oct 1878
John Lee Irwin and Mayfield Wright m. 12 Jun 1914

Orion Clay Michael and Martha Sophia Richardson m. 24 Oct 1894 by Rev. W. A. McDonald at M. E. Church South in Aberdeen, MD

Harry Adolphus Gilbert and Kate Estelle Wright m. 10 Apr 1895 by Rev. W. A. McDonald at M. E. Church South in Aberdeen, MD

Harry Adolphus Gilbert and Edith Chester Irwin, both of Aberdeen, m. 22 Nov 1922

Elizabeth Lee Irwin and Cornelius Farnham Cronin m. 28 Dec ---- [date not given]

Charles Wright Irwin and Jacquelin Kelly m. 6 Aug 1950

Births:
Avarilla Effie Michael, b. 8 Nov 1855
Kate Estelle Michael, b. 28 May 1859
Orion Clay Michael, b. 10 Apr 1861

Edith Chester Irwin, b. 3 Apr 1881
John Lee Irwin, b. 28 Aug 1882
Oliver Perry Irwin, b. 5 Nov 1883

Marjorie Estelle Gilbert, b. 12 Apr 1902
Roger Michael Gilbert, b. 19 Apr 1905
Henry Clay Michael, b. 23 Jun 1828

Adaline Courtney, b. 2 Nov 1813

Ruthen Courtney, b. 2 Nov 1815
Emily Courtney, b. 7 Oct 1816
Sarah Elizabeth Courtney, b. 11 Apr 1820
Mary Courtney, b. 14 Jun 1822
John Franklin Courtney, b. 3 Jun 1824
Avarilla Ann Courtney, b. 26 Nov 1826
Frances Cornelia Courtney, b. 2 Mar 1829
Cyrus Henry Courtney, b. 30 Dec 1831

Estelle Michael Gilbert, b. 28 May 1859

Mayfield Leslie Cronin, b. 20 Mar 1943
Cornelius Charles Cronin, b. 21 Jul 1945
Wendell Lee Cronin, b. 31 Dec 1948
Elizabeth Lyle Cronin, b. 7 Aug 1952
Meredith Cronin, b. 5 Jun 1959

Becky Ava Irwin, b. 13 Sep 1951
Kelly Charles Irwin, b. 4 Apr 1953
Keven Lee Irwin, b. 21 Jul 1959

Deaths:
Ruthen Courtney, d. 11 Nov 1815
Cyrus Courtney, d. 29 Nov 1859, age 70
John Franklin Courtney, d. 12 Jul 1850, age 26

Oliver Perry Irwin, d. 20 Aug 1890, age 6 years and 10 months
Ava E. Irwin, d. 17 Feb 1927, age 72

Orion Clay Michael, d. 23 Feb 1944
Henry Clay Michael, d. 29 Dec 1907, age 79
Frances Cornelia Michael, d. 10 Jun 1916, age 88

Estelle Michael Gilbert, d. 18 May 1920

Cornelius Charles Cronin, d. 5 Oct 1951

Family Records:
Written on a card in Bible: Ava E. Irwin, b. 8 Nov 1855, d. 17 Feb 1827, bur. 20 Feb 1927 at Northwood Cemetery in Downingtown, PA.

Photograph of tombstone pasted in Bible: Sacred to the Memory of Baltsher Michael, a native of Germany, d. 11 Feb 1795; his wife Ann (neé Osborn) d. 10 Aug 1831 [*Ed. Note:* Information transcribed in error: He actually died 14 Feb 1795 and she died 30 Aug 1834].

Marriage certificate: Mr. Henry C. Michael and Miss Cornelia F. Courtney were solemnly united by me on the 18th day of January at her father's residence in the year of our Lord, 1853, conformably to the Ordinance of God and the Laws of Maryland, in presence of their friends and relatives. Signed: Rev. C. C. Cronin.

JACOB MICHAEL BIBLE

Bible published in 1811 by Mathew Carey, No. 122 Market Street, Philadelphia, PA. Family data gleaned from a typescript at the Maryland Historical Society.

Marriages:
Jacob Michael and Mary Everist m. 12 Nov 1795
Jacob Michael and Susanna Crane m. 29 Dec 1808

Births:
Children of Jacob and Mary Michael:
1. ---- Michael (son), b. 12 Oct 1796, d. 12 days old
2. Henry Everist Michael, b. 9 Feb 1798
3. Ethan Michael, b. 20 Oct 1799
4. Anne Mariah Michael, b. 25 Dec 1801

Children of Jacob and Susanna Michael:
1. Semeliann Michael, b. 12 Oct 1809
2. John Osborn Michael, b. 18 May 1811
3. William Harrison Michael, b. 5 May 1813
4. Jacob Jackson Michael, b. 18 May 1816

Deaths:
Mary Michael, d. 29 Mar 1803 in her 31st year
Ann Mariah Michael, d. 10 Sep 1804 in her 3rd year
Susanna Michael, wife of Jacob Michael, d. 26 Sep 1826 in her 51st year
Ann Michael, widow of Balsher Michael, d. 30 Aug 1834 in her 88th year
Jacob Michael, d. 21 Jan 1853 in his 83rd year
Henry E. Michael, d. 3 Jan 1865 in his 65th year

Ethan Michael, d. 10 Sep 1868 in his 69th year
William H. Michael, d. 22 Mar 1878 in his 65th year
John O. Michael, d. 12 Oct 1880 in his 70th year
Jacob Jackson Michael, d. 25 Mar 1892 in his 76th year
Susan Michael, widow of Jacob Jackson Michael, d. 17 Apr 1895 in her 85th year

Semelia Osborn, d. 7 Dec 1810 in her 55th year
John Hanson Osborn, d. 13 Feb 1811 in his 16th year

Semeliann Murphy, d. 1 Nov 1847 in her 38th year

JOHN M. MICHAEL BIBLE

New Testament Bible published by The American Tract Society, 150 Nassau Street, New York (date not given). Inscribed: "John M. Michael Book." Family data gleaned from a typescript of the bible records in the Library of the Maryland Historical Society in 1985. The Michael family resided in Harford County, MD.

Marriage:
John Calvin Michael and Ann Martha Mitchell m. 15 Apr 1856 "at her parents home Mount Felix by the Rev. William Finny who was Pastor at Churchville for 40 years, he married the parents of Mr. & Mrs. Michael."

Births:
John Calvin Michael, b. 10 Sep 1825
Ann Martha Michael [neé Mitchell], b. 6 Nov 1832

[Children of Calvin and Ann Michael]:
1. John M. Michael, b. 16 Feb 1857
2. William Otho Michael, b. 8 Jan 1860
3. Eliza Neoma Michael, b. 24 May 1863
4. Mary Oleita Girtrude Michael, b. 1868

"Brothers of Ann M. Mitchell, now her name is Michael, wife of Calvin Michael":
1. Otho Mitchell, b. 14 Nov 1838
2. William Gashern Mitchell, b. 24 Oct 1841

Deaths:
John Calvin Michael, d. 25 Mar 1895

Otho Mitchell, d. 31 Oct 1842
William Gashern Mitchell, d. 7 Oct 1843

Family Records (Clippings in Bible):
1. In loving memory of my beloved husband, J. Calvin Michael, who died one year ago today, March 25, 1895. Gone but not forgotten. By his wife.

2. In loving memory of our darling, Etta Virginia Kirwan, dau. of Charles R. and Lida Michael Kirwan, who died one year ago today, December 25, 1894.

EDMUND MITCHELL BIBLE

Bible published in 1875 by William W. Harding, Philadelphia, PA. Family data gleaned from a typescript at the Maryland Historical Society.

Marriages:
Edmund Mitchell and Martha Jane Streett m. ---- [*Ed. Note:* Date of marriage was not entered in the bible, but Harford County marriage records indicate "Edward" Mitchell and Martha Jane Streett obtained a license on 4 Dec 1844].

John Paca Mitchell and Matilda Reybold Clark m. 22 Dec 1870
Jacob Edwin Michael and Susan Rebecca Mitchell m. 23 Dec 1875
William D. Osborne and Virginia Sophia Mitchell m. 3 Feb 1880
James Streett Mitchell and Mary Elizabeth Bonn m. 16 Feb 1887
La Mar Mitchell and Victor Baldwin Cain m. 8 Jun 1918
Ruth La Mar Cain and Lee Wilton Anderson m. 27 Nov 1947

Births:
Edmund Mitchell, son of Richard and Priscilla Mitchell, b. 2 Sep 1817
Martha Jane Streett, dau. of James and Margaret Streett, b. 31 Mar 1824

Children of Edmund and Martha J. Mitchell:
1. John Paca Mitchell, b. 24 Oct 1845
2. Margaret Priscilla Mitchell, b. 8 Mar 1850
3. Virginia Sophia Mitchell, b. 15 Apr 1852
4. Susan Rebecca Mitchell, b. 28 Aug 1853
5. James Streett Mitchell, b. 30 Jun 1862

La Mar Mitchell, dau. of James Street Mitchell and Mary Elizabeth Bonn, b. 21 Jul 1889

Victor Baldwin Cain, son of James Henry Cain and Charlotte Baldwin, b. 8 Feb 1890

Ruth La Mar Cain, son of Victor Baldwin Cain and La Mar Mitchell, b. 23 Apr 1923

Matilda Reybold Clark, dau. of Thomas and Ann Clark, b. 11 Jun 1850

Jacob Edwin Michael, son of Jacob and Susan Michael, b. 13 May 1848

Deaths:
Margaret Priscilla Mitchell, d. 23 Jun 1851
Priscilla Mitchell, d. 18 Mar 1856, age 80 years, 10 months and 19 days
Richard Mitchell, d. 7 Oct 1856, age 84 years, 18(?) months, and 28 days

EDWARD T. MONKS BIBLE

Bible published in 1867 by The American Bible Society in New York. Family data gleaned from a typescript at the Maryland Historical Society.

Marriages:
Edward T. Monks and Ellen C. Tredway m. 18 Aug 1866
Harry E. Harkins and Sallie A. Monks m. 8 Oct 1890
William D. Jones and Amy D. Monks m. 28 Apr 1897
Lester Winfield Tucker and Beatrice Harkins m. 2 Nov 1912
Lester Winfield Tucker, Jr. and Nancy Louise Wagner m. 24 Aug 1940
Beatrice Louise Tucker and Don A. Brennan m. 8 May 1942

Births:
Ellen A. Tredway, b. 8 Feb 1830

Edward T. Monks, b. 16 Jun 1831
Amy Drusilla Monks, b. 3 Sep 1868
Sallie Ann Monks, b. 29 Sep 1871

Harry E. Harkins, b. 12 Oct 1866

Beatrice Harkins, b. 1 Sep 1891
Marguerite Elleine Harkins, b. 14 Nov 1895

Lester Winfield Tucker, Jr., b. 3 Mar 1915
Beatrice Louise Tucker, b. 8 Mar 1918

Deaths:
Ellen C. Monks, d. 21 Aug 1879 at quarter past 6(?) o'clock
Edward Treadway Monks, d. -- Sep 1924

Amy Drucilla M. Jones, d. 28 Oct 1898 at quarter of 11 o'clock

Marguerite E. Harkins, d. 31 Mar 1919
Harry E. Harkins, d. 24 May 1929
Sallie M. Harkins, d. 2 Jan 1942

Family Records (Clippings in Bible):

1. Mrs. Sarah J. Grier, widow of Glascow J. Grier of Bel Air, and mother of Fred N., George E., William C., Herbert S. and the late Harry M. Grier, d. in Los Angeles, CA on 19 Dec 1903 in her 62nd year.

2. Mrs. Ellen C. Monks, wife of E. T. Monks, Esq., d. 21 Aug 1879 after a long illness; she was bur. 23 Aug at Mt. Tabor Cemetery in Hickory, MD.

3. James P. Monks, of Abingdon, MD, d. 25 Jan ----, age 78; he m. Mary Treadway of Hickory, MD and raised a large family.

4. Mrs. Amy D. Monks Jones, d. 28 Oct 1898 in her 31st year, a dau. of Edward T. Monks and a granddau. of Rev. Thomas Tredway, late of Harford County; she m. 28 Apr 1897 to William D. Jones; bur. in Rock Spring; article written by S. B. Tredway, Pastor of Bel Air M. P. Church.

5. Mr. J. Benjamin Harkins, of Forest Hill, MD, d. Sun. night ----, age 42; he leaves a widow and six small children; funeral held from his late home and was in charge of Mount Ararat Lodge No. 44; Revs. B. F. Devries and J. L. Sothoron conducted the service and the pallbearers were John G. Rouse, John Harkins, Horace Twining, Samuel Nagle, George L. VanBibber, and J. Wann.

6. Marguerite E. Harkins, dau. of Mr. & Mrs. Harry E. Harkins, of Kalmia, MD, and granddau. of Edward Monks, and a sister of Mrs. Lester Tucker, of Delta, PA;

services were conducted by Revs. Sites and Tucker; she was bur. in Deer Creek Cemetery at Chestnut Hill; pallbearers were Frank Lochary, Allen Hopkins, D. Paul McNabb, Herbert McComas, Benton Gross, and Samuel Galbreath.

7. Edward T. Monks, age 93, d. at the home of his son-in-law Harry E. Harkins at Kalmia, MD; b. 16 Jun 1831 and survived by his dau. Mrs. Harkins, one granddau. Mrs. Lester W. Tucker of Abingdon, MD, and two grandchildren; bur. in Mt. Tabor Cemetery; pallbearers were Howard Russell, Stanley Grier, James Harward, Noble L. Mitchell, John A. Robinson, and James Forwood.

8. Harry E. Harkins, of Kalmia, MD, d. 24 May 1929, a son of the late Capt. Joseph Harkins; survived by his widow, formerly Miss Sallie A. Monks, one dau. Mrs. Lester W. Tucker of Abingdon, MD, four bros. Maurice, Thomas, Wilson and Joseph R. Harkins, and one sister Mrs. James Snodgrass of Bel Air; bur. 27 May at Deer Creek Church with Rev. E. C. Gisriel of Bel Air in charge; pallbearers were Preston M. Barrow, Charles Michael Jr., Samuel W. Galbreath, Malcolm Snodgrass, Calvin Harkins, and Aubrey Harkins; Charles H. McComas sang at the funeral.

9. In memory of Alice E. Johnson who d. 5 Dec 1868, age 19 years, 7 months and 25 days (a poem).

10. Edith C. Michael, youngest dau. of Owen and Mary Michael, d. 17 Feb 1866 of scarlet fever terminating in chronic croup, age 4 years, 9 months and 23 days.

JAMES P. MONKS BIBLE

Bible published by James P. Smith & Company, 27 South Seventh Street, Philadelphia, PA in 1884. Family data gleaned from a typescript at the Maryland Historical Society.

Marriages:
James P. Monks and Mary Amealia Tredway m. 12 Feb 1828
John C. Monks and ---- [blank]. [*Ed. Note:* John C. Monks and Talitha E. Whitaker were married 5 Mar 1857 and the notice appeared in the *Baltimore Sun* on 7 Mar 1857].

Births:
James P. Monks, b. 13 Oct 1800

Mary Amealia Tredway, b. 26 Apr 1811
John C. Monks, b. 23 Feb 1829
Edward T. Monks, b. 16 Jun 1831
Ann Eliza Monks, b. 23 Sep 1833
James H. Monks, b. 78 Mar 1836
William T. Monks, b. 26 Aug 1837
Thomas A. Monks, b. 19 Jul 1839
Lewis W. Monks, b. 7 Apr 1841
Mary E. Monks, b. 20 May 1842
Catherine J. Monks, b. 13 Jul 1843
Sarah M. Monks, b. 22 Sep 1844
Coleman Y. Monks, b. 16 Aug 1845
Olevia C. Monks, b. 22 Jan 1847
A. Coleman Monks, b. 7 Nov 1849
Robert A. Monks, b. 5 Oct 1851
Mary Addie Monks, b. 16 Sep 1854
Sarah Lavinia Monks, b. 1 May 1856

Deaths:
Mary E. Monks, d. 19 Jul 1842
Catherine J. Monks, d. 14 Aug 1843
Sarah M. Monks, d. 22 Jun 1846
Coleman Y. Monks, d. 13 Apr 1848
A. Coleman Monks, d. 27 Aug 1850
Thomas A. Monks, d. 23 Feb 1860
James P. Monks, d. 25 Jan 1878, age 77 years, 3 months, 12 days
Mary A. Monks, d. 17 Feb 1879
Robert A. Monks, d. 4 Oct 1883
Sallie L. Monks, d. 25 Jul 1887 at 2:36 p.m.
Mary Addie Smith, d. 15 Apr 1906 at 12:10 o'clock
Edward Treadway Monks, d. -- Sep 1924

HERRMANN MOOG BIBLE

Bible published in 1873 in New York and dated 1875 in Chicago. This transcript was published in the *Maryland Genealogical Society Bulletin* (Vol. 28, No. 2) in Spring, 1987, noting the bible was in German script and was translated by Mrs. Frederick Gutekunst.

Marriage:
Herrmann Moog and Wilhelmina Emma Zimmerman m. 10 May 1845 in Hymens Fesseln by Pastor Sheib in Baltimore

Births:
Herrmann Moog, son of Johannes Moog, b. 18 Mar 1834 in Warzenbach amt Wetter, Kreis Marburg, Hessen-Cassel

Wilhelmina Emma Zimmerman, b. 19 Apr 1839, 9 o'clock p.m. auf den Fels, near Darmstatd. Father is Christian Zimmerman, forester of Felsberg, son of Postmaster Zimmermann of Bickenbach.

My mother, Mrs. Charlotte, neé Neuffer, born in Wumpfen am Berge

Children of Herrmann and Wilhelmina Moog:
1. Emma Moog, b. Sun., 28 Sep 1857 in Baltimore at 2:45 o'clock in the morning
2. Johan Friedrich Moog, b. Tues., 14 Sep 1858 in Baltimore at 24 minutes past 9 o'clock
3. August Moog, b. 29 Feb 1860 in Baltimore at 5 minutes to 6 o'clock in the morning
4. Emilia Moog, b. 22 May 1865 in Baltimore at 10 minutes before 8 o'clock in the evening
5. Heinrich Robert Alexander Moog, b. Good Friday, 10 Apr 1868 in Baltimore at 10:30 in the evening
6. Christina Augusta Moog, b. Fri., 3 Sep 1869 in Baltimore at 10:30 in the evening
7. Herrmann Moog, b. 14 Aug 1871 in Baltimore at 10:45 p.m.
8. Emil Romeo Wilhelm Heinrich Moog, b. Thurs., 28 Jan 1875 in Chicago at 8:30 in the evening
9. Charlotte Wilhelmina Moog, b. Tues., 1 Apr 1880 in Baltimore at 2:30 in the morning
10. Robert Moog, b. Wed., 20 Apr 1881 in Baltimore at 7:45 o'clock

Death:
Heinrich Robert Alexander Moog, d. Thurs., 28 Oct ---- [blank] in Baltimore at 4:50 p.m., age 1 year, 6 months and 18 days. Recorded by H. Moog, Sr., on Fri., 29 Jan 1875 in Chicago.

THOMAS E. MORGAN BIBLE

Bible published by John Fry and Company, 27 Beekman Street, New York, NY (no date given). Family data gleaned from a typescript at the Maryland Historical Society.

Marriage:
Thomas Elliott Morgan and Laura Jennie Osborn m. 17 Feb 1870

Births:
Thomas Elliott Morgan, b. 30 Jun 1843
Laura Jennie Osborn, b. 6 Jan 1844

Children of Thomas E. and Laura J. Morgan:
1. Elizabeth Elliott Morgan, b. 10 Jan 1871
2. Florence Virginia Morgan, b. 9 Jan 1872
3. Theodora Morgan, b. 18 Mar 1873

Deaths:
Laura Jennie (Osborn) Morgan, d. 8 Dec 1877
Elizabeth A. Morgan, wife of Robert L. Morgan and mother of Thomas Morgan, d. Tues., 1 Nov 1870 in her 52nd year. She was an original member of Grove Presbyterian Church in Aberdeen, MD.

WILLIAM MORRIS BIBLE

Bible published in 1850 in Philadelphia, PA, by John B. Perry for Howard M. Gilbert. Family data gleaned from a typescript at the Maryland Historical Society. "Wm. Morris" was stamped on the front cover of the bible which also contained a page taken from another unidentified Morris Bible.

Births:
Sarah Rebecca Morris, b. 22 Oct 1836
Margaret Ann Morris, b. 25 Jan 1838

Susan Maria Morris, b. 15 Oct 1840 [*Ed. Note:* 1840 was crossed out and 1839 was written in pencil on one page, and another page in the bible indicated 1840 and spelled her name "Sousin"]
John Lloyd Morris, b. 7 Sep 1841
Elizabeth E. Morris, b. 7 Nov 1843
Rebecca Morris, b. 20 Nov 1845

Sarah J. Morris, b. 16 Dec 1847

Deaths:
Sarah R. Morris, d. 20 Nov 1836
Elizabeth E. Morris, d. 22 May 1862
John L. Morris, d. 22 Nov 1862
Rebecca Morris, d. 30 Oct 1865
Sarah J. Morris, d. -- Mar 1866

HAMILTON MORRISON BIBLE

Harding Bible printed in Philadelphia in 1860. Family data gleaned from a typescript of records copied by Jon Harlan Livezey in 1975.

Marriages:
Hamilton Morrison and Elizabeth Ulrich m. 16 Jan 1840 by Rev. Sorien
Philip Strout and Kate Morrison m. 9 Jan 1884 by Rev. Conway

Births:
Children of Hamilton and Elizabeth Morrison:
1. Ellinor Morrison, b. 25 Nov 1840
2. William Thomas Morrison, b. 22 Jul 1843
3. Daniel Edmund Morrison, b. 30 Oct 1845
4. Madora Jane Morrison, b. 12 Sep 1848
5. Osco Bates Morrison, b. 9 Dec 1851
6. James Samuel Morrison, b. 12 Sep 1853
7. Kate M. Morrison, b. 28 Mar 1856
8. George W. Morrison, b. 28 Mar 1856
9. George E. Morrison, b. 1 Jan 1859

Children of Theodore and Kate Strout:
1. Howard M. Strout, b. 7 Oct 1884
2. Lucy Fay Strout, b. 3 Feb 1894

Deaths:
Elizabeth Morrison, d. 20 Jun 1869, age 45
Hamilton Morrison, d. 15 Feb 1881, age 67

Mary Elizabeth Strout, dau. of Theodore and Kate Strout, d. 23 Mar 1902, age 5 years and 2 months

Children of Hamilton and Elizabeth Morrison:
1. Ellinor Jane Morrison, d. 21 Sep 1847, age 6 years, 9 months and 21 days
2. Medora Jane Morrison, d. 26 Aug 1854, age 5 years, 11 months and 13 days
3. Daniel E. Morrison, d. 29 Aug 1854, age 8 years, 9 months and 29 days
4. James S. Morrison, d. 4 Oct 1855, age 2 years and 20 days
5. George W. Morrison, d. 21 Sep 1856, age 6 months and 12 days

Family Records (On Paper Inserted in Bible):
Children of Theodore and Kate Strout:
1. Walter Leon Strout, b. 1 Jun 1891
2. Lucy Fay Strout, b. 3 Feb 1894
3. Mary Elizabeth Strout, b. 14 Jan 1897

"Little Mary Strout died very suddenly of diptheria on the 23d of March, member of Institute Kindergarten and attended school a few days before her death. A similar clipping states Mary was buried at Hopewell Cemetery (error)." [*Note:* 1902 newspaper clippings].

DAVID M. MURRAY BIBLE

Bible published in 1858 (printer and location not indicated). Family data gleaned from a typescript at the Maryland Historical Society.

Marriages:
David M. Murray and Emily L. Harp m. 8 Dec 1859
Charles W. Reid and D. Marion Murray m. 15 Oct 1889
John Monaghan and Ruth Reid m. 11 Oct 1907
Armorel Murray and James M. Morse m. 26 Dec 1911
Charlie Reid and Emmett McClung m. 4 May 1917
James Murray Morse and Velva Taylor m. 27 Oct 1945

Births:
David M. Murray, b. 10 Oct 1835
Emily L. (Harp) Murray, wife of D. M. Murray, b. 1 Mar 1838
Armorel Murray, b. 25 Jan 1891

Children of David and Emily Murray:
1. Green Harp Murray, b. 10 Oct 1860

2. David Marion Murray, b. 17 Jun 1862

Lulu Ruth Reid, b. 14 Jul 1885
Charlie Murray Reid, b. 19 Dec 1893

James Murray Morse, b. 8 Mar 1913
Armorel Morse, b. 5 Jun 1917

Deaths:
David M. Murray, d. 22 Oct 1862
Green Harp Murray, d. 27 Jun 1893
Emily Laura Murray, d. 7 Sep 1914

David Marion Reid, d. 8 Mar 1916
Charles W. Reid, M.D., d. 1 Jan 1946
Mittie Pamelia Harp, d. 9 Jun 1911
Charlie Reid McClung, d. 22 Dec 1917
James M. Morse, d. 15 Nov 1942
Blanche Holmes (Murray) Ford, d. 26 Jul 1945
John Monaghan, d. 17 Apr 1956

MARTIN MYERS FAMILY BOOK

Family records written in a book titled *The Catholic Church Alone* which was published in 1902. A transcript was published in the *Maryland Genealogical Society Bulletin* (Vol. 32, No. 2) in Spring, 1991. Information submitted by Dr. Howard G. Lanham who noted that the Myers family lived in Chase, Baltimore County, MD. The book was owned by Timothy Smith of Westminster, MD in 1991.

Births:
Martin Myers, b. 14 Nov 1849
Rusaltha Ann Myers, b. 6(?) Jun 1857

[Children of Martin and Rusaltha Myers]:
1. Franklin Frederick Joseph Myers, b. 10 Jul 1877
2. Mary Lizer Myers, b. 15 Nov 1880
3. Martin Daniel Myers, b. 17 Jun 1883
4. William Hubanrd *[sic]* Myers, b. 20 Jan 1885
5. James Patrick Myers, b. 27 Jul 1887

6. Augustus Evan Myers, b. 13 Feb 1889
7. John Joseph Elsworth Myers, b. 10 Feb 1892
8. ---- Myers (twins), b. 17 Sep 1894 [no names given]
9. George Anton Myers, b. 27 Feb 1896
10. Stellie Dewer Myers, b. 30 Mar 1899

Annie Francis Myer *[sic]*, b. 26 Jul 1882
Richard Charles Myers, b. 30 May 1915
Martin James Myers, b. 1 Apr 1918
Grome Alexander Myer *[sic]*, b. 10 Sep 1919

Anthony Michel Herfel, b. 20 May 1883
Henry Adam Herfel, b. 23 Jan 1903
George Daniel Herfel, b. 28 Jul 1904
Rusaltha Anna Herfel, b. 11 Mar 1912

Deaths:
Martha M. Myers, d. 28 Sep 1894
Martin Daniel Myers, d. 23 Apr 1903
James Patrick Myers, Jr., d. 5 Jan 1914
Rusaltha Anna Myers, d. 10 Feb 1924
Martin Myers, d. 7 Jul 1924
Carline Myers, d. 7 Jan 1935
Margaret Myers, d. 27 Dec 1936
Augustus Evan Myers, d. 26 Jun 1940
Mrs. Anna Francis Myers, d. 1 Oct 1918 or 7 Oct 191-(?) [page damaged and date was illegibly rewritten]

Harry Leroy Ross, d. 3 Dec 1953
Anthony Michel Herfel, d. 10 Dec 1933

ELIZABETH H. NAGLE BIBLE

Bible printed in 1869 and presented to "Elizabeth R. Hutcheson with the love of her pastor, Julian E. Ingle, St. Paul's, Baltimore, January 26, 1871." Family data gleaned from a typescript at the Maryland Historical Society which noted that Elizabeth Hutcheson's daughter Mary H. Nagle married E. Hall Calder and began the entries in the bible.

Marriage:
Miss Lizzie R. Hutcheson and Thomas F. Nagle m. 26 Jan 1871 by Rev. Julian Ingle

Births:
John Brown Peery, son of John Green Peery and Mary Nagle Calder, b. 4 Apr 1948 at 5:18 a.m. at West Baltimore General Hospital in Baltimore City

Children of E. Hall and Mary H. (Nagle) Calder:
1. Elizabeth Hutcheson Calder, b. 8 Jun 1908 on Thomas Run at Grandfather Nagle's house and bapt. by Rev. S. C. Wasson [date not given]
2. Anna Windom Calder, b. 3 Jan 1910 in Bel Air, bapt. by Rev. H. L. Schlinckle, d. 18 Feb 1910
3. Evelyn Nesbitt Calder, b. 17 Mar 1911 on Thomas Run at Grandfather Nagle's house and bapt. by Rev. H. L. Schlinckle
4. Gladys May Calder, b. 25 Oct 1912 in Churchville
5. Mary Madeline Calder, b. 10 May 1915 in Churchville
6. Thomas Hall Calder, b. 18 Oct 1916 in Churchville
7. Eleanor Harlan Calder, b. 19 Oct 1918 in Bel Air
8. Ruth MacLean Calder, b. 6 Aug 1920 in Bel Air

Children of Charles and Ruth MacLean (Calder) Hrubesh:
1. David Charles Hrubesh, b. 7 May 1942 at Bon Secours Hospital in Baltimore City and bapt. 7 Mar 1943 by Rev. Frank Novak
2. Thomas Franklin Hrubesh, b. 26 Apr 1944 at Bon Secours Hospital in Baltimore City
3. Richard Calder Hrubesh, b. 24 Oct 1945 at Fountain Green Hospital near Bel Air, MD
4. Daniel Allen Hrubesh, b. 9 Nov 1946 at Fountain Green Hospital near Bel Air, MD and d. 27 Aug 1948 [*Ed. Note:* Bible entry mistakenly stated 22 Aug 1938; see newspaper clipping below]
5. Sandra Lee Hrubesh, b. 22 Jul 1948 at Harford Memorial Hospital in Havre de Grace, MD

Children of Frank J. and Eleanor Harlan (Calder) Kilian:
1. Jane Harlan Kilian, b. 16 Jan 1943 at 2:40 p.m. at Union Memorial Hospital in Baltimore City and bapt. 7 Mar 1943 by Rev. Frank Novak
2. Frank John Kilian, b. 16 Jan 1948 at 9:15 p.m. at Union Memorial Hospital in Baltimore City and bapt. 11 Apr 1948 by Rev. E. L. Gettier, Jr. at St. John's P. E. Church.

Children of Robert and Gladyce May (Calder) Brady:
1. Patricia Hall Brady, b. 29 Oct 1940 at Allentown Hospital in Allentown, PA
2. Robert Wilson Brady, Jr., b. 20 Aug 1946 at Allentown Hospital in Allentown, PA

Deaths (Clippings in Bible):
1. Daniel Alan Hrubesh, son of Mr. & Mrs. Charles Hrubesh of Lunch's Corner [Harford County], d. 27 Aug ---- [*Ed. Note:* Year was not given, but it was 1948]; survived by 3 brothers [not named], an infant sister [not named], and grandparents Mr. & Mrs. Charles Hrubesh, Sr. of Lynch's Corner; interment at Mt. Zion; pallbearers were Robert Brady, John Reip, John Peery, and Frank Kilian.

2. John E. Calder, blacksmith, age 73, d. ---- [date not given] at the residence of his son John E. Calder, Jr. in Baltimore City; his wife [not named] d. 26 years ago; interment at Mt. Zion; survived by 5 sons, Charles Lee Calder, E. Hall Calder, John E. Calder, Othos S. Calder, and Archer E. Calder, and 2 daughters, Mrs. Clara McShane and Mrs. Alice Bernard; pallbearers were Charles Everett, William Everett, George C. Calder, and Morris Talbott.

3. Lynn K. Nagle, son of Thomas F. Nagle of Baltimore, formerly of Churchville [Harford County, MD], d. at home in Ripley, TN in Oct ---- [date not given] from 4 days illness of influenza and double pneumonia; he d. 3 weeks before his 3 year old daughter Martha Oleita Nagle; he was born and raised near Churchville, fought in the Spanish-American War, and conducted a successful restaurant and meat marketing business; survived by his widow [not named]; three sons, Thomas F. Nagle, Lynn K. Nagle, Jr., and George A. Nagle; four sisters, Mrs. George K. Livezey of Aberdeen, MD, Mrs. Samuel Gross of Forest Hill, MD, Mrs. Oleita Arthur of Waverly, MD, and Mrs. Hall Calder of Bel Air, MD; and, 3 brothers, Edward R. Nagle and Wallace C. Nagle, both of Churchville, and Stevenson W. Nagle of Thomas Run [Harford County, MD].

4. Annie W. Calder, six week old daughter of Mr. & Mrs. E. Hall Calder, d. at her parents' home on Gordon Street in Bel Air on Fri., ---- [date not given]; interment at Mt. Zion Cemetery, Rev. H. L. Schlincke officiating; pallbearers were masters Hall MacLean, Herbert Wilgis, Kessler Livezey, and Kenneth Livezey.

5. Walter C. Nagle, d. 3 Mar 1913, age 23; funeral from home at Forest Hill; interment in Centre Cemetery.

6. Dorothy E. Calder [misspelled "Caldel"], infant daughter of John E. and Clara O. Calder [misspelled "Caldel"], age 5 months, d. ---- [date not given]; funeral from parents' home at 2103 Smallwood Street.

7. Emmanuel Nagle, age 83, d. Sun., ---- at his home at Thomas Run; survived by widow [not named]; 3 daughters, Mrs. James Blaney, Mrs. Thomas Shannon, and Mrs. Laura E. Butler; 5 sons, Thomas F. Nagle, Samuel O. Nagle, George A. Nagle, John H. Nagle, and Charles C. Nagle; and, 37 grandchildren and 18 great-grandchildren; interment at Emory; pallbearers were 6 grandchildren, Culbert W. Nagle, Emmanuel Nagle, Stevenson A. Nagle, Spencer Nagle, William Blaney, and Clarence Blaney; Rev. S. C. Wasson officiating. [*Ed. Note:* Date of his death was not given, but a later entry stated "died Jan. 7, 1907, Grandmother died July 17, 1908"].

JOHN NAGLE BIBLE

No publication information available. Family data gleaned from a typescript at the Maryland Historical Society. This bible mentions the family history of John Nagle, a resident of Pennsylvania, who brought his large family to Harford County, MD in the late 1830s.

Marriages:
[*Ed. Note:* Some of the marriage entries in the bible only gave one of the names of the parties involved. Some of the other family records in the bible, however, did give both names. They have been gleaned and placed within the following list of marriages].

John Nagle and ---- m. 12 Apr 1835
Rebecke Nagle and ---- m. 30 Sep 1838
Daniel Nagle and ---- m. 28 Mar 1839 [*Ed. Note:* Harford County marriage license issued to Daniel Noggle and Rebecca Buxster on 24 Mar 1839].
Mickel Nagle and ---- m. 4 Mar 1841
Henry Nagle and ---- m. 5 Feb 1842
Leah Nagle and Edward McCue m. 20 Dec 1842
Elizabeth Nagle and ---- m. 19 Jan 1843
William Nagle and ---- m. 9 May 1844
Charlot Nagle and ---- m. 10 Sep 1844

Emanuel Nagle and Debra Shannon m. 15 Oct 1846 [*Ed. Note:* Harford County marriage license issued to Manuel Noggle and Deborough Shannon on 15 Oct 1846].

William Nagle and ---- m. 30 Dec 1849
Mary Ann Nagle and ---- m. 1 Jan 1850
Emanuel Nagle and Elizabeth Howe m. 4 Jul 1850
Miss Sarah Jane Nagle and ---- Billman m. 16 Oct 1859
Miss Ada L. R. Billman and ---- m. 27 Apr 1883
Miss Ella D. Z. Billman and ---- m. 10 May 1883

Births:
Children of John Nagle and Sarah Stumpf:
1. Margrat Nagle, b. 29 Oct 1809
2. John Nagle, b. 4 Aug 1811
3. Rabacka Nagle, b. 22 Dec 1812
4. Daniel Nagle, b. 1 Apr 1814
5. Mickel Nagle, b. 13 Aug 1815
6. Henry Nagle, b. 12 Apr 1817
7. William Nagle, b. 14 Aug 1819
8. Manuel or Emanuel Nagle, b. 14 Nov 1822
9. Eliza or Elizabeth Nagle, b. 12 Mar 1824
10. Lea Nagle, b. 23 Feb 1826
11. Charlot Nagle, b. 27 Apr 1828
12. Maryann Nagle, b. 14 May 1830
13. Sarah Jane Nagle, b. 8 Nov 1831 [*Ed. Note:* One entry spelled her name "Saragain"]
14. Isaac Nagle, b. 18 Jan 1833
15. James Nagle, b. 18 Jun 1835

Sarah Frances Nagle, b. 22 Sep 1847 [*Ed. Note:* One entry spelled her name "Sharah Franacis"]

Children of Emanuel Nagle and Elizabeth Howe:
1. Thomas Franklin Nagle, b. 4 Dec 1851
2. Susan Jane Nagle, b. 2 May 1853
3. Anna Mary Nagle, b. 16 Jun 1855
4. Samuel Owen Nagle, b. 8 Apr 1858
5. George Elexander Nagle, b. 9 Feb 1860
6. William Edman Nagle, b. 15 Mar 1862
7. John Henry Nagle, b. 23 Mar 1864
8. Laura Ellen Nagle, b. 7 Sep 1866
9. Charles Chapman Nagle, b. 27 Jul 1870

Ela. De. Zell. Billman, b. 14 Sep 1860
Ada Taroda Billman, b. 14 Oct 1863

Deaths:
Margaret Nagle, d. 27 Sep 1810
John Nagle, d. 3 Jan 1845
Debrough or Debra Nagle, d. 29 Jul 1849
Sarah Frances Nagle, d. 16 Aug 1849
William Nagle, d. 25 Nov 1866
Mary Ann Nagle, d. 3 Aug 1874
Daniel Nagle, d. 18 Mar 1894
Rebecca Nagle, d. -- Apr 1894
Henry Nagle, d. -- 1894
Emanuel Nagle, d. 7 Jan 1906, age 83
Mrs. Sarah Nagle, d. 8 Sep 1864 [*Ed. Note:* Sarah (Stumpf) Nagle was the widow of John Nagle]

Mrs. Ella D. Z. Voelkel, d. 8 Jan 1890

Family Records:
[*Ed. Note:* Many of the aforementioned entries were repeated on papers inserted in the bible and the following were added at a later time]:
1. Daniel S. Nagle, d. 16 Mar 1894
2. Michael Nagle, d. 1 Sep 1886
3. Charlotte Nagle, d. 1 Sep 1898
4. Eliza Nagle, d. 26 Apr 1899

Handwritten Wedding Invitation:
"Mr. & Mrs. Jacob H. Hess requests your presence at the marriage of their daughter Retta to Mr. Charles C. Nagle, Wed. evening, January 15, 1896 at 7 o'clock p.m., Goodwill U. E. Church, Upper Cross Roads. Reception at bride's home."
The following seven names were written on the back of the invitation:
1. Henry Nagle, d. 2 Oct 1895
2. John Nagle, d. 13 Sep 1896
3. Liza Cloman, d. 26 Apr 1897
4. Charlotte Arnett, d. 3 Sep 1898
5. Mical Nagle, d. 1 Sep 1886
6. Henry Nagle, 366 5th St., Lebanon, PA
7. Mrs. Cole

Elizabeth Howe, second wife of Emanuel Nagle, b. 13 Dec 1827, d. 17 Jul 1908

Thomas Franklin Nagle and Elizabeth Hutchinson m. 26 Jan 1871

Elizabeth Hutchinson Nagle, wife of Thomas, d. 5 Oct 1910

Thomas Franklin Nagle and Capitola McVey m. 2 Nov 1911

Susan Mary Nagle and George W. Blaney m. 2 May 1853

Anna Mary Nagle and George Thomas Shannon m. 16 Jun 1855

Samuel Owen Nagle and Margaret Boyd m. 31 Mar 1881

George Alexandria Nagle and Sarah Finney m. 25 Oct 1880

William Edman Nagle, b. 15 Mar 1826, d. 11 Aug 1865

John Henry Nagle and Florence Livezey m. 4 Aug 1886

Laura Ellen Nagle and Clement G. Butler m. ---- [date not given]

Charles Chapman Nagle and Margaret Heneretta Hess m. 15 Jan 1896

Laura E. Butler, d. 13 Oct 1926, age 60

JOHN H. NAGLE BIBLE

Altemus Bible published in 1884. Family data gleaned from a typescript at the Maryland Historical Society in 1973.

Births:
John H. Nagle, b. 23 Mar 1864
Florence Nagle, b. 12 Nov 1869
Children of John and Florence Nagle:
1. Harry Cramp Nagle, b. 27 Oct 1886 (year altered to 1887)
2. James Stewart Nagle, b. 7 Mar 1889
3. Millard Howe Nagle, b. 23 Dec 1890

4. Sylvania Gertrude Nagle, b. 4 Jun 1892

Death:
Harry Cramp Nagle, d. 15 Aug 1887 (year altered to 1888)

SAMUEL O. NAGLE BIBLE

Parallel New Testament Bible, Revised 1881. Family data gleaned from a typescript at the Maryland Historical Society. Bible originally owned by Samuel Nagle of Harford County, MD.

Marriage:
Samuel O. Nagle and Margaret A. Boyd m. 31 Mar 1881 by Rev. Dice at Salem M. E. Church near Jarrettsville, MD. Marriage certificate was signed by Bro. David Boyd and Rebecca Boughter Ricks.

Births:
Samuel Owen Nagle, b. 8 Apr 1858
Margaret Ann Nagle, b. 19 Sep 1863

Children of Samuel and Margaret Ann Nagle:
1. Della May Nagle, b. 28 Jan 1882
2. Anna Margaret Nagle, b. 29 Sep 1883
3. Ada Ellen Nagle, b. 6 Sep 1885
4. Albert Clinton Nagle, b. 17 Mar 1887
5. Walter Chapman Nagle, b. 8 Dec 1889
6. Willard Sheridan Nagle, b. 5 Apr 1892
7. Owen Wallace Nagle, b. 7 Sep 1897
8. Harry Boyd Nagle, b. 23 May 1899
9. Samuel Owen Nagle, Jr., b. 1 Jun 1904

Deaths:
Children of Samuel and Margaret Ann Nagle:
1. Ada Ellen Nagle, d. -- Apr 1886
2. Owen Wallace Nagle, d. 14 Sep 1897
3. Della May Nagle, d. 5 Jul 1912
4. Walter Chapman Nagle, d. -- Mar 1913
5. Albert Clinton Nagle, d. 23 Feb 1932
6. Samuel O. Nagle, d. 23 Jun 1947

7. Margaret A. Nagle, d. 26 Jul 1947
8. Samuel Owen Nagle, Jr., d. 22 Jul 1952

JAMES NOBLE BIBLE

Bible published by Kimber & Sharpless, No. 50 N. 4th Street, Philadelphia, PA (no date given). Family data gleaned from a typescript at the Maryland Historical Society.

Marriage:
James Noble and Elizabeth Gilbert m. 28 Sep 1837 [*Ed. Note:* James Noble m. 1st to Mary Fletcher circa 24 Jan 1823 (date of license) and he m. 2nd to Elizabeth Gilbert on 28 Sep 1837 (license dated 27 Sep 1837) by Rev. Finney in Harford County, MD].

Births:
James Noble, b. 19 May 1792
Elizabeth Gilbert, b. 5 Apr 1805

[Children of James and Elizabeth Noble]:
1. Mary Frances Noble, b. 20 Jan 1829
2. James Noble, b. 25 Feb 1831
3. William Henry Noble, b. 2 Aug 1838
4. John Thomas Noble, b. 7 Aug 1840
5. George Harrison Noble, b. 5 Aug 1843

Deaths:
George H. Noble, d. 12 Aug 1851, age 8 years and 7 days
Elizabeth Noble, d. ---- [date not given]
James Noble, d. 24 Apr 1871
William H. Noble, d. 14 Jun 1892
John T. Noble, d. -- Jul 1912 [*Ed. Note:* Tombstone in Wesleyan Chapel Cemetery near Aberdeen indicates he died 19 Jul 1912].

Abner Gilbert, d. 6 Apr 1851, age 26 years and 9 months

SAMUEL W. PALMER BIBLE

No publication information available. Family data gleaned from a typescript at the Maryland Historical Society.

Marriage:

Samuel Webster Palmer and Harriet Louisa Numbers m. 30 Oct 1872 in Philadelphia, PA

Births:
Children of S. Webster and H. Louisa Palmer:
1. Ethel June Palmer, b. 26 Oct 1873
2. Mary Alice Palmer, b. 22 Aug 1875
3. William Wallace Palmer, b. 7 Oct 1879
4. Harry Webster Palmer, b. 15 Jan 1884

Deaths:
William Wallace Palmer, d. 10 Mar 1882, age 2 years, 3 months and 3 days

Elizabeth Gunnell, wife of Mahlon Palmer, d. 7 Oct 1894, age 80 years, 4 months and 10 days

PETER PARKS BIBLE

No publication information available. Family data gleaned from a photocopy of the bible records at the Maryland Historical Society.

Marriage:
---- 13 Oct 1790 *[sic]* (apparently a marriage date, although Parks chart gives 11 Sep 1790). [*Ed. Note:* Peter Parks and Precilla Jones obtained a marriage license in Baltimore County on 11 Sep 1790].

Births:
[Children of Peter and Priscilla Parks]:
1. Joshua Parks, b. 29 Aug 1791
2. Elizabeth Parks, b. 29 Sep 1793
3. Mary Parks, b. 9 Oct 1795
4. John Parks, b. 5 Jun 1797
5. Elisha Parks, b. 9 Feb 1799
6. Joseph Parks, b. 16 Feb 1801
7. Peter Parks, b. 10 Jan 1803
8. Ann Parks, b. 12 Mar 1806 (04 lined out)

9. Mary Parks, b. 7 Apr 1808
10. Harriet Parks, b. 16 Apr 1810
11. William Parks, b. 6 Aug 1812

PARSONS-FRENCH BIBLE

Bible published by John C. Winston Company of Philadelphia, Chicago and Toronto (no date given). Family data gleaned from a typescript at the Maryland Historical Society.

Marriages:
William Arthur Parsons and Helen Winfield French m. 15 May 1907 in Richmond, VA by Rev. Dr. R. B. Eggleston, Pastor of the Third Presbyterian Church, in the presence of William Augustus Parsons, Townsend A. Parsons, I. Wray Clarke, and Grace C. French.

William A. French and Lillian N. Coale, dau. of Joseph Atlee Coale and Mary Eliza McFadden, and granddau. of William A. Cole, m. 16 Oct 1888 by Rev. Joseph P. Wilson, Minister of the Gospel, at the residence of the bride's parents in the presence of "parents and families with very many friends."

William Arthur Parsons and Sadie N. ---- m. 19 Apr 1899
William Arthur Parsons and Helen W. ---- m. 15 May 1907
William Arthur Parsons, Jr. and ---- [blank] m. 2 Jul 1930
Ann or Anna Lillian Parsons and William H. Mears m. 28 Sep 1928

Shirley Anne Mears and D. Keith Whitehurst m. 24 Jun 1953

William Arthur Parsons III, son of William Arthur, Jr. and Anne Alsruhe Parsons, and Elizabeth Martindale m. 1 Jun 1957

Helen W. French and ---- [blank] m. 15 May 1907
Grace C. French and C. Wade Yeakle m. 17 Jul 1915

C. Wade Yeakle, Jr. and ---- [blank] m. 9 Dec 1939

Births:
William Arthur Parsons, b. 16 Oct 1872, Goochland C. H., VA

Sadie N. ----, [1st] wife of William Arthur Parsons, b. ----, Charlottesville, VA

Llewellyn A. Parsons, b. 22 Apr 1900, Charlottesville, VA

Helen W. ----, [2nd] wife of William Arthur Parsons, b. 12 Jun 1890, Bel Air, MD

William Arthur Parsons, Jr., b. 6 Feb 1908, Richmond, VA

Ann Lillian Parsons, b. 1 Feb 1910, Baltimore

Shirley Anne Mears, b. 24 Feb 1933, Milford

William Arthur Parsons III, b. 17 Jun 1935, Baltimore

Children of Shirley and D. Keith Whitehurst:
(Both children were born in Baltimore)
1. William Guion Whitehurst, b. 13 Sep 1955
2. Susan E. Whitehurst, b. 15 Jan 1957

Children of William and Elizabeth Parsons:
(Both children were born in Baltimore)
1. Victoria Lee Parsons, b. 8 Oct 1959
2. Stephen F. Parsons, b. 11 Feb 1962

Lillian N. Coale, b. 8 Nov 1868, Bel Air

William A. French, b. 5 Mar 1862, Baltimore
Helen W. French, b. 12 Jun 1890, Bel Air
Grace C. French, b. 27 Aug 1895, Bel Air

C. Wade Yeakle, Jr., b. 23 Jun 1916, Hamilton
C. Wade Yeakle III, b. 5 Sep 1922, Baltimore

Deaths:
William Arthur Parsons, d. 29 Nov 1933
Sadie N. Parsons, d. 26 Jul 1906

William A. French, d. 29 Mar 1915
Lillian N. French, d. 3 May 1942

HENRY CLINT PEDEN, JR. BIBLE

Bible published by The World Publishing Company, 2231 West 110th Street, Cleveland, OH (undated). The bible was presented to Henry C. Peden, Jr., son of Henry Clint Peden and Mary Catherine Frank, on Christmas Day, 1955, by his grandmother Mrs. Ruby Norris Frank (who was born at Aldino in Harford County, MD on 5 Dec 1898, the daughter of Benjamin Brook Cadle and Alice Norris Strong; Ruby died at her home at Poplar in Baltimore County on 25 Jul 1960, the wife of Walter Remington Frank). Bible is presently owned by Henry C. Peden, Jr. of Bel Air, MD.

Marriages:
Henry Clint Peden and Mary Catherine Frank m. 14 Jun 1942

Carol Anne Peden and Loynel Delmore Williams m. 1 Dec 1962

Henry Clint Peden, Jr. and Veronica Ann Clarke were united in Holy Matrimony on 11 Jul 1970 at St. Mary's Star of the Sea Catholic Church in Baltimore City by Rev. William Burke in the presence of Jerry Bowser and Deena Leep.

Linda Marlene Peden and Richard Andrew Noll m. 5 Dec 1970

Carol Anne Williams and Arthur Wayne Michael m. 21 Jun 1975

Births:
Henry Clint Peden, Sr., b. 30 May 1921, Kentucky
Mary Catherine Frank, b. 19 May 1926, Maryland

Children of Henry and Catherine Peden:
1. Carol Anne Peden, b. 16 Mar 1943
2. Henry Clint Peden, Jr., b. 4 Nov 1946
3. Linda Marlene Peden, b. 25 May 1949

Veronica Ann Clarke, wife of Henry Clint Peden, Jr., b. 30 Jan 1950, Baltimore

Henry Clint Peden III, son of Henry Jr. and Veronica Peden, b. 27 Jan 1971

Children of Loynel and Carol Williams:
1. Rebecca Lynn Williams, b. 5 Jul 1964
2. Cynthia Ann Williams, b. 6 Sep 1968

Children of Richard and Linda Noll:
1. Danielle Renee Noll, b. 31 Jul 1972
2. Michelle Maree Noll, b. 24 Mar 1975
3. Lynnelle Marlene Noll, b. 7 Mar 1978
4. William Peden Noll, b. 22 Sep 1984

Walter Remington Frank, b. 1894, Maryland
Ruby Norris Cadle, wife of Walter R. Frank, b. 1898
William Henry Peden, b. 1891, Kentucky
Pearl E. Crenshaw, wife of William H. Peden, b. 1892

Deaths:
Grandparents of Henry Clint Peden, Jr.:
Ruby Norris (Cadle) Frank, d. 25 Jul 1960
Walter Remington Frank, d. 23 Dec 1960
William Henry Peden, d. 24 Feb 1944
Pearl Eugenia (Crenshaw) Peden, d. 15 Oct 1976

RICHARD POOLE BIBLE

Bible published in 1867 by William W. Harding, Philadelphia, PA. Family data gleaned from a typescript at the Maryland Historical Society. The Poole family was apparently from Harford County, MD.

Marriages:
Richard Poole and Florence P. Poole m. 23 Nov 1869 at 11 a.m.

Louie Hankins and Mary Douglas Poole m. 5 Feb 1901 at 2 p.m.

William White Williams and Frances Eleanor Poole m. Sat., 20 Oct 1906 at 10 a.m.
Frederick S. Poole and Mary T. D. Wilson m. 13 Aug 1833

Robert Wilson and Eleanor Shekell m. 1792 [*Ed. Note:* Robert Willson acctually married Eleanor Shekells on 30 Oct 1798 in Prince George's Parish, Montgomery County, MD]

Rev. Walter Williams and Anna Cost Poole m. 14 Oct 1909

William Edward Williams and Rachel Ann Perry m. 23 Oct 1940 at 11 a.m.

Mary Douglas Hankins and T. O. Heinrich m. 10 Jun 1939

Florence Poole Hankins and William Tucker Carrington m. 1 Mar 1930

Richard Poole Hankins and Eleanor Spottswood Turner m. 19 Jun 1940

Births:
Children of Richard and Florence Poole:
1. Mary Douglas Poole, b. Thurs., 10 Aug 1871 at 12? o'clock a.m.
2. Anna Cost Poole, b. Thurs., 27 Aug 1874 at 10 o'clock p.m.
3. Frances Eleanor Poole, b. Sun., 3 Feb 1878 at 5? o'clock a.m.

Frederick S. Poole, b. 19 Jun 1809
Mary T. D. Wilson, wife of Frederick S. Poole, b. 4 Aug 1812

Children of Frederick S. and Mary T. D. Poole:
1. Cumberland Wilson Poole, b. 27 May 1834
2. John Frederick Sprigg Poole, b. 3 May 1836
3. Robert Wilson Poole, b. 15 Mar 1838
4. Frances Eleanor Poole, b. 31 Mar 1840
5. Frederick Sprigg Poole, b. 21 Aug 1842

Robert Wilson, b. 13 Sep 1762
Eleanor Shekell, wife of Robert Wilson, b. 21 Jul 1772

Florence Priscilla Poole, b. 17 Apr 1844

Florence Poole Hankins, b. Fri., 6 Nov 1903 at 4 p.m.
Richard Poole Hankins, b. 25 Mar 1912
Mary Douglas Hankins, b. 10 Aug 1914

William Tucker Carrington, Jr., b. 24 May 1934
Katherine Morton Carrington, b. 8 Oct 1936
Louie Hankins Carrington, b. 23 Mar 1939
Mary Poole Carrington, b. 13 Aug 1942

Richard P. Hankins, Jr., b. 27 Jan 1946

Mary Douglas Heinrich, b. 1 Jan 1941

Elizabeth Dudley Heinrich, b. 6 Jan 1944

Mary Gertrude Poole, b. 10 Mar 1847
Blanche Poole, b. 30 Apr 1848
Wilson Poole, b. 1 Dec 1849
Richard Poole, b. 30 Oct 1843

Richard Poole Williams, b. 9 Sep 1908
William Edward Williams, b. 16 May 1912
William Edward Williams, Jr., b. 3 Oct 1946
Ann Perry Williams, b. 8 Jan 1949

Deaths:
Frederick S. Poole, d. 8 Jun 1888
Mary T. D. Wilson, wife of Frederick S. Poole, d. 23 Jan 1883

Children of Frederick S. and Mary T. D. Poole:
1. Cumberland Wilson Poole, d. 22 Nov 1836
2. John Frederick Sprigg Poole, d. 28 Nov 1838
3. Robert Wilson Poole, d. 13 Dec 1838
4. Frances Eleanor Poole, d. 11 Mar 1860
5. Frederick Sprigg Poole, d. 29 Oct 1843

Robert Wilson, d. 4 Mar 1835
Eleanor Shekell, wife of Robert Wilson, d. 21 Aug 1837

Mary Gertrude Poole, d. 20 May 1853
Blanche Poole, d. 25 Jan 1850
Wilson Poole, d. 20 Jan 1850
Richard Poole, d. Fri., 12 Jan 1906 at 10:25 p.m.
Florence P. Poole, d. 23 Jul 1930

Mary D. P. Hankins, d. 11 Feb 1939
Louie Hankins, husband of Mary, d. 18 Apr 1938

Richard Poole Williams, d. 26 Sep 1910
William White Williams, d. 9 Jan 1926
Frances Poole Williams, d. 8 Feb 1958

WILLIAM PRITCHARD BIBLE

Bible published by The National Publishing Company, Ziegler & McCurdy, Jones Brothers & Company, Philadelphia, PA (no date given). Family data gleaned from a typescript at the Maryland Historical Society.

Marriages:
William G. Pritchard and Christianna Rawhouser, both of Harford County, MD, m. 29 Jan 1857 by Rev. Jonathan Munroe

Mary C. Pritchard, of Aberdeen, MD, and Bernard A. Skinner, of Mansfield, MA, m. 12 Sep 1874

Births:
Joshua Rawhouser, b. 12 Sep 1810 near Dover, York Co., PA
Elizabeth Conn, b. 7 Aug 1814
William G. Pritchard, b. 31 May 1836
Christianna Rawhouser, b. 16 Nov 1837, bapt. by Rev. J. Hempfield

Children of William and Christianna Pritchard:
1. Mary Catherine Pritchard, b. 2 Jan 1858, bapt. by Rev. Robert L. Vinton
2. Joshua R. Pritchard, b. 6 Jan 1859, bapt. by Rev. Robert L. Vinton
3. William Alfred Pritchard, b. 25 Nov 1861, bapt. by Rev. David Shoaf
4. George Edwin Pritchard, b. 22 Feb 1863, bapt. by Rev. David Shoaf
5. Susan Ordella Pritchard, b. 27 Aug 1866, bapt. by Rev. J. McKee
6. Morgan Elliott Pritchard, b. 17 Feb 1872, bapt. by Rev. J. Hagey
7. Charles Arthur Pritchard, b. 3 Jul 1874, bapt. by Rev. Frank Porter

Death:
Joshua Rawhouser, d. 17 Aug 1892, age 82

MITCHEL MARTIN PUGH BIBLE

No publication information available. Family data gleaned from a photocopy of a page of the bible record which was "found on courthouse xerox" (probably Harford County).

Marriage:
Mitchel Martin Pugh and Narcissa Ballow m. 7 Oct 1848

Births:
Mitchel Martin Pugh, b. 9 Apr 1830
Narcissa Pugh, b. 6 Sep 1830

[Children of Mitchel and Narcissa Pugh]:
1. Luticia Pugh, b. 30 Jul 1850
2. James Monroe Pugh, b. 2 Oct 1852
3. Mary Isabel Pugh, b. 23 Feb 1855
4. William Jackson Pugh, b. 22 Jul 1857
5. Malcum Mitchel Pugh, b. 28 Mar 1860
6. Ema Jane Pugh, b. 22 Nov 1862
7. Robert Lee Pugh, b. 28 Jan 1866
8. Louisa Orlean Pugh, b. 3 Apr 1869
9. Rausa Alice Pugh, b. 25 Feb 1873

Deaths:
James Monroe Pugh, d. 20 Mar 1883
Narcissa Pugh, d. 26 Nov 1899, age 69 years and 20 days
Mitchel Martin Pugh, d. 18 Jul 1900
William Jackson Pugh, d. 25 Oct 1919
Malcum Mitchell Pugh, d. 3 Jul 1943

Luticia Spencer, d. 1 Apr 1907
Emma Jane Spencer, d. 9 Jan 1926

Mary Isabel Davis, d. 10 Apr 1919

Louisa Orlean Cornett, d. 31 Dec 1933

ISAAC L. PYLE BIBLE

Bible published in 1851 by John B. Perry Co., 198 Market Street, Philadelphia, PA. Family data gleaned from a typescript at the Maryland Historical Society.

Marriages:
Isaac L. Pyle and Mary E. Welch m. 1 Feb 1849 by Rev. J. Elderdice

Jacob G. Gallion and Edith Gertrude Pyle m. ---- [*Ed. Note:* No date was given in the bible and no record was found in Harford County].

Births:
Isaac L. Pyle, b. 27 Mar 1822 (1823?)
Mary E. Welch, b. 18 Oct 1828

[Children of Isaac and Mary Pyle]:
1. Martha H. Pyle, b. 17 (14?) Jan 1850
2. Robert H. Pyle, b. 12 Jun 1851
3. Amer Montgomery Pyle, b. 31 May 1854(?)
4. Jacob Linley Cromwell Pyle, b. 29 May 1856
5. Isaac Vinton Pyle, b. 24 Apr 1859
6. Nathan Miller Pyle, b. 25 Sep 1861
7. Edith Gertrude Pyle, b. 16 Nov 1862
8. Elnora Pyle, b. 5 Nov 1865
9. Lorenza Hillmen Pyle, b. 10 Mar 1869
10. Granville Putman Pyle, b. 9 Oct 1871

[Children of Jacob G. and Edith G. Gallion]:
1. Helen Zuiletta Gallion, b. 27 Feb 1883
2. Jesse LaRoy Gallion, b. 9 May 1884
3. Ross Leon Gallion, b. 27 Jun 1886
4. Ethel Irene Gallion, b. 15 Nov 1887 [sic]
5. Lester Jay Gallion, b. 24 Nov 1887 [sic]

Deaths:
[Children of Jacob and Edith Gallion]:
1. Jesse LaRoy Gallion, d. 27 Jul 1884
2. Ross Leon Gallion, d. 6 May 1887
3. Ethel Irene Gallion, d. 22 Jul 1887 [sic]
4. Edgar Baxter Gallion, d. 19 Jan 1890

[Children of Isaac and Mary Pyle]:
1. Martha H. Pyle, d. 18 Jun 1851
2. Robert H. Pyle, d. 4 Jul 1853
3. Jacob Linley Cromwell Pyle, d. 23 Mar 1862
4. Isaac Vinten Pyle, d. 22 Jul 1862
5. Nathan Miller Pyle, d. 7 Aug 1862
6. Lorenza Hillman Pyle, d. 20 Mar 1869
7. Mary Elnor Pyle, d. 26 Oct 1870
8. Amor Montgomery Pyle, d. 3 Sep 1882
9. Granville P. Pyle, d. 24 May 1950, age 78

Family Records (On Paper Inserted in Bible):
Children of Granville P. and Viola B. Pyle:
1. Helen Elizabeth Pyle, b. 14 Feb 1897
2. Mary Verna Pyle, b. 7 Apr 1901
3. Lester Baker Pyle, b. 27 Aug 1903
4. Margaret Hanson Pyle, b. 1 Apr 1914

Their grandchildren and great-grandchildren:

Children of Helen Elizabeth (Pyle) Beachboard:
1. Margaret Jean Beachboard, b. 24 Oct 1923
2. John Howard Beachboard, b. 5 Jun 1925
3. Wanda Claire Beachboard, b. 10 Apr 1930

Children of Wanda Claire (Beachboard) Trostle:
1. Karen Lyn Trostle, b. 24 Nov 1951
2. Barbara Ilean Trostle, b. 25 Jul 1954

Children of Mary Verna (Pyle) Livezey:
1. Barbara Louisa Livezey, b. 2 Apr 1933
2. G. Kessler Livezey III, b. 7 Apr 1937

Children of Lester Baker Pyle:
1. Dorothy Ann Pyle, b. 28 Mar 19-- [blank]
2. Richard Granville Pyle, b. 27 Nov 19-- [blank]

Children of Margaret Hanson (Pyle) Jenkins:
1. Marilyn Jenkins, b. 2 Jan 19-- [blank]
2. Carole Sue Jenkins, b. -- Jan 19-- [blank]

JOSHUA HARLAN PYLE BIBLE

Bible published in 1834 by C. Alexander & Co., Athenian Building, Franklin Place. Written on front page: "Joshua H. Pyle's Book. Bought in Baltimore July 16th 1836. Price $2.00." Family data gleaned from a typescript at the Maryland Historical Society.

Marriages:
Harmon Pyle and Ann Thomas m. 9th of 11th month, 1809
Joshua H. Pyle and Gulielma E. Rutledge m. 6th of 10th month, 1847
Elisha R. Pyle and Mary E. Bowen m. 17th of 11th month, 1874
David C. Ely and Mary B. Pyle m. 4th of 5th month, 1880
Lewis T. Pyle and Margaret E. Ely m. 11th of 9th month, 1884
Emery E. Jonson and Susan E. Pyle m. 23rd of 11th month, 1887
John H. Dawson and Ann E. Pyle m. 22nd of 2nd month, 1888
Edwin E. Martin and Kate E. Pyle m. 27th of 3rd month, 1889

Births:
Joshua H. Pyle, son of Harmon and Ann Pyle, b. 14th of 3rd month, 1813 about 5 o'clock in the morning

Gulielma E. Rutledge, dau. of Elisha and Ann L. Rutledge, b. 19th of 9th month, 1829

Children of Joshua H. and Gulielma E. Pyle:
1. Elisha R. Pyle, b. 22nd of 4th month, 1850
2. Harmon Pyle, b. 17th of 8th month, 1852
3. Ann Elizabeth Pyle, b. 30th of 4th month, 1855
4. Mary Bell Pyle, b. 27th of 8th month, 1857
5. Lewis T. Pyle, b. 16th of 2nd month, 1860
6. Kate Elma Pyle, b. 28th of 6th month, 1862
7. Susan Emma Pyle, b. 7th of 10th month, 1866

[Children of Edwin E. and Kate E. Martin]:
1. Harry E. Martin, b. 7th of 11th month, 1894
2. Roberta A. Martin, b. 1st of 12th month, 1895
3. Dorothy L. Martin, b. 9th of 10th month, 1917
4. Harry Ronald Martin, b. 5th of 7th month, 1935

Deaths:
Harmon Pyle, son of Joshua H. and Gulielma E. Pyle,, d. 10th of 10th month, 1852
Joshua H. Pyle, d. 13th of 9th month, 1894, age 81 years and 6 months
Gulielma E. Pyle, d. 8th of 11th month, 1911, age 82 years, 1 month and 18 days
Susan Emma Pyle, daughter of Joshua H. and Gulielma E. Pyle, d. 27th of 11th month, 1938
Mary Ella Pyle, d. 8 Jun 1923, age 67 years and 6 months
Mary Elmira Pyle, d. 5th of 8th month, 1923
Elisha R. Pyle, d. 20 Mar 1928, age 77 years and 11 months

Lewis T. Pyle, d. 2 Jun 1928, age 67 years and 4 months

Edwin E. Martin, d. 6 Apr 1925, age 63
Kate E. Martin, d. 8 Jan 1945, age 82 years, 7 months and 6 days

John H. Dawson, d. 19th of 9th month, 1913, age 55

Mary Belle Ely, d. 19 Jan 1924, age 66 years, 7 months and 8 days
David Ely, d. 21st of 12th month, 1905, age ---- [blank]

JOHN READ BIBLE

Bible published in 1811 by Mathew Carey, No. 123 Market Street, Philadelphia. Family data was published by the St. Mary's County Genealogical Society, Inc. in its newsletter *The Generator* (Vol. 19, No. 10, July-August, 1996). They indicated that the Read family lived in Baltimore City and County and subsequently migrated to Howard County, MD.

Marriages:
John and Catharine Read m. ---- [no date]
Elias and Ann Read m. 29 Nov 1810

Births:
Children of John and Catharine Read:
1. Sarah Read, b. 30 Apr 1773
2. Mary Read, b. 6 Nov 1774
3. Elizabeth Read, b. 17 Jun 1777
4. Hannah Read, b. 27 Feb 1779
5. Deborah Read, b. 18 Jun 1781
6. Elias Read, b. 13 May 1784

Children of Elias and Ann Read:
1. John Read, b. 13 Sep 1811
2. Ruth Read, b. 3 Apr 1813
3. Charles Peregoy Read, b. 8 Feb 1815
4. Catherine Read, b. 4 Feb 1817
5. Elias Joseph Read, b. 27 Jul 1819
6. James Read, b. 25 Sep 1821
7. Maryann Read, b. 5 May 1823

8. Sarah Elizabeth Read, b. 13 Oct 1825
9. Hannah Price Read, b. 26 Nov 1827
10. Nicholas Read, b. 18 Apr 1830
11. Rebecca Jane Read, b. 20 May 1832
12. William Edmonds Read, b. 16 Nov 1836

Charles Peregoy, son of Joseph, b. 18 Dec 1764
Ruth Peregoy, wife of Charles, b. 6 May 1766

Children of Charles and Ruth Peregoy:
1. Elizabeth Peregoy, b. 25 May 1786
2. Sarah Peregoy, b. 23 Dec 1787
3. Ann Peregoy, b. 7 Apr 1789
4. Nicolas Peregoy, b. 12 Sep 1790
5. Helina Peregoy, b. 26 Jun 1792
6. James Peregoy, b. 11 Jan 1794

Deaths:
Elias Read, d. 27 Apr 1857
Ann Read, d. 21 Nov 1862
John G. Read, d. 11 Jul 1870

Children of Elias and Ann Read:
1. Hannah Price Read, d. 16 Feb 1829
2. Nicholas Gorsuch Read, b. 31 May ----
3. Rebecca Jane Read, d. 9 Aug 1834
4. Sarah Kelly, d. 5 Oct 1863
5. Catharine Hutson, d. 16 Apr 1868

WILLIAM H. REASIN BIBLE

Bible published in 1891 by J. A. Wilmore & Company, 43 E. 45th Street (successors to A. J. Johnson & Company, 11 Great Jones Street, New York, NY). Family data gleaned from a typescript at the Maryland Historical Society. Bible originally presented by William H. Reasin to his wife Fannie on 18 Sep 1891.

Marriages:
William H. Reasin and Fannie N. Cole m. 10 Jan 1887
Abraham Cole and Sarah E. Nelson m. 17 Feb 1887
William H. Reasin and Cora D. Gorrell m. 28 Nov 1906

Claude Nelson Reasin and Ruby Arthur m. 9 Dec 1908
Florence Aleine Reasin and W. Russell Hayman m. 7 Apr 1916
Warren Russell Hayman (b. 1 May 1858, son of Warren Benson Hayman) and Hannah Elizabeth Davis (b. Oct. 21, 1862) m. 18 Sep 1892

Births:
Abraham Cole, b. 12 Apr 1809
Sarah Elizabeth Nelson, b. 18 Sep 1821

Cornelius Cole, b. 9 Dec 1848
Henry E. Cole, b. 27 Aug 1851
Fannie N. Cole, b. 1 Sep 1854
Florence M. Cole, b. 19 Apr 1857

William H. Reasin, b. 27 Mar 1853

Children of William H. and Fannie Reasin:
1. Claude Nelson Reasin, b. 29 Mar 1889
2. Florence Aliean Reasin, b. 27 Aug 1892

William Hawthorne Reasin, son of William H. and Cora D. Reasin, b. 7 Aug 1908

Henry Cole Reasin, son of Claude N. and Ruby Reasin, b. 23 Aug 1911

Frances Mary Hayman, dau. of W. Russell and Florence Aliean Hayman, b. 15 May 1918

Deaths:
Abraham Cole, d. 29 Apr 1890 in his 82nd year
Sarah E. Cole, wife of Abraham Cole, d. 16 Mar 1890 in her 69th year

Fannie N. Reasin, d. 17 Jan 1897 in her 43rd year
Hannah E. Reasin, d. 20 Nov 1905
Claude N. Reasin, d. 9 Nov 1912 in his 23rd year
Hannah E. Reasin, d. 20 Nov 1905 in her 84th year
William H. Reasin, d. 6 Aug 1917
Gertrude Reasin, d. 1927

Family Records:
Garrett V. Nelson, son of Aquilla and Frances Nelson, and Hannah Cole, dau. of John B. and Priscilla Cole, m. 2 Dec 1820

Garrett V. Nelson, d. 24 Dec 1850, age 54 years, 4 months and 10 days

Hannah Nelson, wife of Garrett V. Nelson, d. 6 Jan 1862, age 62 years, 10 months and 2 days

Carvelle Douglas Motley (b. 15 Nov 1915, son of Walter Lewis Motley b. 1 Feb 1887 and Lucille Littleton b. 13 Mar 1891, who m. 14 Aug 1912) and Frances Mary Hayman m. 2 May 1942. Issue: Linda Hayman Motley b. 2 Nov 1943, and Walter Russell Motley b. 3 Feb 1947.

REESE-PRICE BIBLE

Bible published in 1845 in Hartford by Sumner & Goodman. Family data gleaned from a typescript at the Maryland Historical Society.

Marriages:
Charles S. Reese and Ann Olivia Diffenderffer, second dau. of Charles and Ann Diffenderffer, m. 17 Oct 1849 by Rev. John S. Reese
James M. Sewell and Annie O. Reese m. 12 Oct 1866 by Rev. Dr. Backus

Henry A. Price and Laura Reese, both of Harford County, MD, m. in 1884 [day and month not given] at the parsonage in Baltimore County by Rev. Messrs. Riley and Black

Births:
Children of Charles and Ann Reese:
1. Laura Reese, b. 28 Oct 1850
2. Charles Reese, b. 20 Sep 1852

Ann Louisa Sewell, dau. of James and Ann, b. 12 Jun 1868

Children of Henry and Laura Price:
1. Charles Henry Price, b. 29 Mar 1885
2. George Diffenderffer Price, b. 29 Dec 1890

Deaths:
Anna Bond, d. 19 Mar 1935 at 3 o'clock

Laura Price, d. 27 Apr 1932
Charles H. Price, d. 4 Jul 1954

James M. Sewell, d. 5 Aug 1869 in his 48th year

Dr. Charles S. Reese, d. 24 Sep 1855, age 37
Charles Reese "died on the 21st age 2 years & 6 months - cronic croup"

Family Records (Clippings Inserted in Bible):
1. Henry Barnett Queen, infant son of A. M. and Sophie Queen, b. 17 Oct 1875, d. 17 Apr 1876 - date line Rockford, WV

2. Died on Wed. 21st Henrietta Dorsey of John and Henrietta D. A. Duer [date not given]

3. Died on 21st at the residence of his grandfather Charles Diffenderffer, Charles Reese age 2 years and 8 months [date not given]

4. Died in Cleveland, OH on 24 Oct ----, Dr. Charles S. Reese, age 37, son of the late Rev. Dr. John S. Reese. Buried at Green Mount Cemetery [year not given]

5. "Another Revolutionary Soldier Gone: It is not often at this day that we are called on to record the death of one of the brave spirits who participated in the war of Independence. Most of those who joined in that great struggle for liberty have long since been gathered to their father, and they only live in the memory of a grateful people. We have now to notice the demise of one who lived nearly a century, and watched the progress of the country from the time the thirteen feeble colonies were acknowledged free until the present period, when it has grown to be among the most powerful and prosperous nations of the earth. Jacob Diffenderffer, another of the well tried heroes who fought so bravely and nobly for the liberty of America, has been gathered to his fathers in the 98th year of his age. He resided in Lancaster County, Pa. One by one his patient band has dropped from among the living until there are but a few to tell the story of the times that tried men's souls." [no date given]

6. George Diffenderffer who lived with his sister, Mrs. Anna Sewell, was buried at Green Mount Cemetery [no date given]

7. Mrs. Fulton, the wife of ---- A. Fulton of Bel Air, d. last Sat. Interment in St.

Ignatius Church Cemetery at Hickory on Tues. [no date given]

8. Mrs. John S. Stonebraker d. at her residence on Thursday last week [no date given]

9. Mr. George M. Diffenderfer, a brother of Mrs. A. O. Sewell of Abingdon, d. at her residence on the 9th [no date given]. He was a native of Baltimore City and was 45 years old.

10. John MacFarland and Mary MacHardy, both of Baltimore, m. at the Presbyterian parsonage, No. 73 Asquith Street, on 12 Feb 1885 by Rev. S. A. Davenport.

11. Charles H. Reese, beloved son of the late Henry A and Laura Reese Price, d. suddenly 4 Jul 1954. Funeral services at McComas Funeral Home, Abingdon, MD on Wed. at 10 a.m. Interment in Cokesbury Memorial Cemetery.

12. Died on the morning of the 20th instant in the 33rd year of his age Charles Diffenderffer Jr. Funeral at his residence Sat. morning [no date given]

13. Died on 19th in her 60th year Mrs. Sophia W. Higinbotham, wife of the late Ralph Higinbotham. Funeral Fri. the 20th from the residence of her son-in-law John B. Egerton, Esq., 143 St. Paul Street [no date given]

14. Died on the 14th John Lewis in his 57th year [no date given]

15. Died on the 19th Frederick C. Cook in his 32nd year [no date given]

16. Died on the 18th Rev. Henry Aisquith, Rector of King & Queen Parish, St. Mary's County, in his 56th year [no date given]

17. Died on the 19th Mrs. Ann E. Hahn at an advance age [no date given]

18. Died on the 18th George Reisinger in his 76th year [no date given]

19. Mrs. Margaret Reese, widow of Rev. John S. Reese, M.D., d. on 31 Mar 1876 at the home of her son Rev. John S. Reese in Baltimore, 83 years old. Funeral on 2 Apr, Dr. A. Webster and Thomas McCormick of M. P. Church presiding, assisted by Rev. William Peterkin of John's Memorial Protestant Church (Church of William Reese and family) with burial at Green Mount, beside her husband. Born in Baltimore County 24 Aug 1793, dau. of George F. and Catherine Spindler.

Married 1 Aug 1816 John S. Reese who was born 7 Mar 1790, the son of David Reese, for many years a citizen of Baltimore. He taught for many years, studied medicine and graduated at Washington University of Baltimore as M.D. and was a local preacher in M. E. Church. They raised 2 sons and 2 daughters.

20. Died 7 Apr 1876 sister Martha Jane Morris, age 50, of hemorrhage of the lungs, born in Madison County, GA on 2 Mar 1826, married to Joseph Morris on 13 May 1841. With her husband and one child emigrated to wilds of Texas in 1843 (rest of article gone) *[sic]*

WILLIAM B. RICHARDSON BIBLE

Bible published in 1853 by John B. Perry in Philadelphia, PA. Notations on front pages: "M. Clara Crevensten 1858" and "Property of W. B. Richardson, formerly belonged to his mother Mrs. M. C. Richardson (1858), 1893." Family data gleaned from a typescript at the Maryland Historical Society.

Marriages:
J. Henry Crevensten and Fannie C. Billingslea m. 23 Feb 1864

William B. Richardson and Mary T. Richardson m. 7 Feb 1895 at Aberdeen Southern Methodist Church

Mary Mildred Hastings Richardson and Ernest Fifer Powell m. 24 Dec 1917 at Trinity Parsonage in Baltimore, MD

"[entry in ball point pen]: Benjamin Richardson married Sophia Green, Dec 20 1817 (Hall of Records Md folio 97)" *[sic]*

Births:
William B. Richardson, son of William J. and Martha C. Richardson, b. 22 Jul 1865

Children of William and Mary Richardson:
1. Mary Mildred Hastings Richardson, b. 31 Mar 1897
2. Clarissa Vaughan Richardson, b. 11 Apr 1900
3. Infant daughter [no name given], b. 14 Sep 1901

Ernest William Richardson Powell, son of Ernest F. and Mildred H. Richardson Powell, b. 23 Aug 1920 (Aberdeen, MD)

Children of Sgt. Ernest William Richardson Powell and Mary Kathryn Matthews Powell:
1. Mary Kay Powell, b. 8 Mar 1944, Mercy Hospital, Baltimore, MD
2. William Terrence Powell, b. 30 Jul 1946, Mercy Hospital, Baltimore, MD

Deaths:
Martha C. Richardson, wife of the late William J. Richardson and mother of Martha S., George A. R., and William B. Richardson, d. 3 Dec 1894

Children of William B. and Mary T. Richardson:
1. Clarissa Vaughan Richardson, d. 16 Jul 1900
2. Infant daughter [no name], d. 14 Sep 1901

Martha S. Richardson Michael, dau. of William J. and Martha C. Richardson, and sister of William B. Richardson, d. Wed., 3 Feb 1937

Japhet Richardson, adopted son of Sophia and ---- Richardson, d. Tues., 2 Sep 1924 at the home of William B. Richardson

Mary T. Richardson, beloved wife of William B. Richardson and mother of Mildred Richardson Powell, d. Sun., 30 Nov 1930

William B. Richardson, son of William J. and M. C. Richardson, husband [record actually stated "wife"] of Mary T. Richardson, and father of Mildred Richardson Powell, d. Wed., 15 Feb 1939

THOMAS M. RICKETTS BIBLE

No publication information available. Family data gleaned from a typescript at the Maryland Historical Society which indicated "Bible dated 12-9-1841, in possession of Miss Irene Ricketts."

Marriages:
Thomas M. Ricketts and Caroline E. Strong m. 28 Jan ---- [*Ed. Note:* Harford County records indicate Thomas M. Rickets and Caroline E. Strong obtained a marriage license on 27 Jan 1824 which was directed to Rev. Richardson].

Samuel J. Ricketts and Belinda Bowen m. 28 Jan 1858
Thomas W. Ricketts and Oneda L. Davis m. 22 Feb 1883
Samuel J. Ricketts, Jr. and Ida Foard m. 15 Jul 1885

Harry G. Ricketts and Nevie E. Miller m. 9 Nov 1885
Louis C. Ricketts and Effie E. Brannan m. 17 Jul 1891
John Edward Ricketts and Dora E. Ford m. 30 Mar 1904
Walter Ricketts, son of John E. and Dora Ricketts, m. 28 Aug 1927 to Josephine Botts

Births:
Children of Thomas M. and Caroline E. Ricketts:
1. Samuel J. Ricketts, b. 6 Mar 1825
2. Thomas Ricketts, b. 18 Oct 1826

[Children of Samuel J. and Belinda Ricketts]:
1. Thomas William Ricketts, b. 28 Oct 1858
2. John C. Ricketts, b. 3 Apr 1860
3. Samuel J. Ricketts, Jr., b. 18 Apr 1862
4. Harry G. Ricketts, b. 2 Jul 1864
5. C. Ricketts, b. 15 Feb 1867
6. Lilly May Ricketts, b. 22 Jan 1870
7. Edward Ricketts, b. 23 Jun 1873
8. Estella Ricketts, b. 22 Jan 1877
9. Walter C. Ricketts, b. 28 Nov 1877

Children of J. Edward and Dora Ricketts:
1. George Walter Ricketts, b. 24 Oct 1905
2. Martha Irene Ricketts, b. 26 Jun 1909

Oneda C. Ricketts, dau. of Thomas and Oneda, b. 17 Dec 1854

Lillie M. Ricketts, dau. of Harry and Nevia, b. 13 May 18--

Joan Virginia Ricketts, dau. of Walter and Josephine, b. 28 Mar 1929

Deaths:
Caroline E. Ricketts, d. 13 Feb 1828
Thomas Ricketts, son of Thomas and Caroline, d. 17 Aug 1827
Thomas Ricketts, d. 6 May 1865
John C. Ricketts, son of Samuel and Belinda, d. 1 Jul 1872
Belinda Ricketts, wife of Samuel, d. 13 Jan 1900
Samuel J. Ricketts, d. 2 Feb 1911

Dora E. Ricketts, wife of John E., d. 1 Jan 1941
John E. Ricketts, d. 2 Feb 1951

Lillie May Baldwin, wife of James H. Baldwin, d. 23 Aug 1930, age 60

Mary E. Smith, d. 12 Feb 1892 at 1:24 a.m.

THOMAS W. RICKETTS BIBLE

No publication information available. Family data gleaned from a typescript at the Maryland Historical Society.

Marriages:
Thomas Ricketts and Oneda Davis m. 22 Feb 1883
Robert S. Myers and Beulah D. Ricketts m. 23 Jan 1900
S. Davis Ricketts and Grace M. Lowry m. 5 Feb 1910
Elizabeth Myers and Philip Kurtz m. 27 Oct 1920
Winsor Myers and Lillian Norman m. 6 Apr 1921
Florence Myers and Edward Franzson m. 23 Jul 1921

Births:
Thomas William Ricketts, b. 28 Oct 1858
Beulah Delamy Ricketts, b. 17 Dec 1883
Samuel Davis Ricketts, b. 19 Jan 1885
Paul Livingstone Ricketts, b. 11 Jun 1913

Oneda L. Davis, b. 14 Sep 1864

William Winsor Myers, b. 12 Sep 1900
Elizabeth M. Myers, b. 24 Jun 1903
Florence McG. Myers, b. 3 Jan 1906
Ranson Lowry Myers, b. 7 Sep 1908
Georganna Estella Myers, b. 29 Dec 1913

Deaths:
Thomas Davis, d. 13 Apr 1890, age 65
Cathrine Davis, wife of Thomas, d. 26 Jan 1910

Caroline E. Ricketts, d. 13 Feb 1828
Thomas Ricketts, son of Thomas and Caroline, d. 17 Aug 1828

Thomas W. Ricketts, Sr., d. 6 May 1865
John C. Ricketts, son of Samuel and Belinda, d. 1 Jul 1872
Belinda Ricketts, dau. of Samuel, d. 13 Jan 1900
Belinda Ricketts, wife of Samuel J. Ricketts, Sr., d. 13 Jan 1900
Samuel J. Ricketts, husband of Belinda, d. 2 Feb 1911
Paul Livingstone Ricketts, d. 2 Jan 1930, bur. 4 Jan 1930

Family Records "Memoranda":

Grace Marie Lowry, wife of S. Davis Ricketts, b. 5 Oct 1888

Ann Tinssell Franzson, b. 7 Sep 1922, dau. of Florence and Edward Franzson
Karl Edward Franzson, b. 31 Oct 1923

Robert Seneca Myers, b. 27 Apr 1916
Dianna V. Myers, b. 9 Feb 1925, son of Robert and Dolly Myers
William Winsor Myers, Jr., b. 2 Oct 1921, son of Lillian and Winsor Myers

Children of Elizabeth and Philip Kurtz:
Oneda Elizabeth Kurtz, b. 6 Sep 1921
Thomas Ricketts Kurtz, b. 16 Jan 1925

HENRY RUFF BIBLE

Bible published in 1867 by The American Bible Society in New York. Family data gleaned from a typescript at the Maryland Historical Society.

Marriages:
Henry Ruff and Elizabeth Warfield Preston m. -- Jan 1844 [*Ed. Note:* Harford County records indicate Henry Ruff and Elizabeth W. Preston were married circa 18 Feb 1845 (date of license) by Rev. Jones]

Mary Elizabeth Ruff and James Amoss m. 3 Jan 1877
James Henry Ruff and Rebecca Riggs Grymes m. 10 Dec 1903
Henry Ruff and Sarah Alethia Streett m. 18 Jun 1857
Henry Ruff and Mary Amelia Syurgeon m. 10 Jun 1930
Elizabeth Ann Ruff and Jerome Morgan Driver m. 18 Aug 1956
James Henry Ruff and Hope Lillian Davis m. 5 Oct 1957

Births:
Children of Henry and Elizabeth W. Ruff:
1. James Henry Ruff, b. 27 Feb 1847
2. Elizabeth Sophia Ruff, b. 25 Jan 1849
3. Mary Elizabeth Ruff, b. 31 Jan 1853
4. Martha Ann Ruff, b. 18 Mar 1859
5. Sarah Augusta Ruff, b. 8 Apr 1861

Children of James H. and Rebecca R. Ruff:
1. Elizabeth Ann Ruff, b. 3 May 1906
2. Henry Ruff, b. 19 Feb 1908
3. ---- Ruff (unnamed son), b. 30 May 1913

James Henry Ruff 3rd, b. 18 Aug 1932
Elizabeth Ann Ruff, b. 15 Jul 1935

Rebecca Marie Driver, b. 8 Nov 1957

Deaths:
Mary Elizabeth Amoss, d. 29 Jan 1901, age 48

Elizabeth Sophia Ruff, d. 6 Aug 1850, age 1 year, 6 months and 12 days
Elizabeth Warfield Preston Ruff, wife of Henry Ruff, d. suddenly -- Oct 1854, age 27 years and 2 months
Martha Ann Ruff, age 7 years and 6 months, and Sarah Augusta Ruff, age 5 years and 5 months, daughters of Henry and Sarah Alethia (Streett) Ruff, d. 4 Aug 1866
Ella Virginia (Findley) Ruff, wife of James Henry Ruff, d. 14 Mar 1900, age 44
Elizabeth Sophia (Mitchell) Ruff, d. 6 Mar 1866 in her 68th year
James Ruff, d. 9 May 1875 in his 84th year
Sarah Alethia (Streett) Ruff, wife of Henry Ruff, d. 18 Mar 1897 in her 74th year
Henry Ruff, d. 15 Jun 1903 in his 86th year
Rebecca Elizabeth Ruff, d. 17 Apr 1907, age 11 months and 14 days
James Henry Ruff, d. 15 Oct 1925 in his 78th year
Rebecca Riggs (Grymes) Ruff, d. 26 Oct 1957 in her 81st year

RUTLEDGE-FITZPATRICK BIBLE

No publication information available. Family data gleaned from a typescript at the Maryland Historical Society.

Marriages:
Jehu Rutledge and Priscilla Fitzpatrick m. 9 Jan 1817
William Rutledge and ---- [blank] m. 1852
Nathan Rutledge and Caroline Commer Fishel, widow of Frank Fishel, m. 7 Mar 1871

Births:
Jehu Rutledge, b. 20 Sep 1789
Priscilla Fitzpatrick, b. 22 Feb 1796

Children of Jehu and Priscilla Rutledge:
1. Ann Eliza Rutledge, b. 23 Dec 1817
2. Joshua Rutledge, b. 15 Oct 1819
3. Ann Eliza Rutledge, b. 19 Feb 1822
4. John E. Rutledge, b. 27 Jan 1824
5. William Rutledge, b. 15 Mar 1825
6. Sophia S. Rutledge, b. -- Oct 1830
7. Nathan Rutledge, b. 23 Mar 1833

Deaths:
Children of Jehu and Priscilla Rutledge:
1. Ann Eliza Rutledge, d. 29 Jan 1822
2. John E. Rutledge, d. 26 Nov 1826
3. Ann Eliza Rutledge, d. 29 Jun 1828

Children of William and ---- Rutledge:
1. John Rutledge, d. 1855
2. Abram Rutledge, d. 1858 [*Ed. Note:* The typescript indicated 1838 as the year of death, but this is an obvious typing error since his parents were not married until 1852 and his father William would have been only 13 years old in 1838].

Jehu Rutledge, d. 16 Dec 1859
Sophia S. Rutledge, d. 20 Oct 1918

Mary Fitzpatrick, d. ---- [blank], in the 88th year of her age
Nathan Fitzpatrick, d. 4 Feb 1848, age 93 on the 12th of March

RUTLEDGE-PRICE BIBLE

No publication information available. Family data gleaned from a typescript at the Maryland Historical Society.

Marriages:
Shelton Price and Ruth Richardson m. 24 Dec 1816
Julia S. Rutledge and C. W. Almony m. 20 Feb 1896
Charles M. Rutledge and ---- [blank] m. 20 Nov 1907

Births:
Lewis C. Rutledge, b. 28 Aug 1852
John Rutledge, b. 14 Mar 1853
Levisa Jane Rutledge, b. 1 Oct 1854
John S. Rutledge, b. -- Jan 1856
William H. Rutledge, b. 21 Feb 1872
Julia S. Rutledge, b. 9 Jan 1875

George F. E. Fishel, b. 23 May 1864

Children of Shelton and Ruth Price:
1. Thomas Price, b. 25 Nov 1817
2. William Price, b. 17 Sep 1819
3. Sara Jane Price, b. 30 Dec 1821
4. Penelope Price, b. 19 Dec 1824
5. Edward Price, b. 26 May 1827

Children of C. W. and Julia S. Almony:
1. Marion Linthicum Almony, b. 29 Sep 1897
2. Lawrence Rutledge Almony, b. 12 Jan 1903
3. Charles Franklin Almony, b. 19 Jun 1906

Deaths:
Margaret Rutledge, d. 8 Jul 1832
Sara Rutledge, d. -- Jun 1842
William H. Rutledge, d. 19 May 1873
Julia S. Rutledge [Almony], d. 12 Sep 1972

"George Bond and Jemima his wife, December 30, 1850 marriage??" [*Ed. Note:* This is the way the typescript was worded; however, George Bond and Jemima Pocock were married for many years before 1850. It would appear, therefore, that they both had died, not married, on 30 Dec 1850].

Children of C. W. and Julia Almony:
1. Marion Linthicum Almony, d. 23 Mar 1902
2. Lawrence Rutledge Almony, d. 22 Feb 1972

George F. E. Fishel, d. 29 Sep 1875(?) [*Ed. Note:* The typescript stated he was born in 1864 and died in 1845, which is an obvious typing error].

THOMAS SCAGGS BIBLE

No publication information available. Family data gleaned from a typescript at the Maryland Historical Society.

Births:
Thomas Scaggs, son of John and Elizabeth, b. 11 Oct 1813
Emeline Roberts, dau. of William H. and Theresa, b. 12 Jan 1819

Children of Thomas and Emeline Scaggs:
1. John Scaggs, b. 26 Sep 1838
2. William H. Scaggs, b. 19 Mar 1841
3. Henry Scaggs, b. 24 Sep 1843
4. Adaline Scaggs, b. 11 Jun 1846
5. Carroline Scaggs, b. 1 Dec 1848
6. Maryelen Scaggs, b. 16 Aug 1851
7. Alphred Scaggs (son), b. 16 Mar 1854
8. Arana Scaggs (dau.), b. 21 Oct 1858

David D. Dutton, son of Isaac and Elizabeth, b. 17 Feb 1797
John Gettman, b. 18 Jan 1839

Deaths:
Emeline Scaggs, wife of Thomas, d. 10 Jan 1859, age 39 years, 11 months and 28 days

GEORGE T. SHANNON BIBLE

Bible published in 1877 by The American Bible Society in New York. Family data gleaned from a typescript at the Maryland Historical Society.

Marriage:

Annie Mary Shannon and George Thomas Shannon m. 8 Aug 1871 [*Ed. Note:*

Harford County marriage records indicate George T. Shannon and Annie M. Nogle obtained a license on 5 Aug 1871 and were married by Rev. Roberts]

Births:
George T. Shannon, b. 7 Apr 1843
Annie M. [Nogle] Shannon, b. 16 Jun 1855

Children of George T. and Annie M. Shannon:
1. Mina Shannon, b. 12 Apr 1872
2. George Edward Shannon, b. 2 Feb 1873
3. John Henry Shannon, b. 16 Apr 1875
4. Mary Frances Shannon, b. 1 Nov 1877
5. Cora May Shannon, b. 13 Mar 1880

Deaths:
Mina Shannon, d. 3 May 1872
George Edward Shannon, d. 13 Feb 1893
George Thomas Shannon (father), d. 18 Feb 1910
Annie Mary Shannon (mother), d. 12 Feb 1922

ASBURY SHERIDAN BIBLE

Bible published in 1851 by George Lane & Levi Scott. Written in flyleaf: "The property of Asbury Sheridan, October 10, 1863. Bot [bought] of Rev. Mr. Vinton." Family data gleaned from a typescript at the Maryland Historical Society.

Births:
Asbury Sheridan, b. 27 Aug 1814

[Children of Asbury and ---- Sheridan]:
1. James Sheridan, b. 20 Feb 1835
2. Margret J. Sheridan, b. 19 Sep 1836
3. Elizabeth Sheridan, b. 14 Mar 1838
4. John Sheridan, b. 3 Mar 1840
5. William Sheridan, b. 25 May 1841
6. Richard Sheridan, b. 28 Nov 1842
7. Telitha Sheridan, b. 28 Feb 1845
8. Luther Sheridan, b. 26 Nov 1846
9. George Sheridan, b. 2 Sep 1848
10. Samuel Sheridan, b. 23 Nov 1852

Deaths:
Asbury Sheridan, d. 23 May 1869
John Sheridan, d. 5 Apr 1903
George Sheridan, d. 11 Nov 1902
Luther Sheridan, d. 29 May 1914

LUTHER SHERIDAN BIBLE

Bible published in 1885 by the American Bible Society. Family data gleaned from a typescript at the Maryland Historical Society.

Marriage:

Luther Sheridan and Mollie E. McCommons m. 29 Dec 1886 by Rev. Litsinger

Births:
Children of Luther Sheridan and first wife ---- Baldwin:
1. Oliver A. Sheridan, b. 15 Nov 1874
2. Mary R. Sheridan, b. 11 Dec 1875
3. Florence N. Sheridan, b. 29 Apr 1877
4. Albert Sheridan, b. 24 Mar 1880

Children of Luther Sheridan and second wife Mollie McCommons:
1. Vernon C. Sheridan, b. 1 Nov 1887
2. Pearly Goldine Sheridan, b. 13 Sep 1889

Daisy Virginia Sheridan, dau. of Vernon C. and Daisy M. Sheridan (neé DeJoy), b. 4 Feb 1914 at Level, MD [Harford County].

Deaths:
Mary E. Sheridan, d. 25 Sep 1896 near Aberdeen
John Sheridan, d. 5 Apr 1903, age 63 years and 1 month
Luther Sheridan, d. 29 May 1914, age 68 years
Florence N. Sheridan, d. 13 May 1897. "She went to Baltimore March 22, 1897. She died at the University hospitte [sic]. She was 20 years and 14 days old."

REBECCA SHERIDAN BIBLE

Bible published in 1878 by William Garretson & Company. "Rebecca A. Sheridan" is embossed on the cover. Family data gleaned from a typescript at the Maryland Historical Society.

Marriage:

Richard Sheridan and Rebecca Ann Gallion, both of Harford County, m. 14 Apr 1875 at Rock Run M. E. Church by Rev. Haskell, pastor. Witnesses were Silas L. Spencer and James H. Bowman.

Births:
Richard Sheridan, b. 28 Nov 1842
Rebecca A. Sheridan, b. 26 Mar 1844

Children of Richard and Rebecca Sheridan:
1. Mary Lavenia Sheridan, b. 9 Feb 1877
2. William Parker Sheridan, b. 14 Apr 1878
3. Twin sons [no names given], b. 10 Mar 1880
4. Lizey Gertrude Sheridan, b. 7 Nov 1881
5. Alfread Fillmore Sheridan, b. 4 Feb 1884
6. Cora R. Sheridan, b. 4 Jan 1887
7. Richard Dallas Sheridan, b. 7 Oct 1890

Deaths:
Sarah Leuvena Sheridan, d. 2 Mar 1891 in her 25th year
Rebecca Sheridan, d. 16 Mar 1893, age 49
Richard Sheridan, d. 16 Dec 1920, age 78 years and 18 days

Family Record:
Funeral Notice: Melvin R. Gallion from James H. Gallion's residence on Wed., August 24, 1892 at 2 o'clock p.m. Interment and services at Rock Run Church.

RICHARD SHERIDAN BIBLE

No publication information available (title page and birth and marriage pages missing). Family data gleaned from a typescript at the Maryland Historical Society.

Marriage:
[*Ed. Note:* The marriage page is missing from the bible; however, Harford County marriage records indicate Richard Sheridan and Margrett Ann Walker were married on or after 4 Feb 1840 (date of license) by Rev. Prettiman].

Deaths:
Thomas L. Sheridan, d. 3 Apr 1862
Richard Sheridan, d. 19 May 1891
Maggie C. Sheridan, d. 5 Sep 1896
Margaret A. Walker Sheridan, d. 5 Sep 1904
Mary L. Sheridan, d. -- Jan 1908
William G. Sheridan, d. ---- [no date]
Ella E. Sheridan, d. 29 Sep 1926
Lizzie Sheridan, d. -- Mar 1920
Richard Coleman Sheridan, d. 8 Feb 1934

JACOB SHERTZER BIBLE

Bible printed by Kimber and Sharpless at their book store, No. 50 North Fourth Street, Philadelphia. No date was indicated, but "Jacob Shertzer Bible 1846" was handwritten on the title page. A transcript was published in the *Maryland Genealogical Society Bulletin* (Vol. 23, No. 2) in Spring, 1982.

Marriage:
Jacob Shertzer and Mary Trege m. 19 Oct 1840

Births:
Jacob Shertzer, b. 15 Jun 1820
Mary Trege, b. 20 Jul 1822
Mary Ann Shertzer, b. 14 Apr 1842 between 11 and 12 p.m.
Abram G. Shertzer, b. 16 May 1844 between 8 and 9 p.m.
Isaac Shertzer, b. 11 Feb 1846 at 8 a.m.
Jacob Shertzer, b. 17 Dec 1846 between 9 and 10 p.m.
David Shertzer, b. 20 Feb 1850 at 4 p.m.
Catherine E. Shertzer, b. 18 Apr 1852 between 4 and 5 p.m.
Anna Elihalah Shertzer, b. 10 Aug 1854 between 4 and 5 p.m.
Benjamin Shertzer, b. 31 Mar 1856 between 12 and 1 a.m.
Hannah E. M. N. Shertzer, b. 8 Nov 1857 between 9 and 10 a.m.
Fannie Priscilla Shertzer, b. 13 Apr 1860 between 3 and 4 p.m.
John Amos Shertzer, b. 27 Apr 1862 between 4 and 5 p.m.
Henry M. Shertzer, b. 2 Aug 1864 between 3 and 4 a.m.
Mary E. Shertzer, wife of Isaac P. Shertzer, b. 16 May 1855
Cleveland Merritt, b. 14 Feb 1885

Deaths:
[*Ed. Note:* There were two lists of deaths in the bible which have been combined below to avoid duplicity of information. The second list was signed "HRS, Phildelphia, Pa., Oct. 5th 1936"].

Anna Elizabeth Shertzer, d. 25 Jul 1856
John A. Shertzer, d. 20 Dec 1863
Fannie Priscilla Shertzer, d. 7 Aug 1897, Philadelphia, PA
Mary Trege Shertzer, d. 25 Mar 1901, Churchville, MD
Jacob Shertzer, d. 17 Nov 1901, Churchville, MD
Mary Ann Shertzer, d. 30 Jun 1910, Churchville, MD
Mary E. Shertzer, d. 25 Aug 1913
Abram Trege Shertzer, M.D., d. 22 Jan 1915, Baltimore, MD
Benjamin Franklin Shertzer, d. 15 Jul 1918, San Francisco, CA
Harry A. Shertzer, d. 15 Sep 1920
Jacob Henry Shertzer, d. 21 Nov 1920, Randlestown, MD
David William Shertzer, d. 4 Feb 1921, Oldham, VA
Isaac Peter Shertzer, Sr., d. 1 Oct 1924, Baltimore, MD
Price I. Shertzer, d. 9 Apr 1957
Anna Elizabeth Shertzer Holman, d. 25 Jan 1917

Fannie Merritt, d. -- Dec 1948
Cleveland Merritt, d. 9 Apr 1975, Baltimore

Walter F. Hoover, Jr., d. 9 May 1975, age 97, Dundalk, MD
Viola Shertzer Hoover, d. 3 Oct 1975, age 95, Dundalk, MD

JOHN H. SHORT BIBLE

Bible published in 1853 by Jasper Harding, Philadelphia. This transcript was published in the *Maryland Genealogical Society Bulletin* (Vol. 28, No. 2) in Spring, 1987.

Marriages:
John H. Short and Elizabeth A. Parker m. 2 Dec 1853 [*Ed. Note:* However, their marriage notice appeared in the *Baltimore Sun* on 4 Dec 1852 and stated they married on 2 Dec 1852].

Harry A. Bersch and Maria Catherine Short m. 28 Dec 1875

Births:
John H. Short, b. 10 Mar 1832
Elizabeth Parker, b. 9 Feb 1832

[Children of John and Elizabeth Short]:
1. Maria Catherine Short, b. 24 Nov 1855 [1853?] at 6 a.m.
2. John Hick Short, b. 4 Feb 1857 at 6 a.m.
3. Mary Augusta Short, b. 28 May 1860 at 2 a.m.
4. William Snyder Short, b. 11 Dec 1861
5. Charles McClendon Short, b. 13 Dec 1864 at 2 a.m.
6. Mary Anna Short, b. 12 Jun 1868 at 1 o'clock

Deaths:
Mary Augusta Short, d. 20 Jul 1862
Elizabeth A. Short, d. 20 Nov 1899
John H. Short, d. 2 Jan 1911
Charles M. Short, d. 31 Dec 1911

Albert C. Adams, b. 25 May 1903

Harry A. Bersh, d. 4 Apr 1900
Maria C. Bersh, d. 24 Jan 1919

GEORGE W. SLEE BIBLE

No publication information available. Family data gleaned from a typescript of records copied by Jon Harlan Livezey in 1974 from the original family record pages from this bible deposited in Filing Case A at the Maryland Historical Society.

Marriages:
George W. Slee and Mary Evans m. 29 Jul 1847
Robert F. Hanna and Florence Slee m. 14 Aug 1867
John Kidd and Mary Lee m. 18 Sep 1874
R. H. S. Slee and Lou M. Barnett m. 25 Nov 1881
N. Tipton Slee and Sadie L. Price m. 6 Jun 1883

Births:
George W. Slee, son of John and Mary Slee, b. 22 Feb 1819
Mary Evans, dau. of John and Mary Evans, b. 26 Dec 1823

Children of George W. and Mary Slee:
1. Albert W. Slee, b. 18 Apr 1848
2. Florence Slee, b. 20 (26?) Feb 1850
3. Robert H. Slee, b. 26 Mar 1853
4. Tipton Slee, b. 29 Dec 1857
5. John Slee, b. 28 Apr 1860

Deaths:
John Evans, d. 20 Sep 1841, age 76
Mary Evans, wife of John, d. 16 Nov 1859, age 72

Julian Lilly, wife of Thomas, d. 21 Jul 1854

John Wakeland, d. 8 Jun 1862, age 44

John Slee, d. 9 Apr 1860, age 82

John Slee, d. 12 Dec 1863, age 3 years
Eliza Slee, d. 20 Dec 1864, age 58(?)
John N. Slee, d. 15 Apr 1866
George W. Slee, d. 15 Aug 1866, age 47
Albert W. Slee, d. 19 Aug 1909, age 61
N. Tipton Slee, d. 19 Nov 1945
Florence Slee, wife of Robert F. Hanna, d. 4 Jan 1926, age 75

John Kidd, d. 13 Jan 1901, age 82
Mary Kidd, wife of George Slee, d. 15 Apr 1905, age 81

JOHN LEWIS UPPERCO BIBLE

No publication information available. The bible records were made available by Leslie M. Upperco of Baltimore County, MD and published in the *Maryland Genealogical Society Bulletin* (Vol. 23, No. 2) in Spring, 1982.

Marriages:
John Lewis Upperco and Ruth Elizabeth VanBibber m. 14 Mar 1852

Lucretia Chew Upperco and William T. Wheat m. 23 Jan 1873

Samuel Nelson Stocksdale and Georgeanna Maria Upperco m. 8 Jan 1874 by Rev.

Christian Lepley

Murray Dixon Upperco and Anna M. Mitten m. 12 Dec 1877

John J. Reighler and Florance Upperco, both of Baltimore County, m. 23 Dec 1879 by Rev. C. Lepley

Guy L. Upperco and Ethel A. Sampson m. 28 Mar 1914 at Fayette Street M. E. Church by Rev. Kenneth G. Murray

Karen Elizabeth Upperco and Leslie Callis Turner m. 16 Dec 1962

Leslie Martin Upperco and Irene Joan Breymaier m. 8 Jan 1964

Karen Upperco Turner and Sgt. Lewis Stanley m. 21 Mar 1969 at Fort Hood, TX

Births:
Jacob Upperco, father of John Lewis Upperco, b. 14 Feb 1788
John Lewis Upperco, b. 9 Oct 1821
Ruth Elizabeth Upperco, wife of John Lewis Upperco, b. 29 Jan 1833

Children of John L. and Elizabeth Upperco:
1. Georgeann Maria Upperco, b. 18 Sep 1852
2. Lucretia Chew Upperco, b. 4 Jun 1854
3. Murry Dickson Upperco, b. 28 Oct 1858
4. John Lewis Upperco, b. 3 Sep 1860
5. Florance Upperco, b. 23 Jun 1863

Bessie Olivia Upperco, b. 1 Mar 1879
Arthur Dickson Upperco, b. 13 Sep 1880
Guy Lee Upperco, b. 18 Apr 1882 at Boering P. O., Baltimore County
Walter Mitten Upperco, b. 6 Mar 1884 at Boering P. O., Upperco, Baltimore County
Guy Lee Upperco, Jr., b. 22 Jan 1916 at 1713 W. Lombard Street [Baltimore]
Martin Thedis Upperco, b. 1 Oct 1917 at 1713 W. Lombard Street [Baltimore]
Susan Roberta Upperco, dau. of Martin T. and Dorothy Upperco, b. 31 Jul 1947 at
    Siania [Sinai] Hospital

Children of Guy Jr. and Marian Upperco:
1. Lee Dickson Upperco, b. 19 Jan 1938 at West Baltimore General Hospital at 5:15
    a.m.

2. Leslie Martin Upperco, b. 25 Oct 1942 at St. Joseph Hospital in Baltimore at 9 a.m.
3. Karen Elizabeth Upperco, b. 8 Mar 1945 at St. Joseph Hospital

Children of Lee D. and Annette H. Upperco:
1. Lee Dixon Upperco, Jr., b. 6 Aug 1956 at Maryland General Hospital
2. Carol Lynn Upperco, b. 20 May 1961 in Elkton, MD at 6:52 a.m.

Children of Leslie C. and Karen U. Turner:
1. Debra Lee Turner, b. 25 Oct 1963 at Franklin, IN
2. Robert Wayne Turner, b. 3 Dec 1965 at MD General Hospital

Children of Lewis and Joan Upperco:
1. Jennifer Irene Upperco, b. 27 Mar 1972 at 8:45 a.m.
2. Jason Leslie Upperco, b. 25 Jul 1975 at Franklin Square Hospital at 9:02 a.m.

Jessica Ann Stanley, dau. of Lewis and Karen Stanley, b. 5 Jun 1974

Deaths:
Jacob Upperco, father of John Lewis Upperco, d. 24 Feb 1867, age 79 years and 10 days

Children of John L. and Elizabeth Upperco:
1. John Lewis Upperco, d. 19 Mar 1861, age 6 months and 16 days
2. Murry Dickson Upperco, d. 15 Jul 1922, age 63, at Boring P. O., Baltimore County

Walter M. Upperco, son of Murray D. and Annie Upperco, d. 29 May 1932; interment in Druid Ridge Cemetery

Annie Phillip Upperco, dau. of Henry and Catherine Mitten, d. 6 Jun 1936; interment in Loudon Park Cemetery

Bessie Upperco Franke, dau. of Dickson and Anna Upperco, d. -- Jul 1936 (b. 1 Mar 1879); interment in Druid Ridge Cemetery

Pearl Brikman Upperco, wife of Walter Upperco, d. 28 Apr 1941; interment in Druid Ridge Cemetery

Ethel A. Upperco, wife of Guy L. Upperco, d. 9 Mar 1951, age 69; interment in

National Cemetery in Baltimore
Guy L. Upperco, Sr., d. 6 Dec 1957; interment in National Cemetery in Baltimore

Arthur D. Upperco, d. 26 Apr 1966; interment in Loudon Cemetery

WILLIAMS-NEILSON FAMILY BIBLE

Bible published in 1841 by G. Lane and P. P. Sandford in New York. Family data gleaned from a photocopy of the records in Filing Case A at the Maryland Historical Society.

Marriages:
John Stump and Cassandra Wilson m. 2 Oct 1779
John Williams and Rosanna Costen m. 2 Jun 1791
James W. Williams and Hannah C. Stump m. 15 Oct 1817
J. Crawford Neilson and Rosa Williams m. 2 Jun 1840
John H. Williams and Antoinette McFadon m. 17 Jun 1844
James A. Williams and Ruth E. Wilson m. 18 Nov 1845

Births:
James W. Williams, b. 8 Oct 1792
Hannah C. Williams, b. 20 Jul 1796

[Children of James and Hannah Williams]:
Rosa Williams, b. 27 Nov 1818
John H. Williams, b. 20 May 1821
James Aldred Williams, b. 14 Apr 1823
Edwin Williams, b. 5 Apr 1825

J. Crawford Neilson, b. 14 Oct 1816

[Children of Crawford and Rosa Neilson]:
Albert Neilson, b. 21 Nov 1841
James Neilson, b. 8 Mar 1845
Virginia P. Neilson, b. 22 Apr 1846
Rosa Neilson, b. 15 Mar 1848

Charles Neilson, b. 19 Jul 1849

[Children of John and Antoinette Williams]:
Rosa Williams, b. 1 Mar 1845
James W. Williams, b. 21 May 1846

[Children of James and Ruth Williams]:
James W. Williams, b. 22 Sep 1846
Edwin Williams, b. 20 Dec 1848

Deaths:
James W. Williams, d. 2 Dec 1842
Rosa Williams, d. 17 Jun 1845
Edwin Williams, d. 1 Jun 1848
James W. Williams, d. 26 Apr 1849
James A. Williams, d. 4 Apr 1850

James Neilson, d. 27 Jun 1845
Virginia P. Neilson, d. 22 Dec 1848

INDEX
to
Maryland Bible Records, Volume 1

Last name missing
----: Alice Cordalia, 167; Amos, 182; Anne, 145; Catharine, 165; Charlott, 137; Cora E., 85; Eliza, 116; Ellen, 155, 181; Emory, 100; George, 116, 181; Hannah, 116; Hazel S., 119; Helen W., 212; John, 116; Kate, 67; Lena, 67; Margaret, 116; Mary, 26; Nellie, 145; Sadie N., 212; Sallie, 116; Sarah, 67; Virgie, 67

AARONSON: Alford E., 1; Alfred E., 1; Alfred Ezra, 2; Ambrose P., 1; Ambrose Palmer, 2; Ann Dickey Jamison, 2; Ann Folwell, 1; Ann Jamison, 1; Anna Elizabeth, 2; Clayton, 1, 2; Edna D., 2; Ezra, 1; Francis Folwell, 1; Frank (Francis), 1; Henrietta Morris, 1; Hope, 1, 2; Jennifer Lynn, 2; Joan R., 2; Martha J., 1; Mary Ann, 1, 2; Mary Elizabeth, 2; Mary Emmeline, 1; Russell T., 2; Russell T., Jr., 1; Russell Taylor, 1; Russell Taylor, 3rd, 2; Russell Taylor, Jr., 1, 2; Samuel Clayton, 2; William, 1; William F., 1; William Folwell, 2

ADAMS: Albert C., 247; Beulah Baker, 20; Catherine, 137; Hannah C., 137; J. Victor, 18, 20; Martha C., 135; William, 135, 137

AIREY: Adelaide, 6; Ann, 3, 5; Beulah, 6; Buelah, 4; Carroll Bell, 4, 5; Charles C., 5; Charles Carroll, 4; Edward, 7; Emma, 3; Emma Jones, 6; Eugene Howard, 6; Francis, 3, 5; Francis A., 3, 5; Francis Asbury, 3, 7; George E., 6; George Washington Wilson, 3, 4, 6; Hyacinth Ella Virginia, 3, 4, 6; James, 3, 4, 5, 6, 7; James K. Polk, 4, 5; Jamess, 5; Jemima, 4, 5, 6; John, 4; John B., 3; John Bond, 4, 5; John William, 4, 5; Joseph, 3, 5, 7; Joseph E., 6; Joseph Edward, 4; Laura, 4, 5; Louisa, 7; Mary, 3, 7; Mary E., 3, 5; Mary Susan, 4; Norma, 6; Norma Valentine, 3, 4; Robert, 7; Samuel, 7; Samuel P., 5; Sinclair, 6; Sinclair C., 6; Sinclair Carroll, 3, 4; Sinclare, 6; St. Clare, 3; T., Rev., 7; Thomas Hill, 3, 7; Thomas, Rev., 7; W. Carroll, 6; William, 4; William Carroll, 3; William Francis, 4, 6; William Howard, 4, 6

AISQUITH: Henry, Rev., 230

AKEHURST: Elzia Agnes, 68; Florence Alvertia, 68; George T., 67, 68; Laura Bertha, 67; Sarah E., 67, 68

ALBAUGH: Mary, 21

ALFORD: James E., 55

ALKIN: Mary Ashbury, 155

ALLEN: John, Rev., 49

ALLISON: Esther, 7, 8; Mary, 9; Patrick, 7, 9

ALMONY: C. W., 238, 239; Charles Franklin, 239; Julia, 239; Julia S., 239; Lawrence Rutledge, 239; Marion Linthicum, 239

AMBROSE: Rena Craig, 23, 24

AMMERMAN: Catherine, 10; Catherine E., 10; Catherine Kinslowe, 10; Daniel, 10; Daniel C., 10; Elmira, 10; Emma, 10; James Y., 10; Josephine, 10; Mary M., 10; Miles G., 10; Oceanna, 10

AMOS: Elizabeth, 11; Elizabeth T.,
11; Garrett, 12; George King, 11;
Hannah, 11; James, 11, 13; James
Oliver, 11; Josephine, 12; Martha,
12; Mary Rebecca, 11; Oliver, 11;
Oliver H., 10; Rebecca Lee, 11;
William, 11, 12; William L., 12
AMOSS: Elizabeth, 12, 236; Elizabeth
A., 12; Elizabeth A. (King), 11;
Garrett, 13; George K., 12;
Hannah, 11; James, 11, 235;
James O., 12; Mary T., 11;
Oliver, 12; Oliver H., 11, 12, 13;
Oliver Huff, 11; Rebecca Lee, 12;
William, 13
ANDERSON: Bessie Mae, 31;
Charles E., 131; Effie O., 31;
Effie Ogilvin, 31; Elwood Lee,
166; J. M., 30; Jane Currie, 31;
Lee Wilton, 190; Levin Feaster,
131
ANTHONY: Aaron, 17; Ann, 17;
Lucretia P., 16, 17
ARCHER: Ann, 14; Augustus C., 63,
64; Catherine Cassandra, 14;
Charles, 43, 172; Cheyney
Hoskins, 63, 64; Edwin
Smallwood, 63; Ethel, 62, 63; F.
Traynor, 172; George, 14, 63, 64,
172; George Trainor, 63, 64;
Hannah, 14, 172; Hannah
Elizabeth, 63, 64; Harold, 172;
Henry Wilson, 14; James, 14,
172; James E., 170, 172; James
H., 172; John, 14, 96, 172; John,
Jr., 14; Joseph F., 172; Joseph W.,
172; Lizzie Jeffers, 147; Louis,
172; Maggie A., 172; Marion, 14;
Mary, 14, 63, 64; Mary I., 96;
Mary Trainor, 63; Maude M.,
171; Robert, 14; Robert H., 96;
Robert H., Maj., 97; Robert
Harris, 96; Theodore, 172;
Traynor, 172; Vernon E., 171;
Walter Henry, 63; Winfield, 172
ARNETT: Charlotte, 207; Netty C.,
66, 67
ARNOLD: Bennett, 1; Ira Fielden, 74;
Laura J., 74; William H., 74
ARTHUR: Oletia, 203; Ruby, 226
ASHBY: Lotta Lee, 58; Lotus Lee, 58
ATWELL: Ann Maria, 15; Catherine,
15; Cathern Leienary, 15; George,
15; James Richard, 15; John, 15;
Joseph Henry, 15; Rebeckah Ann,
15; Sarah Spencer, 142; Sary
Elisibeth, 15; William, 15
AUDD: Edward, 17
AULD: Amanda M., 18; Ann, 18;
Arianna Amanda, 16; Arrianna,
17; Arrianna Amanda, 17;
Arrianna W., 18; Benjamin, 16;
Benjamin F., 15; Benjamin
Franklin, 16; Catherine, 16;
Catherine A., 16; Edward, 16, 17;
Edward Wesley, 16; Elizabeth,
17; Ella Virginia, 16; Haddaway,
17; Hugh, 15, 16, 17; John
Summerfield Deale, 16; Lucretia,
17; Lucretia P., 18; Rowena, 17;
Rowena H., 16; Rowena
Hambleton, 17; Rowena R., 18;
Sally, 17; Sarah, 16, 17; Sarah
Louisa, 16, 17; Sophia, 15;
Thomas, 16, 17, 18; Thomas,
Capt., 18; Washington, 17;
William H., 17; Willson, 17;
Wilson, 16; Wilson C., 16; Z., 18;
Zipporah, 17
AUSTIN: David Lawless, 166;
Elizabeth, 166; Emma L., 1;
Emmalenda, 1; Georgeanna
Mifflin Dallas, 166; James Knox
Polk, 166; Lawless, 166; Martha
Ann, 166; Martha Rebecca, 166;
Mary, 166; Mary Catharine, 166;

Thomas Hart Benton, 166; Thomas Steuart, 166
AYARS: Charles Cronin, 81; L. W., 81; L. Wesley, 81; Maggie R., 81
AYRES: James, 36; Mattie E., 36
BAGGS: Ann, 17; Isaac, 17; Nancy, 17
BAILEY: Asael, 26, 28, 30; Avarilla, 185; Catherine W., 124; Charles L., 28, 30; Elizabeth, 28, 30; George, 128, 172; George M., 171; J. Harvey, 30; James H., 28; Mary, 28, 30; Melvin, 172; Sarah, 26; Silas, 128; William, 28; William A., 30
BAKER: A. Lynn, 18, 20; Ann Elizabeth, 20; Austin Lynn, 19; Barbara, 20; Beulah, 18, 19; C. W., 19; Charles, 20; Charles H., 22; Charles Henry, 22, 23; Charles W., 18, 19, 20; Charles Winfield, 19; E. C., 20; E. R., 19; Edith C., 20; Edmund Monroe, 22, 23; Edythe A., 20; Edythe R., 19; Elizabeth, 21, 22, 23; Elizabeth Ann, 22; Elizabeth Greenland, 21; Elizabeth J., 21; Elizabeth Jane, 21; Emerson, 18, 20; Emma, 19; Emma F., 19, 20; Emma Franklin, 19; F. E., 20; F. P., 23; Frances, 19; Frances Adele, 19; Frank E., 18, 19, 20; Frank Emerson, 19; Frank S., 18; George H., 22; George Hildt, 22, 23; George W., 21; Gwendolyn Wescott, 19; Harry, 23; Helen, 19; Helen Lee, 19; J. H., 21; John C., 22; John Carsins, 22; John H., 20, 21; John Hanson, 21; Katie Kimmel, 21; Lizzie, 21; Margaret Grace, 18, 19; Margaret Littleton, 21; Marion Lynn, 20; Mary, 23; Mary B., 22; Mary J., 22, 23; Mary Jane, 22; Nancy, 20; Neal Pendleton, 20; Nicholas, 22, 23; Nicholas, Jr., 22; P. T., 19; P. Tevis, 20; Patricia Vandergrift, 20; Pendleton Tevis, 18, 19; Reba, 20; Ridgely, 19, 20; Sarah F., 22; Susie E., 20; Viola Estelle, 21; Warren LeRoy, 21; William Reid, 21; Winfield Lee, 22
BALDWIN: Blanche Paxton, 38; Charlotte, 190; E. N., 155; Ed N., 128; Frances, 155, 156; James, 160; James H., 233; Joseph, 39; Joseph S., 37, 38, 39, 40; Joseph Salling, 38; Joseph, Dr., 39; Laura, 152; Lillie May, 233; Margaret B., 21; Nannie, 38, 39; Nannie Bissell, 38; Phebe E., 155, 156; S. T., 156; Samuel T., 155, 156; Sarah, 156, 160; Sarah M., 157; Tyler, 156; Vesta B., 160; Vesty, 160; William J., 21
BALLISTER: Adeline B., 158
BALLOW: Narcissa, 219
BARCLAY: William, 76
BARNARD: Frances, 31
BARNES: Amelia Gertrude, 28; Asail, 27; Beverly L., 25, 28; Charles, 28; Charles F., 26, 28; Clifford C., 26, 28, 29; Clifford Colfax, 23; Edwin, 27, 29; Elizabeth, 29; Elizabeth R., 28; Ellen R., 28, 29; Ellen Randolph, 60; Estelle B., 25, 28; Frances, 28, 29; Frances Cordelia, 27, 29; Frances Eason, 28; Gregory, 29; Gregory, Sr., 29; Hannah E., 28, 29; Mary, 26, 27, 29; Mary E., 29; Mary Elizabeth, 25; Mary Elziabeth, 26, 27; Minnie E., 28; Mordecai, 29; Mordecai G., 29; Polly, 26; R. A., 29; Richard, 26, 27, 29; Richard A., 26, 28, 29; Richard Amos, 25, 27, 29; Richard Randolph, 28, 29;

Richard, Sr., 26, 29; Sarah, 27, 29; Sarah A., 26, 30; Sarahann, 27; Susan, 29; Susanna, 29; Susannah, 27; William Colfax, 25, 28; William Harrison, 27, 29; William Henry, 27, 29; Wilmer, 29; Wilmer L., 26, 28; Wilmer Lewis, 28, 58; Wilmer Noble, 28; Winston, 29
BARNETT: Lou M., 247
BARNS: Ann, 27; Arabella, 27, 28; Averilla, 27; Elizabeth, 27; Elziabeth, 27, 29; Farmer, 27; Ford, 27, 28; Gregory, 27, 28; John, 27, 28; Mary, 27, 29; Mordecai G., 26, 27; Rachel, 27; Richard, 26, 27, 28, 29; Richard, Sr., 27, 29; Sarah, 26, 27, 28, 29; Susannah, 27; Winstone, 26, 27, 29
BARRATT: Frances Louise, 134
BARRETT: Rev., 33; William, 184
BARROW: Cornelia E., 150; Preston M., 193; William, 150
BASE: May, 122
BAUER: Alice French, 167; Alverta, 30, 31; Arthur Lee Clayton, 31, 167; Clara May, 31; Clayton, 167; Effie, 31, 32; George H., 30; Henry, 30, 31, 32; Hettie, 30, 31; Howard Andrew, 31, 167; J. W., 30, 165, 166; James Fulton, 31; John, 30, 31, 32; John Milton, 31; John William, 31; John Wilton, 167; Lawrence Edward, 31, 167; Lawrence S., 30; Lena Jane, 31; Linwood French, 31, 167; Mary, 31; Maryx, 32; Nannie, 30; Nanny, 31; Rebecca May, 31, 167; Sarah Jane, 31, 32; Sarah Jane (Clayton), 31
BAY: Mary A., 51; Mary Ann, 51
BAYARD: Catharine, 168, 169; Catherine, 32, 33; Catherine A., 32, 168, 169; Catherine L., 32; Lewis H., 32, 33, 168, 169; Samuel T., 32, 33, 168, 169; Thomas, 32, 33, 168; Thomas C., 32, 168, 169
BAYLESS: Mary, 26; S. M., 160
BAYLEY: Asael, 26
BEACHBOARD: Helen Elizabeth (Pyle), 222; John Howard, 222; Margaret Jean, 222; Wanda Claire, 222
BEAVEN: Arthur, 33; Emma E., 33; Emma Elizabeth, 33; John S., 33; John Sterrett, 33, 34; John W., 34; John Wood, 34; Margaret, 34; Margaret Rachel, 34; Mary J., 34; Mary Jane, 34; Mary Jane (Sterrett), 34; Sarah Elizabeth, 34; Sterrett Patterson, 33; Walter Crothers, 33
BECHTOL: Carol Ann, 19; Eleanor Marie, 19; Frances, 19; Harry, 19; Harry Addison, 19
BEHR: John, 53
BENDER: Thomas Allen, 1
BERNARD: Alcie, 203
BERSCH: Harry A., 246
BERSH: Harry A., 247; Maria C., 247
BIDDLE: Altossa, 77
BILLINGSLEA: Fannie C., 231
BILLINGSLEY: Alma, 35, 36; Clarence, 36; Daisey L., 36; David G., 36; John, 36; Mattie E., 36; Myrtle, 35; S. Streett, 36
BILLMAN: Ada L. R., 205; Ada Taroda, 206; Ela. De. Zell., 206; Ella D. Z., 205
BINGHAM: Sadie, 84
BIRMINGHAM: Alverda Hawkins, 140
BISHOP: Anna, 172
BISSELL: Benjamin, 37, 38, 39, 40; Bessie, 38; Bessie A., 39; Bessie May, 38; Bessie Webster, 38;

Elizabeth, 37; Elizabeth
Rombaugh, 37; Emma Walker,
38; Fannie Henshaw, 38; Georgia,
38; Harry Reiche, 38; John
Adams, 37, 39; John Adams
Webster, 37, 39; Josephine D.,
37; Josephine Dallam, 40;
Margaret, 37, 39; Margaret Ann,
37; Margaret Webster, 38; Martha
Wilkinson, 37; Mary Jarrett, 37;
Mary Lillie, 38; Mattie, 40;
Nannie, 37, 39, 40; Phoebe Ann,
38; Rachel Virginia, 37; William,
37, 38, 39; William Jacques, 38;
William R., 37, 39; William
Ridgely, 38; William Rombaugh,
37; William T., 40; William
Thomas, 37; Wilson Cleveland,
38
BLAIR: Alexander Ross, 40, 41; Ann
Maria, 40; Eleanor, 41; Eliza
Jane, 40; Esabella Woodward, 40,
41; Hiram Goldsg., 160; Hugh,
40; James, 40; John, 40, 41;
Margaret C., 41; Sarah Catherine,
41; Thaddeus C., 41; William E.,
41
BLAKE: Alma, 24
BLANEY: Betty, 43; Charles Archer,
43; Clarence, 204; Edith Louise,
43; Edith Zachary, 43; Emanuel,
43; Emma, 42; George David, 42;
George W., 42, 43, 207; James,
Mrs., 204; John W., 43; Josias,
42; Julia, 42; Lester C., 42, 43;
Lizzie, 43; Mary, 42; Samuel G.,
43; Stillie W., 43; Susan Jane, 43;
William, 204; William J., 42;
William T., 42
BLEANY: Ann, 42; James W., 42;
Josias, 42; Melissa, 42; Sarah, 42;
Thomas S., 42; William, 42;
William J., 42
BLUMER: Charles E., 117

BOESCHEL: Maurice Julius, 89
BOND: Anna, 228; George, 239;
Jemima, 239; William
Summerfield, 105
BONN: Mary Elizabeth, 190
BOON: William M., 101
BOONE: Clara Dew, 102; Emma,
102, 103; Harriet A., 102; Harriet
Ann, 103; Mabury G., 102; Mary
Ella Shreeves, 102; Walter E.,
Mrs., 172; William Joseph, 102;
William M., 102, 103
BORASTON: George, 49
BORDER: Howard L. A., 31
BORING: Clarra, 44; Corra B., 44;
Edward E., 44; Emma V., 44;
Ephraim, 44; Ephraim A., 44;
Howard, 44; Isaac, 44; Mary, 44;
Mary V., 44; Minia, 44; Minnie,
44
BORNING: Corra P., 44
BOSLEY: Geraldine, 176; Gertrude
Hutchins, 140; John Cole, 139;
Laura May, 139; Milton, 176;
Velma, 176
BOSS: Samuel T., 84
BOTELER: Ellen W., 57; Ellen
Williams, 57; Emma T., 56;
Emma Theresa, 56; Joseph I., 57;
Joseph Isaac, 56
BOTTS: Albert Nelson, 46, 47; Annie
Adelle, 46; Bertha Wheeler, 46,
47; Daisy, 45; Daisy L., 45;
David O., 45; Edgar G., 47; Edgar
Grady, 46; George F., 45; George
Thomas, 46; Irvin C., 45; Isaac
H., 45, 46, 47; Isaac T., 45, 46;
Isaac Thomas, 46, 47; John E.,
45; Joseph G., 45; L. Ellen, 47;
Lovenia, 46; Mary E., 45; Mary
Valeria, 46; Sarah, 46; Susan R.,
45; Theda Mae, 46; William H.,
45

BOWEN: Belinda, 232; Catherine Anne, 88; Clara M., 102; Delila, 88; Delily (Ellender), 88; Eliza Ann, 88; Frederick E., Sr., 88; Harriet R., 102, 103; J. Raymond, 102, 103; Mary E., 222; Mary Ella, 103; Nancy Ann Lenore, 102
BOWMAN: James H., 243
BOWSER: Jerry, 214
BOYD: David, 208; Margaret, 207; Margaret A., 208
BOYDEN: Beatrice Virginia, 103; Donald Galloway, 103; G. A., 103; George A., 103; George Albert, 101, 102, 103; Harriet V., 103; Harriet Virginia, 103; John Calvin, 103; William, 102
BRADFIELD: Alice, 47; Benjamin, 47; Enos, 47; Louisa, 47; Mary, 47; Rebecca, 47; Sammie C., 48; Samuel, 47; William, 47
BRADLEY: Sarah, 71
BRADY: Gladyce May (Calder), 202; Patricia Hall, 202; Robert, 202, 203; Robert Wilson, Jr., 203
BRAMBLE: Dora K. (Davis), 131; Fannie, 131; Forrest, 131; Hattie G., 131; W. Edward, 131; William E., 131
BRANNON: Effie E., 232
BRASHEARS: Elizabeth, 86; John, 86
BRENNAN: Don A., 114, 191; Donna Leslie, 114
BREVITT: Ann, 50; Cassandra, 50; Elizabeth, 49, 50; James, 50; James Wilkes, 50; John, 49, 50; Joseph, 49, 50; Joseph, Dr., 49; Mary, 49, 50; Sarah, 50; Simon, 50; William, 50
BREWER: Richard A., 35
BREYMAIER: Irene Joan, 249
BRIAN: Charles, 100

BRINEY: Howard, 128; Jacob, 128; Ruth A., 128; William, 128
BROOKS: E. Merriman, 148; Rev. Mr., 150
BROTHERTON: Helen C., 136
BROWN: Allison, 8, 9; Allison A., 9; Ann (Perry), 69, 70; Anne (Perry), 68; B. Peyton, Rev., 20; Emily St. Claire, 52, 53; Esther, 8, 9; George, 8, 9; George I., 7, 8, 9; George William, 7, 8; Jane, 8, 9; John Cumming, 8, 9; Robert D., 8; Robert Davison, 8; Rose, 8, 9; Rose Ann, 8, 9; Sidney B., 8; Sidney Buchanan, 8; Susannah D., 68, 69; William, 68, 69, 70
BRUCE: Frank F., 22; Mary Jane, 23
BRUFF: William H., 16
BRUNE: Clara M., 7
BUCHANAN: Jane, 120; Mary, 7, 8
BUCK: Mary E., 108
BULL: Bennett L., 175; Charity, 175; Mary Eliza, 175
BURKE: L. C., Rev., 142; William, Rev., 214
BURKINS: Catharine, 48; Catheren, 49; Claranda, 48; Edward R., 48, 49; Granville S., 48, 49; Jacob, 48, 49; John A., 48, 49; Mamie, 48, 130; Mary E., 48, 49; Nettie, 48
BURNAP: George W., Rev., 8
BURTON: Edward, 51; Emory A., 51; Mary E., 91
BUTLER: Clement G., 207; Laura E., 204, 207
BUXSTER: Rebecca, 204
CADLE: Ruby Norris, 215
CAIN: James Henry, 190; Ruth La Mar, 190; Victor Baldwin, 190
CAIRNES: George R., 51; James, 51; Mary A., 51; William G., 51
CALDER: Anna Windom, 202; Annie W., 203; Archer E., 203; Charles

Lee, 203; Clara O., 203; Dorothy E., 203; E. Hall, 201, 203; Eleanor Harlan, 202; Elizabeth Hutcheson, 202; Evelyn Nesbitt, 202; George C., 203; Gladys May, 202; Hall, Mrs., 203; John E., 203; Mary H. (Nagle), 202; Mary Madeline, 202; Mary Nagle, 202; Othos S., 203; Ruth MacLean, 202; Thomas Hall, 202
CALLAHAN: Anna, 68; Emma, 68; Martha Ann, 68; Michael M., 68
CALWELL: Mary T. (Amoss), 11
CAMPBELL: Alexander, 41; Annie Louisa, 107; Edward, 41; Jane, 40, 41; William Lerue, 107; William Relau, 107; Willim Relau, 107
CANAPP: Nancy B., 35
CANN: Benjamin, 51; Elizabeth, 51; Lloyd, 50, 51; Michael, 51; Nancy (Wamsley), 51; Nathan, 51; Noah, 51; Ruben, 51
CANNON: Mary, 150
CANON: Mary Ann, 150
CAREINS: George, 51, 52; George Richard, 52; James A., 51; James Andrew, 52; Martha Jean, 52; Mary A., 51, 52; Mary A. (Bay), 52; Rebecca Elizabeth, 52; Robert Quilish, 52; William Glasgow, 52
CARLISLE: David, 69; Urath Cromwell (Owings) (Cockey), 70; Worthington C. Cockey, 70
CARMINE: James L., 20
CARNAN: Agnes, 53; Alice Humphreys, 53, 54; Bishop, 52, 53; Catherine, 52; Charles Walter, 52, 53, 54; Charles Walter, Jr., 52, 53; Christopher Bruce, 53, 54; Florence, 53; Lida Valiant, 54; Margaret, 52; Martha Robinson, 54; Walter, 52

CARRICK: Charles Howard France, 55; Emmie Virginia, 55; Gorman, 55; Grace, 55; Louisa Adinia, 55; Lulu, 55; Lydia Charlotte, 55; Mary Elizabeth, 55; R. Minerva, 55; Ridia Minnerva, 55; William Alford Downs, 55; William Isaac, 54; William J., 54, 55
CARRINGTON: Katherine Morton, 217; Louie Hankins, 217; Mary Poole, 217; William Tucker, 216; William Tucker, Jr., 217
CARROLL: Helen, 145; Jemima, 3; John, 3, 6, 13; Susanna, 6; Susannah, 3, 5
CARSINS: Elizabeth, 22; Mary, 182
CARSTENS: Albert J., 111
CARTER: Caroline, 56, 57; Carrie Emma, 56, 57; Charles Wesley, 56, 57; Dale Sandra, 157; Edward Blair, 157; Edward, Mrs., 157; Emma, 56, 57; Emma T., 56, 57; Emma Theresa, 56; Florence Hellen, 56; Grace Addie, 56; J. W., 56, 57; James Garfield, 56, 57; John Edgar, 56; John Wesley, 56; Lewellyn, 56; Milton Irwin, 56; Nettie Estelle, 56; Peter Turner, 157; William H., 56, 57
CASEY: Sallie, 147
CASSELL: Joseph, 45
CHALMERS: John, Jr., 155
CHAMBERS: Jane, 41; John, 41
CHARITON: Alabama Ann, 57; Alabama Louisa, 57; Charles Lewis, 57; Charles Luis, 57; Elizabeth McDonald, 57; Emily Fisher, 58; Emily Jane, 57; Emley Jean, 58; George, 57; George W., 58; George Washington, 57, 58; James Nathaniel, 57, 58; Luisa Fisher, 57; Mary Ann, 58; Ruhanna L., 58; Sarah A., 57; William Henry, 57

CHARSHEE: Reba, 18
CHENWORTH: Bessie, 122
CHESNEY: Ann, 59, 60; Anne, 59; Annie Mollie, 59; Benjamin, 59; Cordelia A., 58, 59; D. B., 59; Daniel B., 58, 60; Elizabeth G., 60; Elizabeth Guest, 59; Ellen R., 26; Ellen Randolph, 58, 59; H. P., 59; Henrietta P., 59; J. R., 59; James, 58, 59; James R., 58, 59, 60; Jesse, 59; Jesse M., 59; John, 59; Lydia R., 58, 59; Marion R., 60; Marion Rebecca, 59; Mary, 59, 138; Mary E., 58, 59; S. R., 59; Sarah R., 59, 60; Susanne, 59; Thomas, 59; William, 59, 138; William H., 58, 59, 60; William, Sr., 59
CHILDS: Clementine, 60; Clementine Adelade, 60; Emma L., 154; Emma Lavanna, 60, 61; Harry E., 154; Harry Ellsworth, 60; Lemuel Levi, 60, 154; Leona Mary, 154; Lulu M., 154; Lulu Maybel, 60, 61; Maria E., 154; Maria Elizabeth, 60; Summerfield, 60, 61, 154; Susanna, 154
CLARK: Ann, 190; Benjamin J., 16; Catherine A. W., 16; Kate A. W., 15; Mary Jane, 16; Matilda Raybold, 190; Thomas, 190
CLARKE: I. Wray, 212; Veronica Ann, 214
CLAYDON: Sarah Jane, 30
CLAYTON: A. L., 64; Anietta, 62; Augustus Lukens, 63; Daniel, 62; Howard Cooper, 63, 64; James, 62; Joseph, 62, 63, 64; Mary, 62, 63; Mary E., 63, 64; Mary Elizabeth, 62, 63, 64; Priscilla, 63, 64; Rebecca, 62; Sarah, 62, 64; Sarah Ann, 62; Sarah Jane, 30; Wells, 62, 63, 64; Wells Orvis, 63

CLEMM: William, 120
CLINE: Laura J., 3; Mary, 108
CLOMAN: Charlotte Rebecca, 66, 67; Charlotte Rebekah, 65; E., 67, 68; Eliza, 65, 66; Elizabeth, 64; Elizabeth Sarah, 66, 67; Elmer Ellsworth, 65; Elmore Ellsworth, 66, 67; Emanuel Edward, 65, 66, 67; George, 65, 66, 67; George Clifford, 65, 66, 67; George Robert, 65, 66, 67; George W., 64, 65; George Washington, 64; James William, 65, 66, 67; Leah Jane, 65, 66, 67; Liza, 207; Sarah Elizabeth, 65; William, 64
COALE: Joseph Atlee, 212; Lillian N., 212, 213
COCKEY: Annie S., 183; Annie Stansbury, 183; Charles, 68, 69, 70; Charles T., 70; Charles Thomas, 68, 69, 71, 72; Edward A., 68, 69, 70; Edward S., 69; Edward, Col., 68, 69; Elinor, 69; Elinor (Pindall), 68; Emela Jane, 69; Emma, 71; Emma Shepherd, 71; Eva Warfield, 70; Joshua Hutchins, 139; Mary A., 69, 70; Prudence, 69; Prudence (Hill), 68; Sallie Ann Warfield, 71; Sally Anne Warfield, 71; Samuel, 69; Sarah, 69; Stephen D., 69; Susanna D., 72; Susannah D. (Brown), 70; Thomas, 68, 69; Thomas B., 68, 69, 70; Thomas Beal, 71, 72; Thomas Beale, 70, 71; Thomas Beale, Jr., 71; Urath, 68, 69, 70; Urath (Cockey), 70; Urath (Cromwell), 68; Urath Cromwell (Owings), 69; Ureth C., 69
COE: Alverdie, 73; Annie C., 72; Annie Cecelia, 73; George Wilford, 73; H. Elmer, 73; Hannah E., 73; Henry Elmer, 73;

Howard Emery, 73; Howard Emory, 73; Laura V., 73; Lizzie, 73; Moses, 73; Moses P., 73; Moses Parlett, 72; Nora Grace, 73; Stella, 73; Victorine, 73; Walter, 73
COLE: Abraham, 226, 227; Cornelius, 226; Elizabeth, 44; Ezikel, 74; Fannie N., 226; Florence M., 226; Frances Emily, 74; Hannah, 227; Harry E., 226; James A., 74; James Amos, 74; James C., 74; John A. Chapman, 74; John B., 227; Larrow (Laura) Jane, 74; Laura J., 74; Mary A., 74; Mary Ann, 74; Mrs., 207; Priscilla, 227; Sarah, 74; Sarah E., 227; Sarah Kezia, 74; William A., 212; William L., 74; William Lewis, 74
CONN: Elizabeth, 218
CONWAY: Rev., 197
COOK: Frederick C., 230; Louisa, 107
COOLEY: Ambrose, 137; Charles, 76; Charles Marvin, 75; Daniel, 137; H. L., 76; Harriet, 137; Hattie (Lord), 75; Hattie L., 75, 76; Helen E., 75, 76; Helen E. (Jones), 75; Helen Leonore, 75; Jessie M., 152; Jno. M., 75; John M., 75, 76; John Marchborn, 75; John Marvin, 75, 76, 152; Lillian G., 75; Lillian Grace, 76; Lillian Grace (Robey), 75; Margaret Anne, 76; Marvin L., 75; Marvin Lord, 75, 76, 152, 153; Susan Lynne, 76; Verneal, 76; Verneal (Kincaid), 75
COOPER: Hannah, 76; Joshua, 76; Nicholas, 76; Sarah, 76
CORD: Thomas, 126, 127
CORNETT: Louisa Orlean, 220
COSNER: Rhoda, 172

COSTEN: Rosanna, 251
COURTNEY: Adaline, 186; Avarilla Ann, 186; Cornelia F., 185, 187; Cyrus, 185, 186; Cyrus Henry, 186; Emily, 186; Frances Cornelia, 186; John Franklin, 186; Mary, 186; Ruthen, 186; Sarah Elizabeth, 80, 186
CRAIG: Bessie, 169; William, 128
CRAM: Clara Lord, 152, 153
CRANE: J. B., Rev., 63; Susanna, 187
CRENSHAW: Pearl E., 215
CRESWELL: Helen M., 152
CREVENSTEN: Addie A., 78; Addie Abercrombie, 77; Clara Elizabeth, 78; Clyde George, 78; Clyde Russell, 78; Emily Isadore, 77, 78; George, 77; George A., 77; George Alexander, 78; George Elliott, 78; Isaac Henry, 77; Isaac Henry Whitfield, 78; J. Henry, 231; Martha, 77, 78; Mary A., 78; Mary Altossa, 77, 78; Mary Florence Reese, 78; Mary Margaret, 77; Robert Greenfield, 77; Robert Greenfield Swan, 78; Sarah J., 77; Sarah Jenness, 78
CROMPTON: Ann, 79; Ann Elizar, 79; Annie E., 79; John G., 79; Stephen John, 80; Stephen John Oliver, 79
CRONIN: Adla Augusta, 80; Benjamin, 80, 81; Benjamin F., 80; C. C., Rev., 187; Cornelius Charles, 186; Cornelius Farnham, 185; Cyrus, 81; Elizabeth, 80, 81; Elizabeth Lyle, 186; Emily C., 81; Fannie B., 81; Fanny Bell, 81; Franklin, 80; J. W., 81; J. W., Rev., 81; John W., 81; John Wesley, 80, 81; Kate, 80; Lydia Hopkins, 129; Maggie R., 81; Margaret Rebecca, 81; Mary Ellen, 81; Mayfield Leslie, 186;

Meredith, 186; Sarah A., 81;
   Sarah Wesley, 81; Wendell Lee,
   186; William Hays, 81
CROSS: John, 152
CUMMINS: Annie, 93
DAME: W. M., Rev., 183
DANBY: Harriett, 163, 164
DAUGHERTY: Sarah Jane, 102
DAVEY: Hugh, 163; Hugh, Capt.,
   163
DAVIS: Alfonzo, 79, 80; Annie, 80;
   Annie E., 79, 80; Catherine, 32;
   Cathrine, 234; Ella, 82; Ella M.,
   82; Ella Marian (Spicer), 82;
   Emma, 32; Frank, 82; Frank
   Rudisill, 82; Hannah Elizabeth,
   226; Harry Russell, 79, 80;
   Hester, 79; Hettie, 79, 80; Hilda
   Herndon, 79; Hope Lillian, 235;
   J. Willard, 82; James S., 82;
   James Willard, 82; Jeff D., 131;
   Jennie T., 80; Jennie Theoba, 79;
   Jesse W., 79, 80; John Harvey,
   79, 80; Lena Leona, 79; Mary E.,
   79, 80; Mary Isabel, 220; Meta
   May, 79, 80; Oneda, 234; Oneda
   L., 232, 234; Onidia, 32; Sarah,
   82; Sarah M., 131; Sarah Sybella,
   82; Thomas, 32, 234; Thomas
   Smithson, 82; Walter Hicks, 82;
   Wilton Howard, 79
DAWSON: John Bernard, 169; John
   H., 223, 224
DAY: Grafton B., 150
DEALE: Arrianna W., 18; William
   G., 18
DECKER: Mary E., 103
DEETS: Frederick L., 141
DeJOY: Daisy M., 242
DeMOSS: Amanda F., 176
DETTUS: John, 53; Margaret, 53
DEVOE: Annie E., 104
DEVRIES: B. F., Rev., 192
DIFFENDERFER: George M., 229

DIFFENDERFFER: Ann, 227; Ann
   Olivia, 227; Charles, 227, 228,
   229; George, 228, 229; Jacob,
   229
DILL: Alexander C., 83; Camilla W.,
   83; Emily H., 83; Frank Eugene,
   83; Jane, 83; Laura H., 83;
   Malcolm, 83; Matthew H., 83;
   William R., 83
DIVERS: Lidie R., 119
DOBBIN: Mary D., 8
DORSEY: Cassander, 84; Elizabeth,
   84; Henrietta, 228; Joshua, 84;
   Mary Ann, 84; Nicholas, 84
DOSH: Ann Elizabeth, 86; Anna E.,
   85, 86; Anna Elizabeth, 85;
   Charles Frederick, 85, 86; Cora
   E., 85, 86; Edgar, 85; George G.,
   85, 86; George Goodlow, 85, 86;
   George Philip, 85, 86; Grant, 85,
   86; Harry Kronenberg, 85, 86;
   Infant, 85; John M., 86; John M.,
   Sr., 86; John Michael, 86;
   Margarett H., 86; Mary Sheaffer,
   85; Rebecca, 86; Rosetta, 86;
   William, 85, 86; William F., 86
DOWNE: Sallie, 12
DRIVER: Jerome Morgan, 235;
   Rebecca Marie, 236
DRUMMOND: Zipporah, 18
DUER: Henrietta D. A., 228; John,
   228
DULANY: Rev., 180
DUNGAN: Abel P., 164; Fanny P.,
   162, 164; Jane, 164
DUNKLE: W. T., Rev., 46
DUTTON: David D., 240; Elizabeth,
   240; Isaac, 240
EARNSHAW: John, 129
EASON: Minnie, 26
ECKELS: J., Rev., 150
EGERTON: John B., 230
EGGLESTON: R. B., Rev. Dr., 212
ELDERDICE: J., Rev., 220

ELLENDER: Charity, 87, 88; Delily (Delila), 87; Eliza, 88; Elizabeth, 87; Elizer (Eliza), 87; Frederick, 87, 88; George, 87; George W., 87; Georgeann(a), 87; Georgeanna, 88; Harriet, 87; July Ann, 87, 88; July Ann (Julia), 87; Mandy E. (Amanda), 87; Mary Ann, 87, 88; Richard, 87; Sarah, 87, 88
ELY: David, 224; David C., 223; Margaret E., 223; Mary Belle, 224
EMMORD: Emilie, 113; George, 113; Harry Oscar, 89; J. Henry, 88; Laura Winifred, 89
ENGEL: Margaret, 123; William, 123
ENGLE: Maggie, 123; Margaret, 123; William, 123
EVANS: Annie Louisa, 106; Battie Blanche, 106; Bessie Alisha, 106; Emma Jane, 107; John, 247; Martha R., 145; Mary, 247, 248
EVERETT: Charles, 203; Florence L., 170; William, 103, 203
EVERIST: Annie, 23; Ava M., 23; Elizabeth, 23, 109; Ellen E., 23; Elmer N., 23; George, 23; George C., 23; George T., 22, 23; Job, 74, 75; Joseph, 109; Kezia, 74; Lily J., 23; Mary, 187; Mary A., 74; Mary Oleita, 23; Thomas C., 75
FARR: Joan Rosemary, 1
FARRER: Eliza, 103
FELTON: C. E., Rev., 163
FERGERSON: Charlotte A., 90; Hellen, 90; John, 90
FERGUSON: Chapin Alexander, 30, 31; Helen M., 91; Henry, 90; Henry J., 90; John, 90, 91; John J., 91; John J., Jr., 91; Louis Albridge, 90; Mary E,, 91; Mary E., 91; Sarah Frances, 31
FIEDLEY: Mildred Grace, 99

FINNEY: Dr., 128; Margaret W., 119; Rev., 209; Sarah, 207; William, Rev., 118
FINNY: William, Rev., 188
FISHEL: Caroline Commer, 237; Frank, 237; George F. E., 238, 239
FITZGERALD: John Michael, 46; John William, 47; Patricia Kathleen, 47
FITZPATRICK: Mary, 238; Nathan, 238; Priscilla, 237
FLETCHER: Elizabeth, 29; Isaac, 58; Mary, 209; Mary E., 60
FOARD: Anna Kate, 47; Bennett S., 47; Carrie V., 47; Charley, 48; Dora E., 47; Ida, 232; Louisa, 47
FOLWELL: Mary Ann, 1
FORD: Albert Malcolm, 47; Blanche Holmes (Murray), 200; Dora E., 232; George, 47; George Michael, 48; James, 48; James F., 150; Malcolm, 47; Martha Louise, 48; Mary, 30; Susannah, 48
FORSYTHE: Ida E., 132; Mary Elizabeth, 77; Samuel, 135
FORWOOD: Amor, 93, 96; Amor S., 94; Elizabeth, 93, 94; Emily B., 96; Eva Grace, 89; George, 93, 94; George W., 96, 97; H. Jennie, 96; Hannah, 92, 93, 94; Hannah J., 97; Hannah Jane, 96; Hannah Jane (Jennie), 96; Harry Maxwell, 92; Helen, 92; Henry, 92; Jacob, 93, 94; James, 192; James G., 96, 97; James W., 92; James W., Sr., 92; James Worthington, 91, 92; Jane Amelia, 93, 94; Jennie, 95; John, 92, 93, 94; John C., 94; John Clark, 93; Julia, 93; Julia A., 97; Julia Ann, 96; Juliann, 92; Lawrence, 95, 96; Lawrence H., 96; Leah, 93, 94; Loammie, 96; Margaret E., 96; Mary, 93, 94;

Mary Isabel, 96, 97; Mary R., 92; Mary Rebecca, 91, 92; Parker, 93; Parker F., 96; Parker Lee, 92; Parker, Dr., 94; Robert, 92, 93, 94, 96, 97; Robert Raymond, 96; Samuel, 93; Samuel W., 96, 97; Sarah, 92, 93, 94, 95, 96, 97; Sarah Margaret, 96; Walter, 96; William, 93, 94, 95, 96, 97

FOSTER: Henry, 58; Rebecca, 168

FOUNDS: Georgianna, 169

FOX: Charles, 164; Charles J., 162, 164, 165; Charles James, 164; Edgar Borrough, 164, 165; Fanny Dungan, 164; H. W., 165; Harriett, 164, 165; Hazel Annabel, 164; Henry W., 164, 165; Henry William, 163, 164; J. Sydney, 164, 165; John, 163, 164, 165; John Morris, 164; John Sydney, 164, 165; Marbury Brewer, 164; Mary Ella, 165; Thomasine, 164; Thomasine M., 165

FRANCE: James, 55

FRANK: Mary Catherine, 214; Ruby Norris (Cadle), 215; Sophia, 93; Walter R., 215; Walter Remington, 214, 215

FRANKE: Bessie Upperco, 250

FRANSON: Edward, 234, 235

FRANZSON: Ann Tinssell, 235; Florence, 235

FRENCH: Alice, 30, 165, 166, 167; Andrew, 165; Catharan, 166; Grace C., 212, 213; Helen W., 212, 213; Helen Winfield, 212; Lillian N., 213; William A., 166, 212, 213

FULFORD: Alexander, 118; Alexander Mitchell, 97; Henry, Jr., 97, 98; Maria, 97, 98; Maria C., 118; Mary, 118; Mary Patterson, 97, 98; William, 97, 98, 118

FULTON: A., 229; Jesse Bruce, 23; Mrs., 229

GALBREATH: Samuel, 192; Samuel W., 193

GALLION: Edgar Baxter, 221; Edith, 221; Edith G., 221; Ethel Irene, 221; Helen Zuiletta, 221; J. B., 128; Jacob G., 220, 221; James H., 243; Jesse LaRoy, 221; Lester Jay, 221; Melvin R., 243; Rebecca Ann, 243; Ross Leon, 221

GALLOWAY: C., 100; Elizabeth T., 99; Ephemia J., 103; Ephemia J. (Eeff Jeremiah), 103; Ephemia Jeremiah, 101; Gouldsmith D., 103; Gouldsmith Day, 101; Harriet, 99, 101, 103; Harriet A., 101, 103; Harriet Ann, 101; Harriet Virginia, 101, 102, 103; Henry Clay, 101; Henry Luther, 102; Isabella, 101; Jemima, 102, 103; John, 101; Martha G., 99, 100; Marthy P., 103; Marthy Presbury, 101; Mary, 99; Mary E., 101, 103; Mary Eliza, 101; Mary Elizabeth, 102; Mary G. D., 99; Moses G., 101, 103; Moses George, 101; Mosses G., 99; ---n C., 99; R. C., 99; Robert C., 99, 100, 101, 103; Thomas B., 99, 100; William A., 101, 102, 103; William Andrew, 101; William George, 102

GALLUP: Ann Elizabeth, 104; Annie Elizabeth, 104; Annie V., 105; Carline Preston, 104; Catharine Martin, 105; Catherine, 104, 105; Catherine Maria, 104; Charles T., 105; Charles Thomas, 104; Daniel, 104, 105; Emily Williams, 104; George W., 104,

105; George Washington, 104; John, 105; John O., 105; John Oliver, 104; Margarett Ann, 104; Marry Louisa, 104; Mary L., 105; Oliver, 104, 105; Oliver Stevens, 105; Permelia, 104; William H., 105; William henry, 104
GARDNER: Mary Ann, 57
GARRET: Edith, 67
GARRETTSON: Aquila, 110; MacDonald, 45, 46; Mary, 110
GARRISON: Alfred, 140; Mary A. Hutchins, 140
GAWTHROP: Alfred, 131
GEIST: Mildred JoAnn, 3
GERLACH: Elizabeth Spicer, 82
GERMAN: Florence, 107; Thomas, 106; Thomas C., 107
GETTIER: E. L., Rev., 202
GETTMAN: John, 240
GILBERT: Abner, 210; Amos, 182; Bennett, 182; Elizabeth, 209, 210; Ellen, 182; Estelle Michael, 186; George, 181, 182; harry Adolphus, 185; Marjorie Estelle, 185; Martha S., 182; Martha Susan, 182; Martin L., 22; Roger Michael, 185; Sarah, 26; Sarah Frances, 23; W., 181; William H., 181
GILDER: Mary Ashbury, 155; Rubin, 155
GILLESPIE: Elizabeth Ann, 107; Emma Jane, 106; Florence, 106; Hatty Brown, 106; Jonathan, 107; Louisa, 106; Mary Ann, 107; Mary E., 106; Mary Elizabeth, 106; Thomas, 106; William A., 106; William Andrew, 106, 107; William James, 106
GILMORE: Louisa Airey, 7
GISRIEL: E. C., Rev., 193
GLENDY: Dr., 8; John, Rev., 120
GODWIN: Mary, 147

GORRELL: Angie V., 132, 133; Cora D., 226; Cordelia A., 60; E. A., Mrs., 128; James Lee, 132; James O., 132, 133; James Oliver, 132; James S., 58; Rose Lyle, 132, 133; S. W., 148; Sarah A., 132
GOUGH: Harry D., 182
GRAFTON: Elizabeth, 115
GRAHAM: Cassander, 87; John, 87
GRAPE: Ann M., 108; Ann Maria, 108; Harry Allen, 108; Harry Winter, 108; Henry Evans, 108; John, 108; John W., 108; John William, 108; Joseph, 108; Laura Janet, 108; Mary Elizabeth, 108; Samuel, 108; Thomas E., 108; Thomas Edward, 108
GREEN: Eliza, 163; John, 163, 202; Marie, 163; Sophia, 231
GREENFIELD: Elizabeth, 109, 110; Henry Austin, 109; Jacob, 109; Joseph, 109; Martha, 77, 109, 110; Mary, 109; Micajah, 109, 110
GREENLAND: Mary B., 22
GREENWOOD: W., 8
GRENINGER: Esther Havilla, 110; Esther Haville, 111; Fannie May, 111; H. N., Rev., 110, 111, 112; Henry Leslie, 110, 111; Henry Noah, 111, 112; John Henry, 110, 111, 112; Leslie, 111; Nellie Catherine, 111; Ruth Caroline, 111; Susanna Graham, 111
GRESSITT: Mary Ella, 163, 164
GRIER: Elwood, 63; Elwood Thomas, 62; Ethel, 63; Fred N., 192; George Archer, 63; George E., 192; Glascow J., 192; Harry M., 192; Herbert S., 192; Jane Thomas, 63; John Walker, 63; Mary Alice, 63; Sarah J., 192; Stanley, 192; William C., 192
GRIFFIN: Cassandra, 112

GROSS: Benton, 192; George, 123; Margaret, 122; Samuel, Mrs., 203
GRYMES: Rebecca Riggs, 235
GUEST: Elizabeth A., 124; George, 125; John E., 125; John W., 124, 125; Lizzie Alexandra, 125; Mary, 125; Mary M., 125
GUNNELL: Elizabeth, 211
GUTHRIE: Susan, 120
GUTTERMUTH: Lena, 145
GWINN: Hugh, 128; Sarah M., 128; William, 128; William R., Rev., 128
HACKNEY: Elizabeth, 165, 166
HAGEY: J. C., Rev., 155; J., Rev., 219
HAHN: Ann E., 230
HAINES: Samuel, 177
HAINS: Daniel, 177
HALLING: Helene, 71
HAMBLETON: Lydia, 17; Rowena, 16; Rowena R., 17; William, 17
HANKINS: Florence Poole, 216; Louie, 215, 218; Mary, 218; Mary D. P., 218; Mary Douglas, 216, 217; Richard P., Jr., 217; Richard Poole, 216
HANNA: Annie May, 112; Carrie G., 129; Cassandra, 112, 128; George T., 112; J. Howard, 112; John R., 112; Lydia Cassandra, 112; Olivia Jane, 112; Robert, 128; Robert F., 247, 248; Robert N., 112; Stephen B., 112; William, 133; William H., 131
HANNA George T., 126, 129
HANSON: Ada Louise, 113; Amelie Sophia, 113; Emelia, 113; Emmord, 113; Herman, 113, 114; Herman William, 113; Mary Irene, 113; Naomi, 113; Ruth, 113; Sophia, 113; Thomas, 113; Thomas Earl, 113
HANWAY: C. Clifford, 119; Harry D., 119, 120; Harry D., Jr., 119, 120; Harry David, 119; Hazel, 120; Hazel E., 119, 120; Hazel W., 120; Lida, 119; Lida R., 120; Lida R., Jr., 120; Lidie R., 119; Lillian, 119; Lillian B., 119; Margaret W., 119; Sarah Grace, 119
HARKINS: Ann E., 148; Aubrey, 193; Beatrice, 114, 191; Calvin, 193; Charles Littleton, 115; Edwin Wilson, 115; Harry E., 114, 191, 192; Henry Edgar, 114, 115; J. Benjamin, 192; Jessie L., 115; John, 192; John H., 116; Joseph A., 115, 116; Joseph R., 193; Joseph Robinson, 115; Joseph, Capt., 192; Lorena S., 116; Lourenna, 115; Marguerite E., 191, 192; Marguerite Eileen, 114; Marguerite Elleine, 191; Marguerite Elline, 114; Maurice, 193; Maurice Stevenson, 115; Mrs., 192; Sallie M., 114, 192; Thomas, 193; Thomas Livingston, 115; Wilson, 193
HARLAN: Edwin, 120; Edwin H. W., 119, 120; Edwin H. W., Jr., 119; Margaret H., 119, 120
HARP: Emily L., 199; Mittie Pamelia, 200
HARPER: Ann, 16; J. C., 18; John C., 16
Harriet CLEMM: Harriet, 120
HARVEY: Florence B. Price, 132
HARWARD: Barbara, 19; James, 192
HASKELL: Rev., 243
HASTINGS: Charles Henry, Mrs., 158; Elizabeth J., 117; Elizabeth Jane, 117; Eurith C., 117; Frances B., 117; John D., 116, 117; John T., 117; John T. H., 117; Mabel

Linda, 158; Mary Elizabeth, 158; Rev., 158; Thelma Louisa, 158
HAWKINS: Edward, 140; Frances, 58; John, 139, 140; Mary Jane, 139, 140; Mary Susan, 140; Thomas, 140; Winifred, 149
HAYES: Frances Marian, 24
HAYMAN: Florence Aliean, 226; Frances Mary, 226, 227; W. Russell, 226; Warren Benson, 226; Warren Russell, 226
HAYS: Archer, 118; Archer, Dr., 118; Hannah, 118; Mary, 118; Mary L., 118; Mary Lorman, 118; Nathaniel, 118; Nathaniel W. S., 98, 118; William, 81, 118
HEARD: John P., Mrs., 157
HEINRICH: Elizabeth Dudley, 217; Mary Douglas, 217; T. O., 216
HELFENSTEIN: Samuel, Rev., 120
HELFRICH: Bruce H., 71; Bruce Hook, 72; Emma Shepherd Cockey, 72; Mary Thomas Warfield, 71; Robert Bruce, 71; Samuel Dalton, 71; Thomas Cockey, 71
HENSHAW: Bessie A., 37
HERFEL: Anthony Michel, 201; George Daniel, 201; Henry Adam, 201; Rusaltha Anna, 201
HERMAN: John, 129; Mary, 129; Samuel, 129
HERRING: Caroline Lowry, 121; Clifford, 121; Eliza, 121; Elizabeth, 120, 121; Elizabeth Rebecca, 121; Emily Virginia, 121; George, 120; George Augustus, 121; H., 120; Henrietta, 121; Henry, 120, 121; Howard McKenzie, 121; Lewis David, 121; Louis David, 121; Louisa, 121; Louisa Lowry, 121; Ludwig, 120; Macolm Lowry, 121; Mary Esther, 121; Mildred Tutts, 121; Rebecca, 121; Sophia DeHaven, 121
HESS: Annie, 123; Benjamin G., 122; Bertha Elnora, 122; Carrie L., 122; Charles B., 122; Clara Irene, 122; George, 122, 123; Henry, 122; Jacob, 123; Jacob H., 206; James Bunyan, 122; John Edward, 122; Lillie A., 123; Mamie, 122; Margaret, 122; Margaret Heneretta, 207; Selda E., 122
HESTON: Mary Ann, 69
HETRICK: Adam, 124; Ann S., 126; Catherine W., 124; Clara, 124; Janie E., 124; Mary Virginia Walker, 124; Theodore, 128; Theodore Jacob, 124; Theordore J., 123
HIGGINS: Albert Sherman, 125; Elizabeth, 125; James, 125; James A., 124; James Albert, 125; Ormond Graham, 125; Robert Elwood, 125
HIGINBOTHAM: Ralph, 230; Sophia W., 230
HILDT: Rev., 180
HINDES: Ann Maria, 108
HOFMAN: Anna Elizabeth, 85; George P., 86
HOHBEIN: Lee B., 35
HOLLAND: --hn, 39; John, 37, 38; Oletia, 38, 39; R. Virginia, 38, 39; Virginia Bissell, 40
HOLLIS: Ella, 152, 153; Susannah, 180
HOLLOWAY: James Anthony, 54; Margarett A., 105; Perme Ann, 104
HOLLWAY: Valerie Leigh, 54
HOLMAN: Anna Elizabeth Shertzer, 245
HOOD: Clara M. Bowen, 104; Eleanor M., 102

HOOPMAN: Carrie G., 126; John N., 126, 128; John Newton, 126; Margaret P., 127
HOOTEN: Susan, 69; William, 69
HOOVER: Viola Shertzer, 246; Walter F., Jr., 246
HOPKINS: Alan L., 153; Allen, 192; Angelina Virginia, 132; Angie V., 132; Ann, 138; Ann Jane, 132; Annie McCausland, 130; Annie S., 124; Austin, 129; Bennett, 131; Bessie A., 132; Caroline, 126; Caroline C., 127; Caroline G., 126, 127; Carroll C., 152; Charlotte M., 126, 127; Charlotter, 126; Edward, 131; Edwin, 152; Eliza, 126; Ella S., 127; Ellen, 132, 133; Ephraim, Dr., 131; Ethel C., 129; Etta, 126, 128; Flordia, 132; Florence B., 132; Fred, 128; George W., 125, 126, 127; Hannah E., 127; Hannah Eliza, 126, 127; Helen Marr, 152; Henry, 138; J., 131; J. F., 152; John E., 126, 127, 128; John H., 138; Joseph, 133; Joseph R., 130; Joseph Reese, 130, 132; Julian, 150; Laetta, 132; Leetta (Miller), 130; Lloyd, 132; Louisa J., 126; Louisa S., 126, 127; Luranna E., 127; Lureanna E., 126, 128; Mamie, 130; Margaret P., 126, 127; Maria, 130; Mary, 127; Mary E., 138; Mary Jane Howlett, 161; Mary McCausland, 130; Mary R., 127, 129; Mary Rebecca, 126; Murray J., 130; Murray Lindley, 130; Roland, 152; Rose, 133; Rose E., 131; Rose Ellen, 132; S. Gover, 129; Samuel, 126; Samuel G., 126, 127; Samuel Parker, 127; Samuel Roland, Col., 153; Samuel W., 152; Sarah A., 127; Sarah Ann, 126, 127, 129; Sophia, 125, 127, 128, 129; Sophia E., 127; Sophia H., 126; Sophia Spencer, 127; T. Kenton, 132; William, 131, 132, 133; William Edward, 126, 127; William J., 132; William Joseph, 132
HORN: Margaret, 123; William, 123
HORST: Christian, 144; Elizabeth, 144; May, 141, 142, 144
HOWE: Elizabeth, 205, 207
HOWLET: Hannah, 135
HOWLETT: Ambrose, 134, 135; Annie, 32, 33; Benjamin Franklin, 134, 135; Catherine, 134, 135; Eliza, 134, 135; Eliza Ann, 134; Elizabeth Taney, 135; Ezekiel, 134; Fannie, 134, 135; Frances Maria, 134, 135; George H., 32; Harry M., 134; James, 134, 135; John, 134, 135, 161; John R., 135; Martha, 134; Martha Caroline, 134; Mary, 134; Matthew, 133, 134, 135; Nancy, 134; Richard, 32, 33; Richard T., 134; Richard Thomas, 134; William, 133, 134, 135
HRUBESH: Charles, 202, 203; Daniel Alan, 203; Daniel Allen, 202; David Charles, 202; Richard Calder, 202; Ruth MacLean (Calder), 202; Sandra Lee, 202
HUBBARD: E. L., Dr., 131
HUDSON: Walter Emory, 142
HUFF: Casander, 136; Casander D., 136; Casander D. (Pyle), 136; Cassie D., 136; Della, 136; Edna, 136; Elizabeth, 136; Ellsworth, 136; Ethel May, 136; Grace E., 136; J. M., 136; John M., 136; John S., 136; Lester, 136, 149; Mabel M., 136
HUGG: Betsy, 163, 164; Eliza, 163; Elizabeth, 163, 164; Elizah, 163;

Ella, 163; Jacob, 163, 164; Jacob H., 163; Jacob Washington, 163; John, 163; Joseph, 163; Maria, 164; Nancy, 163; Sinclare, 164; Sinclare Lancaster, 163, 164; William, 163
HUGHES: A. Hollis, 25; Amanda Melvina Fritzelen, 106; Amos, 137; Amos H., 137; Amos Hollis, 24, 25, 138; Ann, 137; Ann R., 174; Caroline A., 137; Charlott, 137, 138; Charlott C., 137; Clemency, 137, 138; Donald, 25; Elisha Harrison, 106; Elizabeth, 107; Elizabeth Ann, 106; Estelle, 24; Frances Ann, 106; Francis H., 25; Frank Lee, 24, 26; George, 137; George VanBibber, 25; Hannah, 137; Hannah E., 24, 26; Hannah Elizabeth, 23; Harry Edmund, 25; Henry, 107; Jesse B., 25; Jesse Bruce, 25; Jessie Fulton, 25, 26; Jo Ann, 25; John, 137, 138; John Adam, 26; John Adams, 24; John Haul, 137, 138; Joseph Lee, 24, 25; Kate Silver, 24, 25; Kent, 137, 138; Maggie, 107; Martha Ann, 106; Mary, 137; Mary C., 138; Morgan M., 25; Morgan Mitchell, 23, 25; Odessa, 25, 26; R. Leslie, 24; Robert Fulton, 24, 25; Robert Leslie, 24, 25; Rosella Jessie, 25; Sandra Sue, 25; Sarah, 137; Sophia Jane, 106; Susanna E., 138; William Henry, 106; William O., 24; William Oliver, 24, 25, 26; William Oliver, Jr., 24, 25, 26
HULSE: Isabella, 101
HUNTER: Ellen Belle, 24
HUSTED: I. Mapier, Rev., 30
HUTCHESON: Elizabeth R., 201; Fannie Walton, 42; Lizzie R., 201
HUTCHINS: Alverda, 139, 140; Amanda Zana, 139; Annie R., 139; Annie Rebecca, 139, 140; C. Lee, Sr., 140; Charles Lee, 139, 140; Charles Quinby, 140; Estelle, 139; Gertrude, 139; John, 140; John S., 139, 140; John Slade, 139, 140; Laura, 139, 140; Martha J., 139; Martha Jane, 139, 140; Mary, 140; Mary J. Hawkins, 140; Mary Jane, 139; Mary Jane Hawkins, 140; Mary R., 139, 140; Mary Susan, 139; Maude, 139; Nicholas, 139; William, 139, 140; William B., 140; William Beauregard, 139, 140; William Herbert, 139
HUTCHINSON: Elizabeth, 207
HUTSON: Anna D., 141; Anna Deborah, 141, 143; Anna Mary, 141; Bertrand Sherman, 144; Catharine, 141, 143, 144, 225; Catherine, 144; Deborah, 144; Edward, 143, 144; Elis Rachael Elizabeth, 142; Eliza, 142, 143; Ellen, 142, 143; Emory, 141; Frances D., 143, 144; Helen C., 142; James D., 142, 144; James H., 144; James Henry, 143; James Thomas, 141, 142, 144; Joseph, 144; Joseph Emory, 141, 142, 143, 144; Kate Elizabeth, 141; Katherine Elizabeth, 141, 142, 143; Mary, 141, 142, 143, 144; Mary Melvina, 142; Mary Melviney, 143; Michael, 142, 143, 144; Rachael Elizabeth, 143; S. T., 142; Samuel, 141, 143, 144; Samuel T., 141, 144; Samuel Thomas, 142, 143, 144; Sarah A., 144; Sarah Ann, 143, 144; Sophia, 142, 143; Walter, 144; Walter Emory, 141, 143, 144

HUTTON: Emily L., 83; Emily Lathrop, 83; Jesse M., 83; Rebecca L., 83
HYLTON: Dawn Virginia, 3, 4; Hyacinth, 4; Mildred, 4; Ray, 4; Ray Clinton, 3; Ronald, 4; Ronald Dion, 4; Ronald Ray, 3, 4; William Ernest, 4
IMORDE: Lucy, 89
INGLE: Julian E., 201; Julian, Rev., 201
INGLIS: Dr., 8; Rev., 8
IRWIN: Ava E., 186, 187; Becky Ava, 186; Charles Wright, 185; Edith Chester, 185; Elizabeth Lee, 185; Frank M., 185; John Lee, 185; Kelly Charles, 186; Keven Lee, 186; Oliver Perry, 185, 186
ISENOCK: Luara V., 73; Victorine, 73
JACK: Talitha A., 6
JACKSON: Eleanor Jane, 169, 170; W. F., Rev., 8
JAMES: Ellen Jane, 178; Harriet, 178; John, 178; John M., 177; Marietta E., 177; Mary E., 178; Sarah S., 178; William Shewell, 178
JAMISON: Edna Dickey, 1
JARRELL: Ada Lou, 169; Eleanora Leithiser, 169; Joseph, 169
JARVIS: Amos, 138
JEFFERS: Anna, 146; Anne, 147; Annie, 147; Arthur, 146, 147; Bassel, 145, 146, 147; Benjamin, 145, 146, 147; Bertha Elizabeth, 146, 147; Blanche Irene, 146; Clifton, 146, 147; Elwood C., 146; Florence Lillian, 146; George, 145, 146, 147; George Linwood, 146; Grace, 146, 147; Grace Carroll, 146; Henrietta, 145, 146; Howard, 147; James, 145, 146, 147; Johanathan, 146; John Calvin, 145, 146, 147; Joseph, 145, 146, 147; Joseph Lee, 146, 147; Laura, 146, 147; Lena, 146, 147; Lena Marie, 146; Margaret Ann, 146; Marian Lee, 147; Martha, 146, 147; Mary, 146; Mary A., 146, 147; Mary Elizabeth, 145; Mary Helen, 146; Norman, 146, 147; Rebecca, 146; Sally, 147; Sarah, 146; Sarah A., 147; Sarah Jane, 146; Sarah May, 146; Sarah Rebecca, 146; Sarah Wiley, 147; William, 146; William H., 148; William Joseph, 146, 147; William L., 145, 146, 147; William W., 145, 147; William Wesley, 146
JENKINS: Carol Sue, 222; Margaret Hanson (Pyle), 222; Marilyn, 222
JEWELL: Mary E., 103
JOHNSON: Alice E., 193; Ann E., 149; Ann Eliza, 148, 149; Ann M., 150; C. Ellsworth, 149; Carl Ellsworth, 149; Charlotte, 151; Chester C., 122, 148; Cornelia, 151; Ela May, 148; Elisha, 148, 149; Elizabeth, 94; Elizabeth Odessa, 24; Elmer, 148; Emory, 149; Emory E., 148, 149; Emory Ellsworth, 149; Emory Elsworth, 148; F. Heisse, 149; Florence R., 148; Fred Heisse, 149; Frisby, 151; George J., 150, 151; George Monroe, 151; J. Raymond, 149; James, 151; James W., 150; John, 151; John Raymond, 149; Laura B., 150, 151; Lydia, 151; Mabel M., 149; Mabel May, 149; Mable M., 136; Marian, 151; Marion, 150; Melvin P., 149; Sarah E., 150; Susan R., 51; Susie E., 149
JOHNSTON: Ann Eliza, 151; Ann Matilda, 151; Charlotte, 151; Eliza, 151; George Jackson, 151;

James William, 151; John, 150, 151; John Henry, 151; Mary Ann, 151; Miranda, 151; Sarah Elizabeth, 151; Thomas Frisby, 151
JONES: Alice, 167; Amy Drucilla M., 191; Ann Seymour, 152; Braddock, 152; Cordalia M., 168; Dorothy Ann, 143; Elizabeth, 57; Esther A., 152; Esther Ann, 152; Harold Amos, 152; Harry, 143; harry Edwin, 141, 142; Helen Esther, 75, 152; Helen M., 152; Helen Marr, 152; Isabelar, 167; J. Amos, 152; John Amos, 152; John F., 152; John Fletcher, 152; Katherine E., 143; Lovenia Ellen, 46; Lucinda M., 152; Lucy M., 152; Lydia, 30; Lydia E., 30; Mary M., 153; Mary V., 167; Precilla, 211; Wiliam D., 191, 192
JONSON: Emery E., 223
KANE: Rebecca, 64
KAPLAN: Paul Martin, 3
KEBAUGH: Ann D., 2; Ann J., 1; Brendan, 2; Edwin B., 2; Michael Burton, 2
KECK: Clementine, 153; Clementine Addie Lay, 154; Clementine Adelade, 61; John, 153; John A., 60, 153; John Alfred, 60, 61, 153; Lulu Lavanna, 60, 61, 153, 154; Ruth Elizabeth, 60, 61, 153; Walter Winfield, 60, 61, 110, 111, 153, 154
KEEN: Annie L., 124; William J., 124
KEIFFER: W. L., Rev., 131
KEITH: Isaac S., Rev., 7
KELBAUGH: Edwin Burton, Jr., 1
KELLER: B. F., Rev., 110; Fannie E., 110
KELLY: Helen, 19; Jacquelin, 185; John Luke, 19; Mary Lee, 19; P. K., 19; Peter Kendrick, 19; Sarah, 225
KEMP: Bishop, 121
KENNEDY: Marcy, 120; William, 161
KENNELLY: M. A., Rev., 110, 111
KENT: Ann, 155; Emanuel, 155
KIDD: Jewell C., 157; John, 247, 248; Mary, 248
KIEFFER: W. T. L., 133
KILGORE: William, 46
KILIAN: Eleanor Harlan (Calder), 202; Frank, 203; Frank J., 202; Frank John, 202; Jane Harlan, 202
KILTY: William, 155
KIMBLE: A. W., 155; Alfred, 156; Alfred W., 155, 156; Ann, 156; Cynthia Lou, 158; Diana Lynn, 157; Donna Lee, 157; George A., 155, 156; George Finney, 155, 156; George Finnie, III, 157; George Finnie, Jr., 157; Harriet, 155, 156; Harriet Semelia, 155; Harry Kirk, 156; Hattie Semelia, 156; Jennie Sue, 158; Katherine Elizabeth, 157; Lillian Pearl, 155, 156; Mary Frances, 155, 156; Patrick Mary, 158; Phebe, 156; Phebe E., 155, 156; Phebe Evaline, 157; Phebe Loflin, 156; Phoebe Loflin, 155; Robert E., 156; Robert Sheldon, 158; Robert Sheldon, Jr., 158; Samuel A., 156; Samuel Alfred, 155, 156; Virginia Martin, 157; William D., 156
KIMMELL: Edith C., 18
KINCAID: Verneal, 75
KING: Abraham, 11, 13, 159; Abram, 159; Catherine, 159; David, 158, 159; David, Dr., 11; Elisa, 158; Elizabeth, 11, 13, 158, 159; Elizabeth Ann, 10, 158; George, 11, 13, 158, 159; Jane, 11, 159;

John, 158, 159; John C., Hon., 159; Joshua, 159; Mary Elisa, 158; Rebecca A., 158; Rufus, 159; William, 11, 159
KINGHORN: Mary E., 99
KINSLOWE: Katherine, 10
KIRBY: M. M., 125
KIRK: Harry, 156, 157; John, 157; Sarah M., 157
KIRWAN: Charles R., 189; Etta Virginia, 189; Lida Michael, 189
KITTRIDGE: Lola, 35
KLAIR: Ann D., 160; Biard M., 160; Hiram, 160; Howard O., 160; Jesse B., 160; Kenton D., 160; Lewis H., 160; Magie A., 160; Pearson D., 160; Pierson, 160; Pierson D., 160; Vesta, 160
KLUG: Mamie E., 99
KNAUFF: Bruce R., 100; Charles A., 99; Charles Albert, 99; Edna (Klug), 100; Edward E., 99, 100; Edward R., 99, 100; Edward Roston, 100; Elizabeth Deborah, 99, 100; Ella F., 99; Glen Galloway, 100; Helene G., 100; Howard E., 100; Laura V., 101; Laura Virginia, 100; Mamie E., 100; Mary, 99; Mary E., 100; Milton M., 100; Milton W., 99; Robert E., 100; William, 99, 100; William G., 99, 100
KNIGHT: Anne Hughes, 138; G. Leon, 161; George A. B., 161; George Leon, 161; Gover H., 138; James A., 138; James Harry, 161; Jane, 161; Jane Ann, 161; Jeanette M., 161; John, 161; John W., 161; Lola Estelle, 161; Maggie, 161; Mary A., 161; Mary Ann, 135; Mary Eleanor (Nora), 161; Robert H. L., 161; Sarah Ann, 138; Sharlott F., 138;
Thomas A., 138; William, 135, 161; William T., 161
KNOFF: Robert E., 99
KNUAFF: Laura Virginia, 99
KREISEL: Linda, 35
KREPP: Martin W., III, 36; Martin, W., Jr., 35; Patricia Lynn, 36
KUHNS: Florence Maria, 174; Grace Edith, 174, 175; Harvey Eugene, 174; Jane Mary, 173, 175; Jennie M., 174, 175; Joh Theodore, 174, 175; Lillian Gertrude, 174; Milton Lobaugh, 174; Philip U., 174, 175; Philip Uhler, 174, 175
KURTZ: Elizabeth, 235; Oneda Elizabeth, 235; Philip, 234, 235; Ralph, 122
LAGAN: Catharine Elizabeth, 162; John, 162; John Ralph, 162; John S., 162; John Steven, 162; Margaret Mary, 162; Mary, 162; Sarah A., 162; Sarah A. (Terry), 162; Sarah Ann, 162
LaMASON: Anna Elizabeth, 86; Charles Albert, 85; Clifford, Mrs., 85
LAMDIN: Abe Dungan, 164; Amanda Susannah, 164; Ann Marie, 163; Elizabeth Jane, 163; Elizabeth Virginia, 164; Fannie P., 164; Fanny, 164; John Hugg, 163; Nancy, 163; Nicholas, 163; Nicholas Martin, 163; Robert, 164; Robert P., 162, 163, 164; Robert Philip, 164; Thomas Jacob, 163; Thomasine M., 162; Thomasine Morris, 164
LANCASTER: Borneman, 163; Elizabeth, 163; Mary E., 117; Sinclare, 163
LANE: J. H., Rev., 132
LANTZ: Alfred L., 89; Bertha C., 89; Charles H., 89; Edna A., 89; Emma C., 89; George Lewis, 89;

John George, 89; Laura E., 88; Lucy, 113; M. M. E., 89; Mary (Mollie) C., 89
LAUGHLIN: Sarah Ann, 88
LAWDER: Murray V., 31
LAY: Clementine Addie, 153
LEAVERTON: Henrietta Jeffers Shaw, 147
LEE: Amanda Mehynie, 166; Barbara, 12; Benedict, 165, 166; Catharine, 166; Catherine, 168; David, 11, 12, 13; Edmond, 166, 167; Elizabeth, 166; Enoch, 167; Enoch George, 166; George, 166; Harry, 90, 91, 119, 120, 155; Harry H., 156; Hezekiah, 166; John Thomas, 166; Joseph, 24, 25, 146, 147, 166; Lillian Pearl, 156; Martha, 135, 166; Mary, 19, 166, 247; Mary R., 12, 13; Mary R. (Amoss), 12; Miss, 12; Oliver, 12; Otho S., Col., 12; R. Charles, 13; Ralph Charles, 12; Rebecca, 11, 12, 165, 166; Richard D., Dr., 12; Wade, 128; William, 166
LEEP: Deena, 214
LEITHISER: Ada Louise, 169; Annie W., 168; Bayard, 168; Catharine, 168; Charles Austin, 168; Eldon, 169; Eldon Foster, 169; Emma Oneida, 168; Harry Eugene, 168; Hartman, 168; Helen May, 168; Isaac, 168; Isaac I., 168; Lawrence Brett, 168; Myrtle Ruby, 168; Rebecca, 169; Richard Eldon, 169; Richard H., 168, 169; Richard Henry, 168; Salome Ruby, 169; Samuel Lyell, 168; William David, 169
LEMMON: Catharine Ann, 48; Jonathan H., Rev., 48; Mary G. D., 99; Thomas J., 99
LENTZ: Earl, 155; Phebe Loflin, 156

LEPLEY: C., Rev., 249; Christian, Rev., 248
LETTNER: S. C., Rev., 113
LEWIS: Abner K., 84; Henry Dorsey, 84; John, 230, 248, 249, 250; Mary Ann, 84
LIETHISER: Claudia Louis, 168
LIGHTBURNE: W., Rev., 131
LILES: Dick, 18; John Richardson, 20; Margaret Grace, 20; Susan Baker, 20
LILLY: Julian, 248; Thomas, 248
LINABURG: Earl L., 136
LITSINGER: Rev., 242
LITTLE: 1Alexander Jackson, 170; Alexander Jackson, 169; Edward John, 170; Eleanor Chatman, 169, 170; Eleanor Jane, 170; Eleanor Jane Jackson, 170; Harriett Connard, 169, 170; James Burke, 169, 170; James N., 170; james Newton, 169, 170; John Edward, 169, 170; Mary Elizabeth, 169, 170; William Adam, 169, 170
LITTLETON: Lucille, 227
LITTON: Thomas, 163
LIVEZEY: A. Elizabeth, 171; Anna M. C., 173; Barbara Louisa, 222; Charles, 172; Clement S., 171; Clement Sewell, 171; Elizabeth E., 171; Florence, 171, 173, 207; Frances B., 171; G. Kessler, III, 222; George K., 173, 203; Harry K., 173; Jacob, 170, 172; Jacob O., 170, 171, 172; James, 172; James S., 171, 172; John S., 173; Jon Harlan, 1, 74, 75, 77, 152, 180, 197, 247; Kate E. S., 173; Kenneth, 203; Kessler, 203; Margaret E., 173; Mary Ann, 171, 172; Mary J., 170, 171; Mary Verna (Pyle), 222; Paul Victor, 173; Pearl, 172; Pearl H., 171; Robert, 172; Robert H., 171;

Robert S., 170, 171, 172;
Sylvania, 173; Sylvania S., 173;
T. Priscilla, 171; Thomas, 172,
173; Thomas N., 173; Webster,
171, 172; Webster H., 171;
Wilbur, 172
LLOYD: Frances B., 116
LOBACH: Alfred Theodore, 174;
Andrew Jackson, 174; Eliza, 174;
Eliza Ann, 174, 175; Emma
Elizabeth, 174; Florrance Anna,
174; Jane Mary, 174; John T.,
174, 175; John Taylor, 174;
Joseph, 173, 174; Josephine
Laura, 174; Rachael Catharine,
174
LOBAUGH: Alfred T., 174; Jennie
M., 174
LOCHARY: Frank, 192
LOCKARD: James Thomas, 175;
John Amos, 175; Martha Eliza,
175; Mary E., 175; Mary Eliza,
175; Mary Jane, 175; Samuel Lee,
175; William C., 175; William
Henry, 175
LOFFLIN: Charity, 88; Sarah Ann, 88
LOFLIN: Frances, 155, 156; Matilda,
156; Thomas, 156
LOGAN: Jane, 48, 49; Mary Ellen,
48; Patrick, 48
LORD: Hattie, 75, 76, 153; John, 76;
Mary Dearborn, 76
LOWRY: Grace M., 234; Grace
Marie, 235; Louis, 120; Louisa,
120; Mary, 120
LUKENS: Benjamin, 63; Hannah, 63,
76; Mary Elizabeth, 62, 63;
Priscilla, 76
LYNCH: Mabury G., 103
MacDONALD: A. Bruce, 20; Alton
Bruce, 20; Marian Baker, 20
MacFARLAND: John, 229
MacHARDY: Mary, 229
MACKEY: James L., Rev., 40

MacLEAN: Hall, 203
MACREADY: Mary, 41
MAGNESS: Albert, 176; Albert R.,
176; Albert Stanley, 176;
Amanda, 176; Amanda
(DeMoss), 176; Arthur Courtney,
178; Bertha Mae, 176; Charles,
178; Charles E., 177, 178;
Charles Edward, 177; Charles H.,
178; Charles Henry, 177; Clara,
176; Elizabeth, 177, 178; Ellen,
177; Frank, 176; Harriet Ann,
177; Harriet E., 177, 178; Harriet
Edward, 178; Harriett, 178;
Henry F., 179; Henry Farnandis,
179; Ida Mae, 176; Jemima, 177,
178; John R., 178; John
Rockhold, 178; Lawrence
Farnandis, 179; Leonidas M.,
179; Lillie Bell, 176; Lizzie, 176;
Mary, 178, 179; Mary jane, 179;
Nathaniel Parker, 177; Nora Jane,
176; Ramsy Lee, 176; Rhea
Sylva, 179; Susan, 179; Thomas,
177, 178, 179, 180; Thomas H.,
179; Thomas Henry, 177; Thomas
M., 178; Thomas N., 179; Walter
P., 176; Walter Pinkney, 176;
William Henry, 176; William
Parker, 177, 178
MAGRAW: James M., 30
MARKLEY: Irma, 99
MARRIOTT: Ruth, 111; William
Saum, 111
MARSH: John H., Rev., 82; Rev. Mr.,
150
MARSHALL: R. E. L., Mrs., 7
MARTIN: Abraham, 179; Abram,
179, 180; Anna Elizabeth, 105;
Anna Latty, 181; Annie L., 180;
Catherine, 104; Clara, 180; Clara
(Clarissa), 179; Dorothy L., 223;
Edwin E., 223, 224; Eliza Jane,
181; Harry E., 223; Harry Ronald,

223; Henry, 180, 181; Jane L., 181; John, 105; Kate E., 223, 224; Mary, 179, 180; Mary Airey, 7; Mary E., 105; Mary Martha, 180; Myrtle, 155; Roberta A., 223; S. A. (Susan Anne), 179; S. J. (Jane), 179; Susan, 179; Susan A., 179; Susannah, 180, 181; Susannah E. J., 181
MARTINDALE: Elizabeth, 212
MARTINI: A. Lewis, 102, 104; Harriet L., 102
MAXWELL: Carolyn Adele, 54
McCARNS: Hester, 79
McCAULEY: Ann, 58, 59
McCAUSLAND: Ann (Higginbotham), 130; J. W., 131; John, 131; Maria, 130
McCLELLAN: Harriet, 101
McCLUNG: Emmett, 199
McCOMAS: Alexander, 182; Charles H., 193; Dan Preston, 182; Daniel Preston, 182; Ellen, 181; Ellen B., 182; Hannah E., 182; Hannah G., 182; Harry G., 182; Herbert, 192; James P. L., 182; Martha S., 182; Nicholas A., 93, 182; Preston, 182
McCOMMONS: Bessie A., 132; Mollie, 242; Mollie E., 242
McCONKEY: Edward Dawes, 183
McCONKY: Annie S., 182; Edward D., 182, 183; Mary Grafton, 183
McCORMICK: Thomas, 230
McCRONE: Hilda H. (Davis), 80
McCUE: Edward, 204
McDONALD: W. A., Rev., 185
McELVAIN: Annie B., 99
McFADDEN: Mary Eliza, 212
McFADON: Antoinette, 251
McKEE: J., Rev., 219
McKEIN: John, Rev., 84
McMULLEN: Elizabeth, 184; James, 184; Joseph, Jr., 183; Lewis James, 184; Sarah Agness, 184; Teressa May (Wilgus), 184
McMULLIN: Amelia A., 184; Andrew, 184; Clarence, 184; Clarence S., 183, 184; Curtis E., 184; Haslet O., 184; Ivan M., 184; James, 184; Joseph, 183, 184; Joseph Francis, 184; Lewis James, 184; Mary, 184; Mary E., 184; Oscar M., 184; Philip Raftringe, 184; Sarah A., 184; Sarah Agness, 184; Sarah Ann, 184; Teresa, 184; William Andrew, 184
McNABB: D. Paul, 192
McNULTY: Alonzo, 34; Harry Beaven, 34; Margaret, 34; Margaret Beaven, 34
McNUTT: Julia Elvira, 46
McSHANE: Clara, 203
McVEY: Capitola, 207
MEARS: Shirley Anne, 212, 213; William H., 212
MEELER: Elsie, 46; Russell, 46
MERRITT: Cleveland, 245, 246; Fannie, 245
MICHAEL: Ann, 188, 189; Ann Mariah, 188; Ann Martha, 189; Ann Matilda, 151; Anne Mariah, 187; Arthur Wayne, 214; Ava E., 185; Avarilla Effie, 185; Balshar, 188; Baltshar, 187; Calvin, 189; Charles W., 119, 120; Charles W., Jr., 119; Charles, Jr., 193; Charlotte, 150; Edith C., 193; Eliza Neoma, 189; Emma F., 18; Ethan, 187, 188; Grace H., 119, 120; Hannah, 150; Henry C., 185, 187; Henry Clay, 186; Henry E., 188; henry Everist, 187; Jacob, 187, 188, 190; Jacob Edwin, 190; Jacob Jackson, 188; James, 150; John Calvin, 188, 189; John M., 189; John O., 188; John Osborn,

187; Kate Estelle, 185; Martha S.
Richardson, 232; Mary, 187, 188,
193; Mary Ann, 181; Mary Oletia
Girtrude, 189; Miranda, 151;
Naomi, 150; Onion Clay, 185,
186; Owen, 193; Sarah Elizabeth,
119; Semeliann, 187; Susan, 188,
190; Susanna, 187, 188;
Susannah, 151; William, 151;
William H., 188; William
Harrison, 188; William Otho, 189
MICHENER: Sarah Augusta, 81
MIDDENDORF: John W., 122
MIDDLETON: Elizabeth, 155
MILHISER: Mirian, 149
MILLER: Lydia A., 55; Nevie E.,
232; Virginia, 54; Virginia
Rosten, 55
MILLS: Martha F., 22
MITCHELL: Alexander, 98; Ann M.,
189; Ann Martha, 188, 189;
Bertha L., 33; Betsy, 182;
Charlotte, 129; Clemency, 137;
Edith C., 24, 25; Edith Catherine,
24; Edmund, 98, 189, 190;
Edward W., Sr., 172; Eliza, 133,
137; Elizabeth, 98, 133; Elizabeth
Torrance, 118; Ezekiel, 133;
Florence Swartz, 172; George
Torrance, 98; Harry Edmund, 24;
James Street, 190; James Streett,
190; John, 137; John Paca, 190;
La Mar, 190; Mabel C., 24; Maria
C., 97; Martha J., 190; Mary, 127,
133; Morgan, 23, 25; Noble L.,
192; Otho, 189; Patrick Henry,
98; Priscilla, 190; Richard, 190;
Robert P., 137, 138; Samuel
Rickey, 24; Shirley Blake, 25;
Susan Rebecca, 190; Virginia
Sophia, 190; William, 127, 137;
William Gashem, 189; William
Maitland, 98

MITTEN: Anna M., 248; Catherine,
250; Henry, 250
MONAGHAN: John, 199, 200
MONKS: A. Coleman, 194; Amy D.,
191, 192; Amy Drusilla, 191; Ann
Eliza, 193; Catherine J., 194;
Coleman Y., 194; E. T., Esq.,
192; Edward, 192; Edward T.,
114, 191, 192, 193; Edward
Treadway, 191, 194; Ellen C.,
191, 192; Ellen Treadway, 114;
James H., 193; James P., 192,
193, 194; John C., 193; Lewis
W., 193; Mary A., 194; Mary
Addie, 194; Mary E., 194; Olevia
C., 194; Robert A., 194; Sallie A.,
191, 192; Sallie Ann, 114, 191;
Sallie L., 194; Sarah Lavinia,
194; Sarah M., 194; Thomas A.,
193, 194; William T., 193
MONROE: Rev. Mr., 150
MOOG: August, 195; Charlotte
Wilhelmina, 195; Christina
Augusta, 195; Emil Romeo
Wilhelm Heinrich, 195; Emilia,
195; Emma, 195; H., 195;
Heinrich Robert Alexander, 195;
Herrmann, 194, 195; Johan
Friedrich, 195; Robert, 195;
Wilhelmina, 195
MOORE: Elizabeth, 169; F. X., Rev.,
33; George, Mrs., 128; John, 12;
Mary, 12; Paul A., 35, 36; Paul
C., 35
MORGAN: Clarence, 171, 172;
Elizabeth A., 196; Elizabeth
Elliott, 196; Estelle, 24, 25, 26;
Florence Virginia, 196; Laura J.,
196; Laura Jennie (Osborn), 196;
Robert L., 196; Theodora, 196;
Thomas, 169, 196; Thomas
Elliott, 196
MORISON: Nathaniel Holmes, 8

MORRIS: Elizabeth E., 197; Ellen, 131, 132; Henry Presbery, 133; John L., 197; John Lloyd, 197; Joseph, 230; Lloyd, 132, 133; Margaret Ann, 196; Martha Jane, 230; Rebecca, 132, 133, 197; Sarah J., 197; Sarah R., 197; Sarah Rebecca, 196; Susan Maria, 197; Thomas Francis, 157
MORRISON: Daniel E., 198; Daniel Edmund, 197; Elizabeth, 197, 198; Ellinor, 197; Ellinor Jane, 198; George E., 198; George W., 198; Hamilton, 197, 198; James S., 198; James Samuel, 197; Kate, 197; Kate M., 197; Madora Jane, 197; Medora Jane, 198; Osco Bates, 197; William Thomas, 197
MORSE: Armorel, 199; James M., 199, 200; James Murray, 199
MOTLEY: Carvelle Douglas, 227; Linda Hayman, 227; Walter Lewis, 227; Walter Russell, 227
MOUNT: Clarence Jackson, 150; James A., 150; Laura, 150
MOXLEY: Ida A., 145
MUNROE: Jonathan, Rev., 218
MURPHY: Semeliann, 188
MURRAY: Armorel, 199; D. Marion, 199; David M., 199; David Marion, 199; Emily, 199; Emily Laura, 199; Green Harp, 199
MYER: Annie Francis, 200; Grome Alexander, 200
MYERS: Anna Francis, 201; Augustus Evan, 200, 201; Carline, 201; Dianna V., 235; Dolly, 235; Elizabeth, 234; Elizabeth M., 234; Florence, 234; Florence McG., 234; Franklin Frederick Joseph, 200; Georganna Estella, 234; George Anton, 200; James Patrick, 200, 201; John Joseph Elsworth, 200; Laura A., 179; Lillian, 235; Margaret, 201; Martha M., 201; Martin, 200, 201; Martin Daniel, 200, 201; Martin James, 200; Mary Lizer, 200; Ranson Lowry, 234; Richard Charles, 200; Robert, 235; Robert S., 234; Robert Seneca, 235; Rusaltha, 200; Rusaltha Ann, 200; Rusaltha Anna, 201; Stellie Dewer, 200; William Hubanrd, 200; William Winsor, Jr., 235; Winsor, 234, 235
NAGLE: Ada Ellen, 209; Albert Clinton, 209; Anna Margaret, 209; Anna Mary, 205, 207; Benjamin, 64; Charles C., 204, 206; Charles Chapman, 206, 207; Charlot, 204, 205; Charlotte, 66, 206; Charlotte R., 68; Culbert W., 204; Daniel, 66, 67, 68, 204, 205, 206; Daniel S., 206; Debra, 206; Debrough, 206; Della May, 209; Edward R., 203; Eliza, 205, 206; Eliza Agnes, 64, 67; Elizabeth, 42, 66, 68, 204, 205; Elizabeth Hutchinson, 207; Emanuel, 42, 66, 68, 205, 206, 207; Emmanuel, 204; Florence, 208; Frank, 67; George A., 203, 204; George Alexandria, 207; George Elexander, 205; Harry Boyd, 209; Harry Cramp, 208; Henry, 66, 204, 205, 206, 207; Isaac, 66, 205; James, 66, 205; James Stewart, 208; John, 64, 66, 67, 204, 205, 206, 207, 208; John H., 204, 208; Laura Ellen, 206, 207; Lea, 205; Leah, 66, 204; Lynn K., 203; Manuel, 205; Margaret, 206; Margaret A., 209; Margaret Ann, 208, 209; Margarette, 66, 67; Margrat, 205; Martha Oletia, 203; Mary Ann, 66, 67, 205, 206; Mary H., 201; Maryann, 205;

Mical, 207; Michael, 66, 206; Mickel, 204, 205; Millard Howe, 208; Mrs., 67; Owen Wallace, 209; Rebecca, 66, 67, 68, 206; Rebecke, 204; Samuel, 192, 208, 209; Samuel O., 204, 208, 209; Samuel Owen, 205, 207, 208, 209; Sarah, 64, 67, 206; Sarah (Stumpf), 206; Sarah Frances, 205, 206; Sarah Jane, 66, 205; Spencer, 204; Stevenson A., 204; Stevenson W., 203; Susan Jane, 42, 205; Susan Mary, 207; Sylvania Gertrude, 208; Thomas, 207; Thomas F., 42, 201, 203, 204; Thomas Franklin, 205, 207; Wallace C., 203; Walter C., 203; Walter Chapman, 209; Willard Sheridan, 209; William, 66, 67, 204, 205, 206; William Edman, 206, 207
NAGLE.: Mr., 67
NATCHER: Mary Janet, 174, 175
NAYLOR: R. D., Rev., 60
NEELY: D. T., Rev., 142
NEILSON: Albert, 251; Charles, 252; Crawford, 251; J. Crawford, 251; James, 251, 252; Rosa, 251, 252; Virginia P., 251, 252
NELSON: Aquilla, 227; Belle, 51; Frances, 227; Garrett V., 227; George Alfonso, 104; Sarah E., 226; Sarah Elizabeth, 226
NEUFFER: Charlotte, 195
NICOL: Aggie, 99
NICOLL: William, 57
NOBLE: Elizabeth, 210; Frances, 26, 210; George H., 210; George Harrison, 210; James, 209, 210; John T., 210; John Thomas, 210; William H., 210; William Henry, 210
NOGGLE: Daniel, 204; Eliza, 65, 66; Manuel, 205

NOGLE: Annie M., 240
NOLL: Danielle Renee, 215; Linda, 215; Lynnelle Marlene, 215; Michelle Maree, 215; Richard, 215; Richard Andrew, 214; William Peden, 215
NORMAN: Lillian, 234
NORTHAMER: Lillie A., 123; Lilly A., 122; W. T., 123
NOVAK: Frank, Rev., 202
NUMBERS: Harriet Louisa, 210; Martha J., 1
OLIVER: S. R., 68
OPPERMAN: Agnes E., 90, 91; Frederick Hugo, 91; Harry Lee, 90, 91; Hugo Frederick, 90; Lulu E., 90; Richard, 91; Richard T., 90
ORR: Rebecca, 41
OSBORN: Aberilla, 109; Ann, 187; Cordelia, 109; Cyrus, 109; Frances, 109; John Hanson, 188; Laura Jennie, 196; Martha R., 58; Mary, 109; Sarah, 109; Semelia, 188; Susannah, 26; William, 109
OSBORNE: William D., 190; Wilson, 82
OWENS: Elmore Hazlett, 169; Sarah Ann, 183; Thomas Morgan, 169
OWINGS: Ruth (Cockey), 68, 69, 70; Samuel, 68, 69, 70; Urath Cromwell, 68
PALMER: Ethel june, 210; H. Louisa, 210; Harry Webster, 210; Mahlon, 211; Mary Alice, 210; S. Webster, 210; Samuel Webster, 210; William Wallace, 210, 211
PARKE: Samuel, Rev., 64
PARKER: Elizabeth, 246; Elizabeth A., 246; Mary, 126, 127; Mary V., 26
PARKS: Elisha, 211; Elizabeth, 211; Harriet, 211; John, 211; Joseph, 211; Joshua, 211; Mary, 211;

Peter, 211; Priscilla, 211; Samuel, Rev., 67; William, 211
PARSONS: Ann Lillian, 213; Anna Lillian, 212; Anne Alsruhe, 212; Elizabeth, 213; Helen W., 213; Llewellyn A., 213; Sadie N., 212, 213; Stephen F., 213; Townsend A., 212; Victoria Lee, 213; William, 213; William Arthur, 212, 213; William Arthur, III, 212; William Arthur, Jr., 212; William Augustus, 212
PASTRE: Betty Yeager, 85
PATTERSON: Belle A., 51; Elsie A., 33
PAYNE: Ann, 3, 7
PEARCE: Estelle Hutchins, 140; Harry Thornton, 139; John Myers, 139; Maude Hutchins, 140
PEDEN: Carol Anne, 214; Catherine, 214; Henry Clint, 214; Henry Clint, III, 214; Henry Clint, Jr., 214, 215; Henry Clint, Sr., 214; Linda Marlene, 214; Pearl Eugenia (Crenshaw), 215; Veronica, 214; William H., 215; William Henry, 215
PEERY: John, 203; John Brown, 202; John Green, 202
PENICK: D. Allen, 77
PENNINGTON: Annie J., 1
PEPPLER: Alexander, 123; Annie C., 122
PEREGOY: Ann, 141, 225; Charles, 224, 225; Elizabeth, 225; Helina, 225; James, 225; Joseph, 225; Nicholas, 225; Sarah, 225
PERGOY: Ollie, 99
PERRY: Rachel Ann, 216
PETERKIN: William, Rev., 230
PETERS: T. E., 149
PHILLIPS: Mary A., 58; Mary Ann, 57, 58; Nathaniel, 58; Samuel, Rev., 174

PICKERT: Bruce Gordon, 157; Richard Martin, 157; Robert Wellington, Jr., 157; Robert, Mrs., 157; Sally Lynn, 157
PILKEY: Elizabeth, 174
PININO: Florence H--ton, 131
PIPINO: Hattie G., 131
PITT: Elizabeth, 7
PLUMMER: Annalizer, 143; Deborah, 142, 143; Edward C., 143; Eliza, 143; Eliza (Hutson), 144; Fayet, 142, 143; George, 143
POE: Bridget, 120; David, 120; Eliza, 120; Elizabeth, 120; jacob, 120; Maria, 120
POITS: Ann, 62; Isaac, 62; William, 62
POOLE: Anna Cost, 216; Blanche, 217; Cumberland Wilson, 216, 217; Florence, 216; Florence P., 215, 218; Florence Priscilla, 216; Frances Eleanor, 215, 216, 217; Francis Herbert, Dr., 30; Frederick S., 216, 217; Frederick Sprigg, 216, 217; John Frederick Sprigg, 216, 217; John Knox, 31; Mary Douglas, 215, 216; Mary Gertrude, 217; Mary T. D., 216, 217; Richard, 215, 216, 217, 218; Robert Wilson, 216, 217; William Clayton, 31; Wilson, 217, 218
PORTER: Frank, Rev., 219; Jemima, 101, 103
POWELL: Ernest F., 231; Ernest Fifer, 231; Ernest William Richardson, 231; Mary Kathryn Matthews, 231; Mary Kay, 231; Mildred H. Richardson, 231; Mildred Richardson, 232; William Terrence, 231
POWER: John, 49
PREGOY: Ruth, 225

PRESTON: Cora Edna, 122; Elizabeth W., 235; Elizabeth Warfield, 235; John F., 47
PRETTIMAN: Rev., 244
PRICE: Agnes Elizabeth, 90; Albert W., 91; Albert Wesley, 90; Charles H., 228; Charles Henry, 228; Charlotte A., 91; Edward, 239; George, 90; George Diffenderffer, 228; Harry A., 90; Harry G., 91; Harry Gilmore, 90; Henry, 228; Henry A., 90, 91, 228, 229; Howard Lee, 90; John F., 90; Joseph A., 91; Laura, 228; Laura Reese, 229; Lulu, 90; Penelope, 238; Raymond, 90; Raymond Wesley, 90; Routh, 90; Ruth, 238; Sadie L., 247; Sara Jane, 238; Shelton, 238; Thelma Reese, 90; Thomas, 238; William, 238; William, Mrs., 12; Winnie, 90
PRIGG: Robert E., 153
PRITCHARD: Austin Bernard, 78; Charles Arthur, 219; Christianna, 218; Clara Frances, 78; Emily I., 78; Ethel Estelle, 78; George E., 78; George Edwin, 77, 218; George Ray, 78; Guy Edwin, 78; Joshua R., 218; Mary C., 218; Mary Catherine, 218; Mary Kathryn, 78; Morgan Elliott, 219; Ross Elliott, 78; Sadie Christiana, 78; Susan O., 18; Susan Ordella, 219; William, 218; William Alfred, 218; William G., 218
PUGH: Ema Jane, 219; James Monroe, 219, 220; Louisa Orlean, 219; Luticia, 219; Malcum Mitchel, 219; Malcum Mitchell, 220; Mary Isabel, 219; Mitchel Martin, 219, 220; Narcissa, 219, 220; Reusa Alice, 219; Robert Lee, 219; William Jackson, 219, 220
PYLE: Amer Montgomery, 220; Amor Montgomery, 221; Ann, 223; Ann E., 223; Ann Elizabeth, 223; Casander, 136; Cassander D., 136; Dorothy Ann, 222; Edgar W., 136; edith Gertrude, 221; Edith Gertrude, 220; Elisha R., 222, 223; Elnora, 221; Ely, 136; G. P., 21; Granville P., 21, 221; Granville Putnam, 221; Gulielma E., 149, 223; Harmon, 222, 223; Helen Elizabeth, 21, 221; Isaac L., 220; Isaac Vinten, 221; Isaac Vinton, 221; Jacob Linley Cromwell, 220, 221; Joshua H., 149, 222, 223; Kate E., 223; Kate Elma, 223; Lester Baker, 221, 222; Lewis T., 223, 224; Lorenza Hillman, 221; Lorenza Hillmen, 221; Margaret Hanson, 222; Martha H., 220, 221; Mary, 220, 221; Mary B., 223; Mary Bell, 223; Mary Ella, 223; Mary Elmira, 223; Mary Elnor, 221; Mary Verna, 221; Nathan Miller, 221; Richard Granville, 222; Robert H., 220, 221; Susan E., 223; Susan Emma, 223; Susie E., 148, 149; Viola B., 221; Viola E., 21
QUADE: Joseph, 6; Joseph (Joe), 4; Joseph McKinley, 3; Melody Page, 4; Melody Paige, 6; Nancy Carroll, 3, 4; Norma, 4
QUEEN: A. M., 228; Henry Barnett, 228; Sophie, 228
QUINBY: Frances Lorvma, 139
RAMPLEY: Mary, 139
RAMPLY: Mary, 140
RASMUSSEN: Ann Baker, 19; Emma, 19; Kai, 19; Kai, Jr., 19
RAVEN: Ann, 100

RAWHOUSER: Christianna, 218; Joshua, 218, 219
RAY: Jane, 40
REACE: Rev., 145
READ: Ann, 224, 225; Catharine, 142, 224; Catherine, 225; Charles Peregoy, 224; Deborah, 224; Elias, 224, 225; Elias Joseph, 142, 225; Elizabeth, 224, 225; Hannah, 224; Hannah Price, 225; James, 225; John, 224; John G., 225; Mary, 224; Maryann, 225; Nicholas, 225; Nicholas Gorsuch, 225; Rebecca Jane, 225; Ruth, 224; Sarah, 224; William Edmonds, 225
REASIN: Claude N., 226, 227; Claude Nelson, 226; Cora D., 226; Fannie, 226; Fannie N., 227; Florence Aleine, 226; Florence Aliean, 226; Gertrude, 227; Hannah E., 227; Henry Cole, 226; Ruby, 226; William H., 226, 227; William Hawthorne, 226
REED: C., Rev., 131; William T., Rev., 145
REELY: Lee, Mrs., 15
REESE: Ann, 228; Annie O., 228; Charles, 228; Charles H., 229; Charles S., 227, 228, 229; John S., 227, 229, 230; Laura, 228; Rev., 145
REGESTER: Eva Warfield Cockey, 72; Henry S., 70
REGISTER: Henry Slicer, 72
REID: Charles W., 199, 200; Charlie, 199, 200; Charlie Murray, 199; David Marion, 199; Ruth, 199
REIGHLER: John J., 249
REIP: John, 203
REISINGER: George, 230
REMBOLD: Mary, 145
REVES: Cooper, 158
RHOADS: Charles Grant, 3

RHODES: A. Churchill, 6; Augustus Churchill, 4; Charles Grant, 6; Helen, 4; Helen Hayes, 3; W. Edgar, 31
RICHARDSON: Benjamin, 231; Charlotte E., 39; Charlotte R., 39; Clarissa Vaughan, 231; E. Hall, 39; E. Hall, Dr., 13; E. R., 39; Elihu Hall, 38, 39; Elizabeth, 38, 39, 117; Elizabeth R., 39; Eurith B., 117; Frances M., 117; George A. R., 231; George J., 117; George J. T., 117; Infant, 231; Japhet, 232; John M., 117; John R., 117; John W., 117; Lizzie Judson, 117; M. C., 232; Martha C., 231, 232; Martha S., 231; Martha Sophia, 185; Mary, 231; Mary Mildred Hastings, 231; Mary T., 231, 232; Mary Thomas, 117; Matilda, 117; Minnie Belle, 117; Rev., 232; Ruth, 238; Sophia, 232; W. H., 39; William, 38, 39, 117, 231; William B., 39, 231, 232; William J., 231, 232; William S., 37, 39
RICKETS: Thomas M., 232
RICKETTS: Belinda, 233, 234, 235; Beulah D., 234; Beulah Delamy, 234; C., 233; Caroline, 233; Caroline E., 232, 233, 234; Dora, 232, 233; Dora (Ford), 48; Dora E., 233; Edward, 233; Estella, 233; G. Walter, 48; Harry, 233; Harry G., 232, 233; J. E., 48; J. Edward, 233; Joan Virginia, 233; John C., 233, 234; John E., 232, 233; John Edward, 232; Josephine, 233; Lillie M., 233; Lilly May, 233; Louis C., 232; Martha Irene, 48, 233; Nevia, 233; Oneda, 233; Oneda C., 233; Paul Livingstone, 234, 235; S. Davis, 234, 235; Samuel, 233;

Samuel Davis, 234; Samuel J., 232, 233, 235; Samuel J., Jr., 232; Thomas, 233, 234, 235; Thomas M., 232; Thomas W., 232, 234; Thomas William, 233, 234; Walter, 232, 233; Walter C., 233
RICKS: Rebecca Boughter, 208
RIDGELY: Ethel Lee, 18; Vernon N., Rev., 142; Washington, 142
RIEGER: Mary Margaret Elizabeth, 89
RIGDON: Alexander, 95; Benjamin, 93, 95; Elizabeth, 95; Ely, 95; George B., 93; George Sankey, 95; Hannah, 95; John Forwood, 95; Lacy, 95; Laomi, 95; Lillie, 95; Samuel Forwood, 95; Sarah Ann, 92, 95; Stephen, 95; Thomas Baker, 95
RILEY: Rev., 228
ROBERSON: Jennie A., 90
ROBERT: Mary B., 9; Sanderson, 8, 9
ROBERTS: Emeline, 239; Rev., 240; Theresa, 239; William H., 239
ROBEY: Lillian G., 75; Lillian Grace, 152
ROBINSON: Alverta, 73; Benjamin, 120; Charles Littleton, 116; Christine, 115; Elizabeth, 115, 116; Emma Jannette, 115; Hester Jane, 115, 116; John A., 192; John Cameron, 116; Lorena, 115; Lourenna S., 115; Margaret Lucinda, 115; Mary Ann, 115; Rebecca Adelia, 115; Sarah Elizabeth, 115; Thomas, 115, 116; Thomas Jefferson, 115
ROCKHOLD: Jemima, 177, 178; Mary Ann, 177
ROGERS: Edythe, 18; Ettie, 129; Evans, 13
ROSS: Harry Leroy, 201; Jane, 41; Mary M., 152; William, 41
ROTH: O. C., 124
ROUCH: Mary Henrietta, 145; R. S., 41
ROUSE: John G., 192
ROUSS: Charles Broadway, 12
ROWAN: Jane, 83
ROYER: Ida, 124
RUBY: Salome, 168
RUFF: Elizabeth Ann, 235, 236; Elizabeth Sophia, 236; Elizabeth Sophia (Mitchell), 236; Elizabeth W., 236; Elizabeth Warfield Preston, 236; Ella Virginia (Findley), 236; Henry, 235, 236; James, 236; James H., 236; James Henry, 236; Martha Ann, 236; Mary Elizabeth, 235, 236; Rebecca Elizabeth, 236; Rebecca R., 236; Rebecca Riggs (Grymes), 236; Sarah Alethia (Streett), 236; Sarah Augusta, 236
RUSSELL: Howard, 192
RUTLEDGE: Abram, 238; Ann Eliza, 237; Ann L., 223; Charles M., 238; Elisha, 223; Gulielma E., 222, 223; Jehu, 237, 238; John, 237, 238; John E., 237; John S., 238; Joshua, 237; Julia S., 238, 239; Levisa Jane, 238; Lewis C., 238; Margaret, 239; Nathan, 237; Priscilla, 237; Sara, 239; Sophia S., 237, 238; William, 237; William H., 238, 239
RYLAND: C. W., Rev., 62
SANK: James H., 181; Jane L., 181
SCAGGS: Adaline, 240; Alphred, 240; Arana, 240; Carroline, 240; Elizabeth, 239; Emeline, 240; Henry, 240; John, 239, 240; Maryelen, 240; Thoams, 239; Thomas, 240; William H., 240
SCARF: Samuel, 116
SCARFF: Rebecca Hawkins, 140
SCHEIB: Henry, Rev., 88
SCHLINCKLE: H. L., Rev., 202

SCHRADER: Helen Gertrude, 24
SCHROEDER: Helen Gertrude, 24; Hugo, Rev., 33
SCHULTZ: J. R., Rev., 132
SCOTT: Elizabeth, 161; Jane, 161; Jane Ann, 135, 160, 161; Wakeman H., 132
SEARS: Arianna Amanda, 18; John L., 16, 18
SEWELL: A. O., 229; Ann, 228; Ann Louisa, 228; Anna, 229; Charles Smith, 157; Hattie S., 157; James, 228; James M., 228; Lillian Phebe, 157; Nena Semelia, 157; Rebecca, 62; Richard, 62; Robert D., 122; Sarah, 62; William H., 155, 156, 157; William Kimble, 157
SHANNON: Annie M., 240; Annie M. (Nogle), 240; Annie Mary, 240, 241; Cora May, 241; Deborough, 205; Debra, 205; George Edward, 240, 241; George T., 240; George Thomas, 207, 240, 241; John Henry, 241; Mary Frances, 241; Mina, 240, 241; Thomas, Mrs., 204
SHAW: Rebecca E., 83; Rebecca Lathrop, 83
SHAY: Alice, 48; Bennett, 48; Martha Louisa, 48
SHEIB: Pastor, 194
SHEKELL: Eleanor, 216, 217
SHEKELLS: Eleanor, 216
SHEPHERD: Thomas J., Rev., 70, 71
SHERIDAN: Albert, 242; Alread Fillmore, 243; Asbury, 241; Cora R., 243; Daisy M., 242; Daisy Virginia, 242; Elizabeth, 241; Ella E., 244; Florence N., 242; George, 241, 242; Infant, 243; James, 241; John, 241, 242; Lizey Gertrude, 243; Lizzie, 244; Luther, 241, 242; Maggie C., 244;
Margaret A. Walker, 244; Margret J., 241; Mary, 45; Mary E., 242; Mary L., 244; Mary Lavenia, 243; Mary R., 242; Oliver A., 242; Pearly Goldine, 242; Rebecca, 243; Rebecca A., 243; Richard, 241, 243, 244; Richard Coleman, 244; Richard Dallas, 243; Richard, Mrs., 128; Samuel, 241; Sarah Leuvena, 243; Telitha, 241; Thomas L., 244; Vernon C., 242; Will, 128; William, 241; William G., 244; William Parker, 243; William, Mrs., 128
SHERMAN: Helen, 141; Helen C., 141; Hellen C., 142
SHERTZER: Abram G., 245; Abram Trege, M.D., 245; Alma, 35; Alma Mildred, 35; Anna Elihalah, 245; Anna Elizabeth, 245; Benjamin, 245; Benjamin Franklin, 245; David, 245; David William, 245; Debra Lee, 35, 36; Denise L., 35; Denise Lynn, 36; Diane Lisa, 36; Fannie Priscilla, 245; Hannah E. M. N., 245; Harry A., 245; Henry M., 245; Isaac, 245; Isaac P., 245; Jacob, 244, 245; Jacob Henry, 245; John A., 245; John Amos, 245; Leslie Norman, 36; Marian E., 35; Marian Elizabeth, 35; Mary Ann, 245; Mary E., 245; Mary Trege, 245; Nancy, 36; Norman, 36; Norman Edward, 36; Norman L., 35; Price I., 35, 36, 245; Price L., 35; Price Leslie, 35; Theodore P., 35; Theodore Price, 36
SHINNICK: Blanche W., 92; O. W., 92
SHIPLEY: E. E., Rev., 84
SHOAF: David, Rev., 218

SHORT: Charles M., 247; Charles McClendon, 246; Elizabeth, 246; Elizabeth A., 246; John H., 246; John Hick, 246; Maria Catherine, 246; Mary Anna, 246; Mary Augustus, 246; William Snyder, 246
SHREEVES: Rev., 3
SILVER: George B., 137; George Bartol, 138; Samuel, 137; Sarah, 137
SINCLARE: Miss, 163
SINGLETON: Ruth, 141
SISCO: Ronald Emmett, 157
SITES: Rev., 192
SKATT: Elizabeth, 49
SKINNER: Bernard A., 218
SLEE: Albert W., 247, 248; Annie L., 180; Annie Mary, 180; Cicero C., 180; Cicero Columbus, 180; Coleman, 180, 181; Eliza, 248; Florence, 247, 248; George, 248; George Henry, 180; George W., 247, 248; Harold Martin, 180; John, 247, 248; John Bay, 180; John N., 248; Letitia, 180; Mary, 180, 247; N. Tipton, 247, 248; R. H. S., 247; Robert H., 247; Susie Frost, 180; Tipton, 247; Warren Hudson, 180; William, 180
SMALL: Cassandra M., 40; Elizabeth (Hopkins), 130; Frederick, 130; Harry, 130; James, 130; John, 130; Noah, 130; Sylvester, 131
SMILEY: William H., 141
SMITH: Ann, 181; Augustus, 128; Basil L., 181; Bayla, 99; E. J., 20; Elizabeth, 21; Elizabeth jane, 21; J. Holmes, Mrs., 159; Jane L., 180; Jess, 142; Joseph F., Rev., 118; Livingstone, 128; Lizzie J., 20; Margaret B., 21; Margaret Hand, 21; Mary Addie, 194; Mary E., 233; Nathaniel, 126; Otha, 128; Ross W., 56; Sarah, 45; Thomas, 126, 127; William J., 21
SMITHSON: Anna Louisa, 93; Annie, 94; Cassandra G., 95; Elizabeth, 94, 95; Emma Julia, 93; Franklin, 94; George, 94; George W., 94; Henry, 94; James, 94; Julia, 92; Juliann, 94, 95; Louisa, 93; Louisa A., 95; Margaret, 94; Mary, 94; Priscilla F., 94; Sallie Ann, 94; Sarah, 94; Sophia, 93; William, 92, 93, 94, 95; William Jr., 93; William Preston, 93
SNODGRASS: James, Mrs., 193; Malcolm, 193
SNYDER: Elizabeth, 174
SORIEN: Rev., 197
SOTHORON: J. L., Rev., 192
SPALDING: Basil Dennis, 38; Elizabeth Rombaugh, 38; Hargraves, 37, 38, 40; Margaret Webster, 38; Martha, 38; Martha Bissell, 38
SPARKS: Clara Dew, 103; Mr., 8; William E. E., 102; William Everett Edward, 103
SPARROW: Elizabeth, 40
SPENCER: Emma Jane, 220; Ethel Harlan, 149; Hermon, 128; John W., 129; Luticia, 220; Rebecca K., 129; Silas L., 243; Sophia, 126, 127; William T., 129
SPIAGHT: Joseph, 155
SPICER: Elizabeth, 82; Ella M., 82; Ella Marian, 82; James A., 51, 82, 251, 252
SPINDLER: Catherine, 230; George F., 230
SPRANKLIN: B. J., 130; Samuel, Rev., 130
STANDFIELD: Simpson, Rev., 142
STANLEY: Jessica Ann, 250; Karen, 250; Lewis, 250

STANSBURY: Edward J., 106; Emerson Eugene, 106; Florence Vernon, 107; Mary Elizabeth, 107
STAPLEFORD: Sarah A., 145
STEBBING: Emma Elizabeth, 33, 34
STEEL: J. W., Rev., 132
STEPHENSON: Ann P., 129; James, 126, 127; Priscilla, 128; William, 128, 129; William B., 128
STERRETT: John, 33, 34; Mary Jane, 34
STEVENS: Annie Virginia, 104; Sarah, 142; William, Rev., 150
STEVENSON: Robert Caruth, 3
STEWARD: Edward, 99
STEWART: Sylvania, 172, 173
STIFLER: Thomas E., 122
STOCKHAM: Lidia A., 150
STOCKSDALE: Samuel Nelson, 248
STONEBRAKER: John S., 229
STORMS: Lester, Mrs., 157
STOUT: Catherine, 41; Charity, 41; Daniel, 41; John, 41; John, Sr., 41; Josuf, 41; Mary, 41; Polley, 41; Richard, 41; Ruth, 41
STREETT: Charles, 139; James, 190; Margaret, 190; Martha Jane, 189, 190; Mary, 42; Mary Susan Hutchins, 140; Sarah Alethia, 235
STROBEL: Margaret, 163
STRONG: Caroline E., 232
STROUT: Howard M., 198; Kate, 198; Lucy Fay, 198; Mary, 198; Mary Elizabeth, 198; Philip, 197; Theodore, 198; Walter Leon, 198
STUMP: Ann, 14; Hannah C., 251; John, 251
STUMPF: Sarah, 205
SULLIVAN: Mary Frances, 156; Matthew, 155
SUSEMIHL: Doris May, 33
SUTCH: Fannie May, 110

SWARTZ: Florence O., 170; james, 170; Mary Ann, 171; Mary S., 170
SYURGEON: Mary Amelia, 235
TAGGART: Jane, 40
TALBOTT: Morris, 203
TANEY: Catherine, 133; Elizabeth, 133, 135; Samuel, 133
TAYLOR: Catherine, 151; Catherine A., 150; David, 158; Eliza, 173, 174; Elizabeth, 11, 13, 159; Frances Belck, 150; Frank, Mrs., 12; James, 150; Jane, 159; John, 11, 13, 159; Mary Amanda, 151; Mary Ann, 150; Mary Manda, 150; Maryan, 150; Velva, 199
TEANEY: Elizabeth, 133
TERRY: Sarah A., 162
THOMAS: Ann, 222; Gertie, 155; J. Robert, 152; L. Allie, 152
THOMPSON: Amanda M., 16; Harry L., 119; Harry Lee, 119, 120; Lillian (Hanway), 120; Lillian H., 119; Lillian Hanway, 119; Sarah, 120; Sarah R., 58; Susan, 139
THOMSON: Mary, 7
TIBBETT: Charles B., Rev., 108
TIFFANY: Francis, 8, 9
TINDAL: Norman Earl, 24
TOWNSEND: Ann C., 79
TOWNSLEY: Annie Cecelia, 73; James O., 72; Mora Grace, 73
TOY: John, 93; Louisa, 94
TREADWAY: A. E., 30; Aquila E., 26, 28, 29, 30; Clayton Seward, 28, 30; Ellen B., 28; Ellen Barnes, 30; Sarah A., 28, 30; Sarah Ann, 29
TREDWAY: Elizabeth, 178; Ellen A., 191; Ellen C., 191; Ellen Cornelia, 178; John Edward, 178; Mary Amealia, 193; S. B., Rev., 192; Thomas, 177, 178, 192; Thomas Magness, 178

TREGE: Mary, 244, 245
TROSTLE: Barbara Ilean, 222; Karen Lyn, 222; Wanda Claire (Beachboard), 222
TROUTNER: Mary E. (Mollie), 153
TUCKER: Beatrice Louise, 114, 191; Edward Buckley, 114; James Wagner, 114; Julia, 93; Lester W., Mrs., 192, 193; Lester Winfield, 114, 191; Lester Winfield, III, 114; Lester Winfield, Jr., 114, 191; Lester, Mrs., 192; Rev., 192
TURNER: Debra Lee, 250; Eleanor Spottswood, 216; Karen U., 250; Karen Upperco, 249; Leslie C., 250; Robert Wayne, 250
TWINING: Horace, 192
ULRICH: Elizabeth, 197; Lena Leona, 80
UPPERCO: Anna, 250; Annette H., 250; Annie, 250; Annie Phillip, 250; Arthur D., 251; Arthur Dickson, 249; Bessie Olivia, 249; Carol Lynn, 250; Dickson, 250; Dorothy, 249; Elizabeth, 249, 250; Ethel A., 250; Florance, 249; Georgeann Maria, 249; Georgeanna Maria, 248; Guy L., 249, 250, 251; Guy Lee, 35, 249; Guy, Jr., 249; Jacob, 249, 250; Jason Leslie, 250; Jennifer Irene, 250; Joan, 250; John Lewis, 248, 249, 250; Karen Elizabeth, 36, 249, 250; Lee D., 250; Lee Dickson, 249; Lee Dixon, 36; Lee Dixon, Jr., 250; Leslie Martin, 36, 249; Lewis, 250; Lucretia Chew, 248, 249; Maria, 249; Martin T., 249; Martin Thedis, 249; Murray D., 250; Murray Dixon, 248; Murry Dickson, 249, 250; Pearl Brikman, 250; Ruth Elizabeth, 249; Susan Roberta, 249; Walter, 250; Walter M., 250; Walter Mitten, 249
VALIANT: Lida, 52, 53, 54
VANBIBBER: George L., 192; Ruth Elizabeth, 248
VANZANT: Curtha Emily, 122
VINTON: Rev. Mr., 241; Robert L., Rev., 218
VOELKEL: Ella D. Z., 206
WAGNER: Nancy Louise, 114, 191
WAKELAND: John, 248
WALKER: Christian H., 124; Cornelia A., 124; Ethel, 169; George W., 126; Hannah Elizabeth, 72; J. Reese, 129; Jesse, 72; John Reese, 126; Lizzie H., 73; Margrett Ann, 244; Mary R., 129; Mary Rebecca Hopkins, 127; Mary Virginia, 123; Mr., 8; Mr. H., 8; Robert J., 127, 129; Robert James, 126; Sarah S., 129; Victorine, 72; Winfield S., 124
WALLACE: James M., Rev., 142
WALTERS: Buelah, 3
WALTHAM: Sarah Hughes, 138; --sas, 109; Thomas, 109
WAMSLEY: John, 51; Nancy, 51
WANDERFORD: Alexander, 100
WANN: J., 192
WARD: Isabelar, 168; John Amos, 167
WARFIELD: Charles Thomas, 71; Emma Shepherd, 71; Eva, 70, 71; Evan W., Dr., 71, 72; Mary T., 71; Mary Thomas, 70, 71, 72; Sallie Anne, 71, 72; Sally Anne, 71; Thomas Beal, 71
WASSON: S. C., Rev., 202, 204
WATKINS: Anna, 143; Charles Bryan, 143; Katharine Elizabeth, 143; Richers, 142, 143
WATSON: Elizabeth T., Mrs., 159; Susan Airey, 6; William T., 12

WATTERS: Charles Edward, 177; Charles Howard, 177, 178; Emily B., 97; Florance Virginia, 177, 178; Henry R., 97
WAYMAN: Catharine, 165, 166; Elizabeth, 166; Hezekiah, 166
WEBSTER: A., Dr., 230; Cassandra, 50; Elizabeth, 38; Margaret, 37
WEIDEMEYER: Lloyd H., 112
WELCH: Mary E., 220
WELLENER: Basil S., 181; Elizabeth, 181; Isabella, 181; Thomas, 181
WELLS: Avarilla, 75; Benjamin N., 74, 75; John, 63; Joseph, 74; Libbie, 22; Martha L. C., 22; Mary A., 74; Mattie C., 22; Sarah, 62, 63; Susannah, 63
WELSH: Isaac P., 78; Robert W., 77, 78; Sarah, 77, 78; Sarah J., 77; Sarah Jenness, 77
WERTH: M. F. Maury, 71; Matthew Fontaine Maury, 71, 72; Sallie Ann Warfield Cockey, 72; Sallie Anne Warfield, 71; Virginia Lee Maury, 71
WESCOTT: Helen, 19
WEST: Clarkson H., 40
WESTAWAY: William Henry, 142
WHEAT: William T., 248
WHITAKER: Talitha E., 193
WHITE: Earl, Mrs., 172; Hyacinth Ella Virginia, 6; Raymond B., 3
WHITEFORD: Mary Jain, 178; Mary Jane, 177
WHITEHURST: D. Keith, 212, 213; Shirley, 213; Susan E., 213; William Guion, 213
WHITING: William Linus, 77
WHITMORE: Marion, 154
WILEY: Sarah, 145
WILGIS: Herbert, 203
WILGUS: Tressa May, 183
WILIGON: Ann, 134

WILKES: Ann, 49
WILKINSON: Harriet Ann, 102, 104; James, 101, 102, 104; John N., 37, 38; John Nicholas, 38; Joseph Levey, 102; Mary, 102; Mary Alice, 102; Mary Archer, 38; Mary Bissell, 40; Mary J., 38; Samuel George, 102
WILLEY: Charles, 126, 127; Hannah Eliza, 129
WILLIAM: Frederick, 89; Frederick, Sr., 89
WILLIAMS: Ann Perry, 217; Antoinette, 252; Carol, 215; Carol Anne, 214; Cynthia Ann, 215; Edwin, 251, 252; Ellen, 56; Frances Poole, 218; Hannah, 251; Hannah C., 251; James, 251, 252; James A., 251, 252; James Aldred, 251; James W., 251, 252; John, 251, 252; John H., 251; Loynel, 215; Loynel Delmore, 214; Rebecca Lynn, 215; Richard Poole, 218; Rosa, 251, 252; Ruth, 252; Walter, Rev., 216; William Edward, 216, 217; William Edward, Jr., 217; William White, 215, 218
WILLNER: Brian Lee, 4; Charles, 4; Charles Frederick, Jr., 3; Dawn, 4; Glenn Alan, 4; JoAnn Gail, 4; Wayne Lawrence, 4
WILLSON: Robert, 216; Zipporah, 16
WILSON: Cassandra, 251; Frances E., 149; J. E., Mrs., 159; Joseph P., Rev., 212; Joshua, Dr., 13; Mary T. D., 216, 217; Rebecca, 13; Robert, 203, 216, 217; Ruth E., 251; S. H., 158; Susan G., 128
WINN: Charles McIntyre, 54; Washington Carlyle, 53; Washington Carlyle, III, 54
WOLFE: Alice, 141; Alice V., 141; C. N., Rev., 42

WOLMSEY: John, 51
WOODLAND: Cassandra, 49;
    Jonathan, 50
WOODS: Rev., 55
WORTHINGS: Ann, 69, 70; John, 69
WORTHINGTON: Ann, 70;
    Emerson, 20; Jane, 13; Joan, 20;
    John, 69, 70; June, 70; Mary, 20;
    Mary A., 68; Mary Anne, 69;
    Nancy, 18; Penelope, 69;
    Thomas, 69, 70
WRIGHT: Kate Estelle, 185;
    Mayfield, 185; William, Dr., 53
WYATT: Rev. Dr., 121; Rev. Mr.,
    121; William E., Rev., 121;
    William W., Rev., 121; William,
    Rev. Dr., 7
YEAGER: Mary Sheaffer, 86
YEAKLE: C. Wade, 212; C. Wade,
    III, 213; C. Wade, Jr., 212, 213
YOUNGER: John, 61; Lemuel, 61;
    Maria, 61; Susanna C., 61, 154
ZIMMERMAN: Christian, 195;
    Lillian, 111; Postmaster, 195;
    Wilhelmina Emma, 194, 195

Heritage Books by Henry C. Peden, Jr.:

*A Closer Look at St. John's Parish Registers
[Baltimore County, Maryland], 1701–1801*

A Collection of Maryland Church Records

*A Guide to Genealogical Research in Maryland:
5th Edition, Revised and Enlarged*

*Abstracts of Marriages and Deaths in Harford County,
Maryland, Newspapers, 1837–1871*

*Abstracts of the Ledgers and Accounts of the Bush Store
and Rock Run Store, 1759–1771*

Abstracts of the Orphans Court Proceedings of Harford County, 1778–1800

Abstracts of Wills, Harford County, Maryland, 1800–1805

Anne Arundel County, Maryland, Marriage References 1658–1800
Henry C. Peden, Jr. and Veronica Clarke Peden

Baltimore City [Maryland] Deaths and Burials, 1834–1840

Baltimore County, Maryland, Overseers of Roads, 1693–1793

Bastardy Cases in Baltimore County, Maryland, 1673–1783

Bastardy Cases in Harford County, Maryland, 1774–1844

Bible and Family Records of Harford County, Maryland, Families: Volume V

Cecil County, Maryland Marriage References, 1674–1824
Henry C. Peden, Jr. and Veronica Clarke Peden

Children of Harford County: Indentures and Guardianships, 1801–1830

Colonial Delaware Soldiers and Sailors, 1638–1776

*Colonial Families of the Eastern Shore of Maryland
Volumes 5, 6, 7, 8, 9, 11, 12, 13, 14, 16, and 19*
Henry C. Peden, Jr. and F. Edward Wright

*Colonial Families of the Eastern Shore of Maryland
Volume 21 and Volume 23*

Colonial Maryland Soldiers and Sailors, 1634–1734

Colonial Tavern Keepers of Maryland and Delaware, 1634–1776

Dorchester County, Maryland, Marriage References, 1669–1800
Henry C. Peden, Jr. and Veronica Clarke Peden

Dr. John Archer's First Medical Ledger, 1767–1769, Annotated Abstracts

Early Anglican Records of Cecil County

*Early Harford Countians, Individuals Living in
Harford County, Maryland in Its Formative Years
Volume 1: A to K, Volume 2: L to Z, and Volume 3: Supplement*

Family Cemeteries and Grave Sites in Harford County, Maryland

First Presbyterian Church Records, Baltimore, Maryland, 1840–1879

*Frederick County, Maryland, Marriage References
and Family Relationships, 1748–1800*
Henry C. Peden, Jr. and Veronica Clarke Peden

Genealogical Gleanings from Harford County, Maryland, Medical Records, 1772–1852
Winner of the Norris Harris Prize from MHS for the best genealogical reference book in 2016!

Harford (Maryland) Homicides

Harford County Taxpayers in 1870, 1872 and 1883

Harford County, Maryland Death Records, 1849–1899

Harford County, Maryland Deponents, 1775–1835

Harford County, Maryland Divorces and Separations, 1823–1923

Harford County, Maryland, Death Certificates, 1898–1918: An Annotated Index

Harford County, Maryland, Divorce Cases, 1827–1912: An Annotated Index

Harford County, Maryland, Inventories, 1774–1804

Harford County, Maryland, Marriage References and Family Relationships, 1774–1824
Henry C. Peden, Jr. and Veronica Clarke Peden

Harford County, Maryland, Marriage References and Family Relationships, 1825–1850

Harford County, Maryland, Marriage References and Family Relationships, 1851–1860
Henry C. Peden, Jr. and Veronica Clarke Peden

Harford County, Maryland, Marriage References and Family Relationships, 1861–1870
Henry C. Peden, Jr. and Veronica Clarke Peden

Harford County, Maryland, Marriage References and Family Relationships, 1871–1875

Harford (Old Brick Baptist) Church, Harford County, Maryland, Records and Members (1742–1974), Tombstones, Burials (1775–2009) and Family Relationships

Heirs and Legatees of Harford County, Maryland, 1774–1802

Heirs and Legatees of Harford County, Maryland, 1802–1846

Inhabitants of Baltimore County, Maryland, 1763–1774

Inhabitants of Cecil County, Maryland 1774–1800

Inhabitants of Cecil County, Maryland, 1649–1774

Inhabitants of Harford County, Maryland, 1791–1800

Inhabitants of Kent County, Maryland, 1637–1787

Joseph A. Pennington & Co., Havre De Grace, Maryland, Funeral Home Records: Volume II, 1877–1882, 1893–1900

Kent County, Maryland Marriage References, 1642–1800
Henry C. Peden, Jr. and Veronica Clarke Peden

Marriages and Deaths from Baltimore Newspapers, 1817–1824

Maryland Bible Records, Volume 1: Baltimore and Harford Counties

Maryland Bible Records, Volume 2: Baltimore and Harford Counties

Maryland Bible Records, Volume 3: Carroll County

Maryland Bible Records, Volume 4: Eastern Shore
Maryland Bible Records, Volume 5: Harford, Baltimore and Carroll Counties
Maryland Bible Records, Volume 7: Baltimore, Harford and Frederick Counties
Maryland Deponents, 1634–1799
Maryland Deponents: Volume 3, 1634–1776
Maryland Prisoners Languishing in Goal, Volume 1: 1635–1765
Maryland Prisoners Languishing in Goal, Volume 2: 1766–1800
Maryland Public Service Records, 1775–1783:
A Compendium of Men and Women of Maryland
Who Rendered Aid in Support of the American Cause
against Great Britain during the Revolutionary War
Marylanders and Delawareans in the French and Indian War, 1756–1763
Marylanders to Carolina: Migration of Marylanders to
North Carolina and South Carolina prior to 1800
Marylanders to Kentucky, 1775–1825
Marylanders to Ohio and Indiana, Migration Prior to 1835
Marylanders to Tennessee
Methodist Records of Baltimore City, Maryland: Volume 1, 1799–1829
Methodist Records of Baltimore City, Maryland: Volume 2, 1830–1839
Methodist Records of Baltimore City, Maryland: Volume 3, 1840–1850
(East City Station)
More Maryland Deponents, 1716–1799
More Marylanders to Carolina: Migration of Marylanders to
North Carolina and South Carolina prior to 1800
More Marylanders to Kentucky, 1778–1828
More Marylanders to Ohio and Indiana: Migrations Prior to 1835
Orphans and Indentured Children of Baltimore County, Maryland, 1777–1797
Outpensioners of Harford County, Maryland, 1856–1896
Presbyterian Records of Baltimore City, Maryland, 1765–1840
Quaker Records of Baltimore and Harford Counties, Maryland, 1801–1825
Quaker Records of Northern Maryland, 1716–1800
Quaker Records of Southern Maryland, 1658–1800
Revolutionary Patriots of Anne Arundel County, Maryland, 1775–1783
Revolutionary Patriots of Baltimore Town and Baltimore County, 1775–1783
Revolutionary Patriots of Calvert
and St. Mary's Counties, Maryland, 1775–1783
Revolutionary Patriots of Caroline County, Maryland, 1775–1783
Revolutionary Patriots of Cecil County, Maryland, 1775–1783
Revolutionary Patriots of Charles County, Maryland, 1775–1783
Revolutionary Patriots of Delaware, 1775–1783
Revolutionary Patriots of Dorchester County, Maryland, 1775–1783

Revolutionary Patriots of Frederick County, Maryland, 1775–1783
Revolutionary Patriots of Harford County, Maryland, 1775–1783
Revolutionary Patriots of Kent and Queen Anne's Counties, 1775–1783
Revolutionary Patriots of Lancaster County, Pennsylvania, 1775–1783
Revolutionary Patriots of Maryland, 1775–1783: A Supplement
Revolutionary Patriots of Maryland, 1775–1783: Second Supplement
Revolutionary Patriots of Montgomery County, Maryland, 1776–1783
Revolutionary Patriots of Prince George's County, Maryland, 1775–1783
Revolutionary Patriots of Talbot County, Maryland, 1775–1783
Revolutionary Patriots of Washington County, Maryland, 1776–1783
Revolutionary Patriots of Worcester and Somerset Counties, Maryland, 1775–1783
St. George's (Old Spesutia) Parish, Harford County, Maryland Church and Cemetery Records, 1820–1920
St. John's and St. George's Parish Registers, 1696–1851
Survey Field Book of David and William Clark in Harford County, Maryland, 1770–1812
Talbot County, Maryland Marriage References, 1662–1800
Henry C. Peden, Jr. and Veronica Clarke Peden
The Crenshaws of Kentucky, 1800–1995
The Delaware Militia in the War of 1812
Union Chapel United Methodist Church Cemetery Tombstone Inscriptions, Wilna, Harford County, Maryland